James Broughton Edge, William Hardy

On the Management of a Parliamentary Election

A practical Guide

James Broughton Edge, William Hardy

On the Management of a Parliamentary Election

A practical Guide

ISBN/EAN: 9783337154295

Printed in Europe, USA, Canada, Australia, Japan

Cover: Foto ©Lupo / pixelio.de

More available books at **www.hansebooks.com**

ERRATUM, page 27, from line 23 to 26 inclusive.

IN A COUNTY :—
For more than one Central Committee Room, and one Committee Room, for each Polling District, but when the number of Electors in a Polling District exceeds 500, one additional room for every complete 500 electors.

ADDENDUM, page 126, after line 20.

Since the present Edition of this work was printed, the 48 and 49 Vic. Chap. 56 has been passed, which declares that it shall not be illegal for an employer to permit persons in his employ to absent themselves from their employment for *a reasonable time* for the purpose of voting at a Parliamentary Election without having any deduction made from their salaries or wages on account of such absence, if such permission is so far as practicable without injury to the business of the employer, given equally to *all persons alike, who are at the time in his employment*, and if such permission is not given with a view of inducing any person to record his vote for any particular Candidate at such Election, and is not refused to any person for the purpose of preventing such person from recording his vote for any particular Candidate at such Election.

ON THE

MANAGEMENT

OF A

PARLIAMENTARY ELECTION:

A

PRACTICAL GUIDE,

WITH ALL THE NECESSARY FORMS, INSTRUCTIONS, NOTICES,
CIRCULARS, &c., REQUIRED IN THE FORMATION OF
COMMITTEES, AND IN THE CANVASS,
NOMINATION, AND ELECTION.

SECOND EDITION.

BY

JAMES BROUGHTON EDGE AND WILLIAM HARDY, ESQRS.,

OF THE MIDDLE TEMPLE, BARRISTERS-AT-LAW.

1885.

PREFACE TO THE FIRST EDITION.

———o———

THE object of the writer of this little book is to place in the hands of persons unacquainted with the *modus operandi* of an election a general plan of the work to be done preliminary to and at an election, with such details as will enable such general plan to be carried out without difficulty.

It is hoped that the work may also be found useful to more experienced electioneerers, who will be able to add to or modify its recommendations, to suit their own plans of procedure.

It may be stated here that the instructions, forms, &c., contained in the book, are in the main such as have been frequently used in both borough and county elections, and everywhere with the best results. They have also been seen and approved of by some of the leading election agents in England.

The writer has, as much as possible, confined himself to a bare detail of the *practical work* of an election. No attempt has been made to discuss mere points of law, but references have been given, where it has been thought necessary, to standard legal works and Acts of Parliament, which may be consulted when requisite.

A copy of the Ballot Act, 1872, and extracts from various Acts of Parliament bearing upon elections, will be found in the appendix. A copious *index* is also added.

In conclusion, the writer cannot hope to have avoided errors, or to have provided a plan which will meet the views of every experienced agent. He trusts, however, that his errors will be few, and that his plan, carefully worked out, will be a good guide, where a better does not exist.

J. BROUGHTON EDGE.

5, St. James' Square, Manchester,
   November, 1873.

PREFACE TO THE SECOND EDITION.

THE first edition of this work was very extensively used during the General Election of 1874, a copy having been sent gratuitously by the Conservative Central Council, to every principal Conservative Agent then engaged in a contested election.

The author of that edition has every reason to believe the book was found most useful, as numerous applications were subsequently received from all parts of the country for further copies; but the edition was soon exhausted, and the book became out of print.

The extensive alterations made in Parliamentary Election Law by the Corrupt and Illegal Practices Act, 1883, rendered a re-writing of the work necessary, and this has been done.

Many opinions expressed are, in the absence of judicial decisions, necessarily those of the authors alone, who are solely responsible for them. The greatest care, however, has been exercised in forming them, and they are, as far as possible, based on the *dicta* of Judges and the decisions of Election Committees.

It will be seen that in one or two instances instructions are given on matters which, it is suggested, should be altogether avoided, if possible. The question of refreshments to persons actually engaged in the carrying on of the election is one of these. *If it be possible*, refreshments should not be given to anybody, at any time, as the *danger* of a breach of the law is, owing to the indiscretion of over-zealous and reckless workers, very great. At the same time, it may be found impossible in large towns and wide country districts to obtain that constant attention during the extended hours of polling which is necessary to the getting up of voters to the poll, unless some provision is made for refreshments to the persons employed in the work, and in such a case it is better to devise a plan which, if *strictly* carried out, is perfectly legal, than to leave the matter to be dealt with, on the spur of the moment, by each individual election agent, who might not have time to think out what precautions ought to be taken to prevent the law being violated.

It is *strongly recommended* that in using the book the Election Agent should read up a few chapters in advance of his work, as this will not only explain some matters not, perhaps, perfectly plain to him at the moment, but will enable him to have all his preparations well in hand.

J. B. E.
W. H.

3, Plowden Buildings, Temple, E.C.,
and
5, St. James' Square, Manchester.
MAY, 1883.

TABLE OF STATUTES.

			Page.
6 Vict., c.	18, s. 85		153
30 & 31 „	102, s. 11		153-154
31 & 32 „	125, ss. 1, 2, 3, 4	…	154-155
35 & 36 „	33 (Ballot Act, 1872)		155-175
„ „	(Schedules)		176-194
„ „	(Abstract)		195-206
38 & 39 „	84 (Returning Officers Act, 1875)		207-216
46 & 47 „	51 (Corrupt Practices Act, 1883)	…	217-263
„ „	(Schedules)	…	264-280
47 & 48 „	34 (Hours of Poll Act, 1884)	…	281-282

ON THE MANAGEMENT

OF A

PARLIAMENTARY ELECTION.

—:o:—

THE CANDIDATE.

THE first duty of the election agent is to see whether any valid objection can be made to the status of any of the candidates. If any objection can be made to his own candidate, he should, at once, take steps to remove it, if possible. If it cannot be removed, then the sooner he informs his principal of the fact the better. If there is a good objection to the opposite candidate, it should, on no account, be made known until after the nomination, and then only as directed under that head.

No qualification by *property* is now required from either Borough or County Members. But a candidate must be—

1. A natural born subject.[1]
2. Of the full age of 21 years.[2]

And he must *not* be—

1. A peer (unless of Ireland, and *not* one of the Irish representative peers in the House of Lords).
2. A judge of the Superior Courts in England, Ireland, or Scotland.[3]
3. A County Court judge.[4]
4. The judge of the Admiralty Court.[5]
5. A police Magistrate for the Metropolitan District.[6]

Qualifications of a candidate.

Disqualifications of a candidate.

---

[1] As to what constitutes a natural born subject, see 12 and 13 William 3, cap. 2; 7 Anne, cap. 5; 4 Geo. 2, cap. 21 & 13 Geo. 3, cap. 25.
 7 & 8 Wm. 3, c. 25, s. 8.
[3] It is said the Master of the Rolls may sit in the House of Commons.
[4] 10 & 11 Vic. c. 102, s. 18.
[5] 3 & 4 Vict., c. 66. See 20 and 21 Vict. c. 77. s. 10.
[6] 3 & 4 Wm. 4, c. 19.

B

Disqualifications of a candidate.

6. A Commissioner of the City of London Police,[1] or a Justice of the Peace, or Receiver appointed under the 10 Geo. 4, c. 44, s. 18.
7. Registrar or Deputy-Registrar of deeds for the County of Middlesex,[2] or of the North,[3] West,[4] or East[5] Ridings of the County of York.
8. A priest or deacon of the Church of England, or a minister of the Church of Scotland.[6]
9. A person in holy orders in the Church of Rome.[7]
10. A person holding an office or place of profit under the Crown created *since* the 20th October, 1705.[8]
11. A holder of a pension from the Crown during pleasure,[8] or for a term of years certain.[9]
12. A contractor for the public service.[10]
13. A bankrupt.
14. A convicted felon or misdemeanant convicted of fraud.
15. A candidate at a *municipal* election, reported by an election court, *or any person* convicted on indictment or information, or adjudged to pay a penalty for any *corrupt* practice at a parliamentary or municipal election, during seven years after the date of such report, conviction, or judgment.[11]

A candidate who answers any of the above descriptions is *absolutely* disqualified; may be objected to on *nomination*, and though a majority of votes are given in his favour, his election is void.

Disqualifications of a candidate as to a particular place. A candidate may not be wholly disqualified, and yet be disqualified *within a certain district*, thus :—

1   2 & 3 Vict., c. 94.
2   7 Anne, c. 20, s. 21.
3   8 Geo. 2, c. 6, s. 37.
4   2 & 3 Anne, c. 4, s. 22.
5   6 Anne, cap. 35, s. 32.
6   41 Geo. 3, cap. 63.
7   10 Geo. 4, cap. 7, sec. 9.
8   6 Anne, cap. 7, s. 25, which specifies some old offices which also disqualify, and see Rogers on "Elections and Registrations," 11th edition, pp. 220—241, for a list of offices which do and which do not disqualify.
9   1 Geo. 1 stat. 2, c. 56.
10 22 Geo. 3, cap. 45, sec. 1. As to the meaning of "contractor," see Royse v. Birley, 20 L. T. Reports N. S. 786.
11 Corrupt Practices Act, 1883, sec. 6, and Municipal Corporations Act, 1882, secs. 78-9.

A Recorder cannot be elected for the Borough for which he is appointed.[1]

A Sheriff or Returning Officer for the County or place for which he acts.

A Revising Barrister for the place, &c., for which he was appointed, within 18 months after his appointment.[2]

A Candidate at a previous election, reported by an Election Court as having *knowingly consented* or been party to the commission of any *corrupt practice* other than treating or undue influence, *or* as having *personally* been guilty of *treating* or *undue influence* at *such* election, can never be elected or sit for the County or Borough to which the report refers.[3]

A Candidate may also be absolutely disqualified or disqualified within a particular district, *for a certain time* thus:—

A candidate at a previous election who has been guilty of one or other of the offences mentioned in the last paragraph, incurs the further punishment of being subject to the same incapacities as if at the date of the report he had been convicted on an indictment of a corrupt practice, *i.e.*, he is *absolutely* disqualified from becoming a candidate for any place for seven years from the date of the report.[3]

A candidate at a previous election, reported by an Election Court as guilty *by his agents* of any *corrupt* practice at *such* election cannot be elected or sit in the House of Commons for the County or Borough to which the report refers, for *seven years* after the date of such report.[3]

[1] 5 & 6 Wm. 4, c. 76, s. 103.
[2] 6 Vict., c. 18, s. 28.
[3] Corrupt Practices Act, 1883, sec. 4

A candidate at a previous election reported by an Election Court as having *knowingly consented* to the commission of any *illegal* practice at *such* election cannot be elected or sit in the House of Commons for the County or Borough to which the report refers for *seven* years after the date of such report.[1]

A candidate at a previous election reported by an Election Court as guilty *by his agents* of any *illegal* practice at *such* election, cannot be elected or sit in the House of Commons for the County or Borough to which such report refers *during the Parliament* for which such election was held.[1]

It would appear that if the corrupt practice, &c., was committed when the person committing it was not himself a candidate, no disqualification would attach to him after the expiration of seven years from his conviction, either with respect to the same or any other County or Borough.

Must appoint an Election Agent

The candidate *must* on or before the day of nomination appoint either himself or some other person his election agent, and must notify the same to the Returning Officer, not later than that day. He must also give an address, where claims, notices, &c., can be served on him.—See "Election Agent."

If he names himself as his Election Agent he will have to appoint Clerks, Messengers, Polling Agents, &c., &c., and will have to make certain returns of his receipts and expenditure, as to which see the various heads following.

Special agent to attend candidate.

If the candidate personally undertakes any part of the canvass, a special agent should always accompany him. This agent should either be a professional man or a man of high character, *who should never leave the candidate alone* whilst canvassing. The latter, if not his own election agent, should pay nothing, order nothing, and employ no one,

---

[1] Corrupt Practices Act, 1883, sec. 11.

except through the election agent, to whom every applicant should be referred. Looking at the severe penalties now imposed for even a trifling breach of the law, this precaution should never be omitted.

The candidate may pay any *personal expenses* incurred by him in connection with the election, not exceeding £100. He may, of course, incur further expenses on his personal account, if he chooses, but everything beyond the £100 must be paid by his election agent.[1]

<small>Personal expenses of candidate.</small>

A written statement of the *amount* of personal expenses paid by the candidate must also be sent to the election agent within 14 days after the declaration of the poll.[2]

<small>Statement of to be sent election agent.</small>

Personal expenses are defined to be the reasonable travelling expenses of a candidate and the reasonable expenses of his living at hotels or elsewhere for the purposes of and in relation to the election.[3] It may be added that they form no part of the election expenses proper, and are not to be reckoned as part of the expenses limited by the Corrupt Practices Act, 1883.[4]

<small>What are "personal" expenses.</small>

Subscriptions towards the expenses of the election may be received by the candidate, and it is open to argument whether he is bound, as the election agent is, to specify the sources from which they have come. No positive direction can, in the absence of judicial decisions, be given, but unless there is some very strong reason why the names of the individual subscribers should not be disclosed, it will be better that subscriptions should be sent to the election agent direct.

<small>Subscriptions to expenses of election.</small>

The expressions "candidate at an election" and "candidate" respectively, mean *unless the context otherwise requires,*

<small>Definition of candidate.</small>

1. Any person *elected* at such election.

<small>1 Corrupt Practices Act, 1883, sec. 31.   2 Ibid, sec. 29.
3 Corrupt Practices Act, 1883, sec. 64, and see Rogers on Elections, 13th edn., p. 324.
4 Corrupt Practices Act, 1883, Schedule 1, Part 4.</small>

2. Any person *nominated* as a candidate at an election.

3. Any person declared by himself, *or by others* to be a candidate *on* or *after* the issue of the writ, or after the dissolution or vacancy, in consequence of which the writ is issued.[1]

It will thus be seen that a man may be declared a candidate by other persons, and may be nominated and elected without taking any active part in the election. In such a case some person would have to name an Election Agent "on behalf" of such candidate,[2] and the person signing his nomination paper would, if he did not consent to be nominated, be liable for the Returning Officer's charges.[3]

Candidate may withdraw. A candidate may withdraw, or, if abroad, be withdrawn, by his proposer on a written notice to the Returning Officer during the time appointed for the election, *i.e.*, during the time appointed for the delivery of nomination papers, but not afterwards.[4]

Death of candidate before poll. If a candidate die between the nomination and the poll, the Returning Officer must countermand the poll, and the election must commence afresh, just as if he had *received the writ* on the day when the death of the candidate was duly *proved*, except that no fresh nominations are necessary for the candidates already nominated.[5]

There is no provision for the case of a candidate dying immediately before or during the time appointed for the election.

---

1 Corrupt Practices Act, 1883, sec. 63.
2 Ibid, sec. 24.
3 38 and 39 Vic., c. 84, sec. 2.
4 35 and 36 Vic., cap. 33, sec. 1.
5 Ibid.

THE ELECTION AGENT.

On or before the day of nomination a person shall be named by *or on behalf* of each Candidate as his Agent for such election.[1] *An election agent must be appointed.*

It will be observed that *each* candidate appoints *one* election agent only. Two or more candidates may appoint the same agent, or each may appoint a different person.[1]

A candidate may name *himself* as acting on his own behalf.[1] *Candidate may be.*

In either case the name and address of the election agent *or* of the candidate acting as his own election agent must be declared in writing to the Returning Officer *not later* than the day of nomination.[2] *Name and address to be given to returning officer.*

At the *same time* the address of an office, where claims, notices, &c., may be sent, and which must be within the County or Borough where the election is proceeding, or within any County of a City or Town adjoining, must be declared to the Returning Officer.[3] *Also address of office or place where claims, &c., may be sent.*

The following form may be used:— *Form.*

FORM No. 1.

.........................Parliamentary Election, 18 .

To   Esq., Returning Officer for the...................of.......................

I, ...of &c., ...being a Candidate at the above Election, do hereby nominate and declare that Mr.
of   is my Agent for such Election, and that the office or place to which all claims, notices, writs, summonses, and documents relating to such Election may be sent is at ....

Dated this   day of   18 .

N.B.—This notice must be given to the Returning Officer *not later* than the day of nomination.

---

1 Sec. 24, Corrupt Practices Act, 1883.   2 Ibid.   3 Sec. 26, Ibid.

Form, where candidate his own agent.
If the candidate names himself as his election agent the above form may be modified accordingly.

Duty of returning officer.
It is the duty of the Returning Officer to forthwith publish the names and addresses of the election agents, and of the situation of their offices or places where claims, &c., may be sent, and neither the candidate or his agent will incur any responsibility if he fails to do this.

Appointment of agent may be revoked,
The appointment of an election agent may be revoked at any time by the candidate, or if the candidate has declared himself to be his own agent, and from any cause desires to retire from that position he may do so, but in either case, or in case of the death of his agent, another agent must *forthwith* be appointed, and his name and address and the address of his office declared in writing as before. This new appointment must be made whether the vacancy has arisen before, during, or *after* the election, so long as anything remains to be done in reference to the election.[1]

Paid election agent cannot vote.
A *paid* election agent, if an elector of the County or Borough where the election is for, cannot vote.[2]

Who may not be an agent.
No person who has within seven years previously been found guilty of any corrupt practice by any competent legal tribunal, or been reported guilty of any corrupt practice by a Committee of the House of Commons, or by the report of an election judge or election inquiry commissioners, can be engaged as an *agent* for the management of an election or as a *canvasser*.[3]

Penalty of employing such.
If any person is engaged in such capacity by the candidate personally, with a knowledge of this disqualification, the election of the latter, if elected, is void.[3]

Agent's duty.
As a candidate may be seriously compromised by the acts of his agent, and the latter incur severe penalties by any breach of the law, the agent should take the greatest

---

1 Corrupt Practices Act, 1883, sec. 24.   2 Ibid., schedule 1, part 1.
3 31 & 32 Vict. c. 125, sec. 44.

care, on his employer's account as well as his own, that he engages in no *questionable* proceeding whatever. Agents are continually importuned by over zealous and not over prudent friends to do things which, if not absolutely illegal, approach very near to the border line. The agent's duty is firmly to refuse participation in advising or even listening to suggestions of the nature referred to. Agent's duty.

An agent should constantly bear in mind that *his* business is *superintendence*; he should personally do *no* work that can be done by others. He should accustom himself to a calm and quiet manner; should never be hurried with his work, however much he hurries others; and, above all, he should never allow himself to become excited during the progress of the contest.

It is his duty to organise the various committees and hire committee rooms; to appoint polling agents, clerks, and messengers; to draft all circulars and direct the preparation of all necessary books, papers, forms, &c.; to make all payments on account of the election; to daily examine the general returns of the canvass; to arrange for the candidate addressing meetings &c.; and generally to superintend the whole machinery of the election.

His place of business should be at the central committee rooms, where he should have a room to himself, with a special messenger at the door to take in the names of all who desire to see him. No person except members of the central committee should be allowed to enter this room without the agent's permission being first given. His place of business.

The election agent may in counties appoint *one* deputy election agent (in the Act called sub-agent) and no more, to act within *each polling district* in his county or division.[1] Sub agents in counties.

---

[1] Corrupt Practices Act, 1883, sec. 25.

Defaults of sub-agent. All acts, omissions, and defaults, by a sub-agent *in his district* will be deemed the acts, &c., of the election agent—except, of course, such as entail penal consequences upon the sub-agent personally.[1]

Name and address, &c., to be sent to returning officer. The name and address of every sub-agent, with the address of an office, or place, *within his district*, must be declared by the election agent to the Returning Officer one *clear* day, *i.e.* not later than the day but one, before the day of *polling*.[2]

This appointment is not revoked by the election agent ceasing to be such. It may, however, be revoked from time to time, in which case, notice of any new appointment must be *forthwith* given to the Returning Officer.[3]

Form. The appointments may be in the following form:—

Form No. 2.

Parliamentary Election, 18 .

To   Esq., Returning Officer
for the county of

I   of   being the
Election Agent of   Esq.,
a Candidate at the above Election, do hereby declare that the following persons have been appointed by me as my Deputy Election Agents to act respectively within the Polling District set opposite their respective names, and that the address of the office or place to which claims, notices, writs, summonses, and documents relating to such election within each district may be sent, is set opposite the name of such district.

Name of Polling District.	Name of Sub-Agent.	Address of Sub-Agent.	Address of Office or Place where Claims and Notices may be sent.

Dated   day of   , 18
                                    Election Agent.

N.B.—This List must be delivered to the Returning Officer not later than the day *but one* before the day of poll.

---

1 Corrupt Practices Act, 1883, sec. 25.   2 Ibid.   3 Ibid.

It need scarcely be said that the utmost care must be exercised in the choice of Sub-Agents, as almost any illegal act on the part of a Sub-Agent will void the election. If it is possible to secure the services of professional men in such a capacity, it will be most desirable to do so. It is feared, however, that the limited amount which can now be expended in election expenses will, in many cases, prevent this being done, as it will be impossible to pay them adequate fees, but in other cases, men may be found who will either give their services or accept a nominal fee merely. *Care in the selection of sub-agents.*

A sub-agent, if paid, cannot vote. *Sub-agent, if paid, cannot vote.*

As it is almost impossible under the stringent rules laid down by the Corrupt Practices Act 1883, for an election to be conducted without some infringement of the law for which an application to the High Court of Justice, under the 23rd section of the Act, will be necessary, the election agent and sub-agents in their respective districts, should take "all reasonable means for preventing the commission of corrupt and illegal practices" in the full spirit of the 22nd section of that Act. *Agents to take every means to prevent corrupt practices.*

To this end the election agent and sub-agents should *immediately after their appointment* print and publish in the newspapers of their districts, or otherwise, a notice to the following effect:— *Notice in Newspapers, &c.*

FORM No. 3. Form.

..............................Parliamentary Election, 188 .
I, the undersigned, being the appointed Election Agent (or *sub-Election Agent*) for .... Esq., a Candidate at the above Election, hereby give notice that in view of the provisions of the Corrupt and Illegal Practices Act, 1883, the said Candidate will not be answerable or accountable for any payment for goods supplied, services rendered, or expenses incurred by any person acting or claiming to act on his behalf, unless such purchase, service, or expense has been previously authorized in writing under my hand.

Signed..
Of..
Dated...........................188 .

A notice to the same effect should also be printed on every "order" form sent out, as hereafter mentioned, and should be posted up in each committee room.

Notice on "order" forms, and in committee rooms.

It should be clearly borne in mind that every penny of expenditure, except the candidate's "personal" expenses, must be under the entire control of the election agent, who will be responsible that the maximum amount allowed by law is not exceeded.

Expenditure to be under absolute control of election agent.

If a candidate or election agent of a candidate (including sub-agents in counties) causes any bill, poster, or placard, having reference to the election, to be printed, published, or posted, without the name and address of the printer and publisher on the face of it, he will be guilty of an illegal practice. The printer and publisher will be liable to a fine of £100.[1]

Name and address of printer to be on all placards.

The election agent should therefore require a "proof" of every bill, poster, and placard to be sent to him before it is published or posted, and should carefully see that this provision of the law is complied with. It would also be a prudent thing to do, to serve a notice on every printer employed requiring him to place his name and address on every bill, &c., ordered, and warning him of the penalties of a breach of the law.

Agent to examine same.

The further duties of the election agent and sub-agents in reference to the expenses of the election; the employment of clerks, polling agents, and messengers; the hire of committee and other rooms, &c.; will be detailed under the various heads which follow.

---

1 Corrupt Practices Act, 1883, sec. 18.

ELECTION EXPENSES.

Part I.—APPORTIONMENT.

One of the most difficult matters with which the Election Agent will have to deal will be the apportionment of the *maximum* sum allowed by law for the expenses of the election, under the different heads of expenditure necessary to the carrying of it on. [Apportionment of sum allowed for.]

Much *gratuitous* aid can, in many cases, be obtained, and this should be earnestly asked for from trustworthy friends, not only because the expenses of the election generally will be thus kept down, but because the election agent will be enabled to spend more on other matters connected with the election, especially in the event of something unforeseen happening which requires it. [Gratuitous aid to be sought.]

The apportionment should be made, if possible, *prior* to the *commencement* of the election, and a record of it kept for use at any moment. After an election has taken place, the actual cost of it should be apportioned in the same manner, and a record kept for future reference. [Apportionment to be made prior to election.]

The first step, therefore, to be taken by the agent is to ascertain what sum can be legally spent in the election. [Amount which can be legally spent.]

This amount is limited by Part 4 of Schedule 1 of the Corrupt Practices Prevention Act, 1883, and is as follows:—

If the number of Electors on the *Register*	The *maximum* amount allowed shall be	In a Borough.
Does not exceed 2000	£350	
Exceeds 2000	£380	
	And an *additional* £30 for every *complete* 1000 electors above 2000.	

In Ireland—

If the number of Electors on the Register	The *maximum* amount shall be
Does not exceed 500	£200
Exceeds 500 but does not exceed 1000	£250
Exceeds 1000 but does not exceed 1500	£275

<small>In a County.</small>

If the number of Electors on the Register	The *maximum* amount shall be
Does not exceed 2000	£650 in England and Scotland. £500 in Ireland.
Exceeds 2000	£710 in England and Scotland. £540 in Ireland. And an *additional* £60 in England and Scotland, and £40 in Ireland for every *complete* 1000 Electors above 2000.

<small>What sum covers.</small>

This maximum sum is to cover the *whole* cost of the election, *except* the Candidate's "personal" expenses, *and* the charges of the Returning Officer, which latter are regulated by the 38 and 39 Vic., c. 84, and are not to be reckoned in the above sums.

<small>Excepted Boroughs.</small>

In the case of the boroughs of East Retford, Shoreham, Cricklade, Much Wenlock and Aylesbury, the provisions of Parts 2, 3 and 4 of the First Schedule of the Corrupt Practices Act 1883, are to apply as if each of such boroughs was a county.

<small>Joint Candidates.</small>

Where there are two *joint* candidates, the maximum amount of expenses allowed shall, for *each* candidate, be reduced by *one-fourth*; if there are more than two joint candidates, by *one-third*. It may thus be advisable, where other considerations are equal, to run two candidates instead of one, so as to get the benefit of ample funds for more thorough organization, and especially may this be the case if the other side will gain any advantage by having two candidates.

If one candidate may expend £1,000, two joint candidates may expend £1,500. This may be of material importance in securing the success of the first candidate, where, even, there is but a faint chance of carrying the second.

For the purposes of limiting and regulating the *expenses* of the election, candidates shall be deemed joint candidates. *(Who are to be deemed joint Candidates.)*

1.—Where *the same election agent* is appointed by them or on their behalf;
2.—Where they, by themselves, or any agent or agents, *hire or use the same committee-rooms;*
3.—Or, employ or use the services of the *same sub-agents, clerks, messengers, or polling agents;*
4.—Or, publish a *joint address* or *joint circular* or *notice* at the election.[1]

It is provided, however, that if the employment and use of the same committee-room, sub-agent, clerk, messenger, or polling agent, is accidental or casual, or of a trivial and unimportant character, they are not to be deemed of themselves to constitute persons joint candidates.[1]

A candidate may, of course, come out as an independent candidate, and may, at any time during the election, become a joint candidate with another or others, and in like manner he may, if a joint candidate, cease to be such and act independently. In either of these cases, if the maximum sum allowed as expenses for one of two or more joint candidates be exceeded, by reason of his becoming or ceasing to be a joint candidate, then such an excess shall not be considered an illegal practice, as it otherwise would be, provided such excess is not more than under the circumstances is reasonable, and the *total* expenses of such candidate do *not exceed* the maximum amount allowed for *a separate* candidate. The allowance of such excess by the High Court or Election Court, as hereafter mentioned, will, however, have to be obtained.[1] *(Candidates may become or cease to be joint Candidates.)*

---

[1] Corrupt Practices Act, 1883, schedule 1, part 5.

The agent having ascertained the maximum amount which can be legally spent in the election, the next thing is to apportion it to the different departments in their order of importance. If a copy of the accounts of a previous election in the same county or borough can be obtained, much valuable assistance may be derived in compiling this estimate of expenses, though in most cases the sums which have hitherto been expended will have to be considerably reduced.

The items of expenditure will generally fall under the following heads:—

  Agent's and sub-agent's fees.
  Clerk's and messenger's wages.
  Polling agent's fees.

The above are the *only* persons who can be *legally* employed for *payment*.

  Printing and stationery.
  Bill posting.
  Advertising.
  Postage and Telegrams.
  Hire of committee-rooms.
  Expenses of public meetings.
  Miscellaneous.

From the widely differing character of the constituencies, the compactness or otherwise of the constituency, the uncertain duration of the contest, the amount of voluntary and gratuitous help obtainable, and the circumstances of joint-candidatures, &c., it is impossible to lay down any rule as to the amount which is absolutely necessary in each case.

Fee to election agents. The fee to be paid to the election agent, and in counties to the sub-agents, should be settled, if possible at the beginning of the election, either at a certain fixed sum or on the basis of a certain sum per day or week during the election, inasmuch as the sum to be paid will not only have to be taken into account in apportioning the expenses of the election, but *so far as circumstances admit*, these claims for remuneration will have to be sent in to the Returning Officer in like manner as other claims and payments.[1]

It is difficult to say what is the precise meaning of the words above italicised, but probably they mean that the election agent's claim is to include only such charges as are properly chargeable against the election fund for conducting the election up to the date of the return, and do not include charges for work which may be required to be done subsequently, and was unforeseen when the return was made, Ex. gr: many of the claims sent in to the Candidate or Election Agent may be disputed, and the latter may have much trouble in investigating them, or getting them allowed or rejected, and, for the time and labour *bonâ fide* expended, it is assumed the agent can afterwards legally charge, and these charges will not be " on account of or in respect of the conduct or management of the *Election*."

The amount of the fee should also depend upon the election agent (including sub-agents in counties) confining the expenditure within the legal limits. If the expenditure exceeds the maximum sum allowed by the Act, the agent's fee should be reduced accordingly. The experience derived from the Borough Elections which have taken place since the Act came into force shows that this *can* be done; and as the agent has the entire control of the expenditure, it will not be difficult for him to prevent any excess.

---

[1] Corrupt Practices Act, 1883, sec. 32.

In Counties sub-agent may act for *two or more* districts.	A sub-agent need not be appointed for every polling district of a county or division. The same agent may act for *two* or more polling districts, but he should be *separately appointed* for each, and his address in each polling district given.
WAGES to clerks and messengers.	The number of clerks and messengers who can be retained for *payment* is limited by the Corrupt Practices Act, 1883.
If *paid*, cannot vote.	They may be voters or non-voters, but the former *cannot* vote, and on this account should not be employed, if it can be avoided.
Unpaid clerks and messengers	Much gratuitous assistance may frequently, however, be obtained from zealous friends and their sons, clerks, &c., who will gladly give their assistance for a few hours in the evening, when their services can generally be made available. A list of these volunteers, with their addresses, should be prepared, so that they may be sent for on an emergency. The list should also be headed with a declaration of the persons named in it to give their services gratuitously, and should be signed by each.

The following form may be used:—

FORM No. 4.

..........................Parliamentary Election, 18......

Messrs. SMITH and JONES.

List.	List of Volunteer Clerks (or *Messengers*).

We, the undersigned, do hereby respectively place our services at the disposal of Mr.........................., the election agent of the above candidate, as clerks (*or messengers*), without payment or promise of payment of any kind.

Name.	Address.	Signature.	Date.

There is, of course, no limit to the number of clerks or ^{Can vote.} messengers who can thus be employed, and they can, if voters, vote at the election.

The number of *paid* clerks and messengers allowed by ^{Number of paid clerks and messengers allowed.} the statute are as follows:—

IN BOROUGHS.

Where 500 electors and *under*	1 clerk, 1 messenger.
Above 500, and not exceeding 1,000	2 clerks, 2 messengers.
Above 1,000, and not exceeding 1,500	3 clerks, 3 messengers.
Above 1,500, and not exceeding 2,000	4 clerks, 4 messengers.

And so on, one clerk and one messenger being allowed for every *complete* 500 electors, and for any *remaining* electors over and above the last complete 500.

IN COUNTIES.

For the *Central* Committee Room	1 clerk, 1 messenger.
Where *above* 5,000 electors	2 clerks, 2 messengers.
Where *above* 10,000 electors	3 clerks, 3 messengers.
Where *above* 15,000 electors	4 clerks, 4 messengers.

And so on, one clerk and one messenger being allowed for every *complete* 5,000 electors, and for any *remaining* electors above the last complete 5,000.

For *each Polling* District.

The *same number* of clerks and messengers as if the polling district was an *independent borough.*

The boroughs of East Retford, Shoreham, Cricklade, Much Wenlock, and Aylesbury are to be treated as if each borough was a county.

It is to be observed that no provision is made for a *Central* Committee Room in *boroughs,* and consequently for clerks and messengers to serve therein. Probably, however, ^{May be used in any part of borough.} the number allowed will permit of a Central Committee Room, with clerks and messengers being provided; but if any difficulty arises the Committee Room of the most central ward can be used for the purpose.

In counties it is expressly provided that the clerks and ^{Or county.} messengers allowed for the *whole* county may be employed in *any* polling district where their services may be required.[1]

List of paid clerks and messengers.

A list of the *paid* clerks and messengers should be prepared, and may be in the following form:—

FORM No. 5.

.... Parliamentary Election, 188...

Messrs. SMITH and JONES.

List of *Paid* Clerks (*or Messengers*).

We, the undersigned, do hereby acknowledge that we have been engaged by Mr............................, election agent for the above candidates, to act under his instructions for the remuneration set opposite our respective names; that our appointment will cease and determine at the close of the poll, unless sooner determined by [*one*] day's notice; and that we are to provide our own refreshments and to make no charge for any overtime, unless engaged after 11 p.m. or before 7 a.m., when such overtime is to be paid for at double the rate per day.

Name.	Address.	Amount per day.	Date Engaged.	Signature.

Each clerk and messenger should sign his name to the sheet in the presence of the election agent (or sub-agent), who is the only person legally entitled to employ him, and who should place his initials opposite each signature, as evidence of his assent to the employment.

No further appointment will then be necessary.

Election agents' and Law Stationers' clerks.

It is submitted that the election agent may employ his own regular staff of clerks to assist him in matters connected with the election, but the remuneration to these persons must be included in his fee and not charged to the

[1] C. P. Act, 1883, schedule 1, part 1, sub-sec. 6.

candidate. Such clerks, however, should not be placed in charge of ward or district committee-rooms, and must not be engaged specially for the election. Upon the same principle a law stationer may be employed to address envelopes, send out circulars, prepare canvass books, and generally to do copying work usually done in his business; and in many cases this course will be cheaper and speedier than employing clerks. His clerks will not be considered "clerks" within the Act of Parliament, which seems to apply to clerks in charge of committee-rooms, and specially engaged for the election on behalf of the *candidate*. His bill will not, of course, be for the services of specified clerks, but for so much work done by him. These clerks, May vote. if voters, will not be debarred from voting.

The paid clerks may be used in any part of the borough May be used in any part of borough or district. or district, and may, therefore, be first employed in the central committee-room to send out the candidates' addresses, and prepare the canvass books and other papers, and then drafted off to the ward or district committee-rooms, as required.

The number of polling agents is limited to *one* for each Fees to polling agents. polling station.[1] It will be seen under the head of "Polling Agents" what are the duties of the office, and Duties of office. what sort of men should be selected to perform them. Much *gratuitous* aid may be obtained from zealous friends, Gratuitous aid. as their duties are limited to the day of election only. The election agent must, however, arrange his list of polling agents as early as possible, as the fees to those requiring to be paid must be taken into account in estimating the expenditure.

The usual fee, where the agent resides near to the Usual fee. polling station, is half a guinea. A *paid* agent cannot Paid agent cannot vote. vote.[1]

---

[1] C. P. Act, 1883, schedule 1, part 1.

Expenses of Printing and Stationery.

The expense of printing is one of the most important items in the cost of an election, and, unless kept down by care and forethought and unceasing control, may upset all the calculations of the election agent, and land him in the serious position of having spent most of the sum allowed for the election long before the day of poll.

It should be a cardinal maxim with the election agent—1st, to dispense with as much printing as possible; and, 2nd, to limit that which must be done to what is absolutely necessary. As many of the forms used in elections are only required in small quantities, it is better to procure these ready printed; or where one or two only are required to copy them out on foolscap paper. A glance at the list of forms will show these, and the election agent can generally obtain them, by a return of post, at a less cost than any single form can be procured in the ordinary way. Of course, if a great number of forms are necessary, it will be cheaper to have them printed with the headings, &c., inserted.

Arrangements with other side as to placards and advertisements.

In many cases arrangements may be come to with the other side for only a limited number of candidates' addresses, placards, &c., being used, and that they should not be interfered with when posted. A similar arrangement might also be made with reference to the length and number of advertisements.

Number required.

The first question will be as to the *number* of forms, placards, handbills, &c., which will be required, and these will, of course, vary according to the numbers of the constituency and the extent of the borough or district. A few more than is necessary at first should be ordered, as some will require replacing from time to time.

Tenders.

In every case a tender should be obtained, and, if there

is time, from more than one person. It is an exceedingly good plan to obtain tenders from time to time, somewhat in the following form, the same to be in force for a year from date:—

FORM No. 6.

I, the undersigned, hereby offer to supply the various printed matter, hereinafter mentioned, at the prices quoted, and with all reasonable and prompt despatch. Quantities to be not less than one-half those mentioned, and quotations to be in force for 12 months from the date hereof. The amount of printing on each document not to be strictly limited to that on the specimens, but to be within reasonable limits of the same.

No. of Specimen.	Description of Document.	No likely to be required.	Size.	Price. £ s. d.	
1	Headed Note Paper	1 ream	8vo.		per ream
2	Candidate's Address	500	3 Sheet Double Demy		per 100
3	Do. do. (small)	10,000	Demy 8vo.		per 1000
4	Do. Meetings	300	Double Demy		per 100

And so on.

Night work ... ... per cent. extra.

Coloured ink or paper ... do. do.

Dated this 1884.

Signed,

The following is a list of prices for the ordinary requirements of an election, and it may serve as a guide to an agent in making his contracts. They have been based upon estimates supplied by several firms, and include a fair and even liberal profit to the Printer :—

PRICES FOR ORDINARY HANDBILLS, PLACARDS, AND POSTERS.

Quantity.	Demy 8vo. 8½ × 5½ in.	Demy Folio 17¼ × 11¼ in.	Demy 17¼ × 22¼ in.	Dble. Demy 35¼ × 22¼ in.	8-sheet Dble. Demy 67¼ × 35¼ in.
100	3 6	10 6	17 6	27/-	80/-
250	5/-	16 -	25 -	35 -	100/-
500	8 -	22 -	32 -	63/-	180/-
1000	12/-	30 -	50/-	95 -	—
5000	32 6				
10,000	50 -				
20,000	80/-				
Every additional 100		25 -	45 -	80 -	—

Red Ink   (Say) 30 per cent. extra.
Other Colours   ,, 10 ,, ,,
Coloured Paper   ,, 10 ,, ,,
Night Work   ,, 50 ,, ,,

The cost of composition in the case of Election Addresses and other Placards requiring a larger amount of type would be additional.

Bill posting.   It is an *illegal* practice to *pay* or *contract* to pay an elector for the *exhibition* of any address, bill, or notice relating to the election, unless it is the ordinary business of the elector to exhibit bills, &c., for payment, and such payment or contract is made in the ordinary course of his business.[1]

Free of charge.   In most cases, except in large towns where hoardings have a certain value, and are usually hired by bill posters, whose ordinary business it is to let out spaces for hire, the election agent will have little difficulty in procuring per-

[1] Corrupt Practices Act, 1883, sec. 7.

mission to have the election addresses, bills, and notices posted on fences and the walls of barns, stables, outhouses, &c., without charge. Most innkeepers and beersellers will also permit bills to be exhibited in their houses or in the windows in like manner; and the election agent will, of course, take care that they are plentifully exhibited in the windows and about the doors of committee rooms, party clubs, &c. If, however, there is a lack of suitable places, rough boards may be nailed together and the addresses, &c., posted upon them, and permission sought to exhibit them in gardens or other enclosed spaces of friends.

A list of the places where they can be thus exhibited gratuitously should be made as early as possible, and a copy given to the bill poster. List to be made.

A notice should also be placed on every posting station, of which the use is specially granted, to the following effect:—

FORM No. 7.

Notice is hereby given that this posting station is *private property*, and any person posting bills, or tearing down, defacing, or otherwise injuring bills posted thereon without my permission first obtained, will be prosecuted according to law.

Dated this   day of   188 .

....

Election Agent for &c.

Similar arrangements should be made for each polling district of a county. In counties.

Payment will, of course, have to be made for advertising, but it can only be made under the same conditions applying to bill posting, *i.e.*, payments and contracts can only be legally made to and with electors whose *ordinary business* it is to receive advertisements for payment.[1] Advertising.

1 Corrupt Practices Act, 1883, sec. 7, sub-sec. 3.

The advertisements necessary for the election campaign should be carefully considered beforehand, and the charges for the same arranged.

The following form may be useful to the election agent in settling the expenditure under this head:—

FORM No. 8.

Name of Newspaper.	Description of Advertisement.	Number of Insertions.				No. of Lines (about).	Cost (about).		
		1st week.	2nd.	3rd.	4th.		£	s.	d.
	Candidates' addresses.								
	List of committees.								
	List of committee rooms.								
	Notice by Election Agent.								
	Notices of public meetings.								
	Notices to voters removed.								

In counties

In counties a similar estimate must be obtained for each district.

Postages and telegrams.

In cases where the candidates' addresses, circulars, &c., are sent by post, they may be sent under cover of a halfpenny wrapper, but in cases where a circular is enclosed, which the voter is requested to return, the latter must bear a *penny* stamp.

Telegrams are an expensive mode of communication, and should never be resorted to except for matters of great urgency. Post cards can, in many instances, be safely used.

In a borough constituency of nearly 11,500 electors the cost of postage was £82 10s., or less than 2d. per head. The election lasted three weeks, and the candidate's address and the voting cards were sent by post, but no return circulars were enclosed. In another borough, with nearly 8,000 electors on the register, the cost was about 1½d. per head.

The arrangements for committee rooms should be made *as soon as possible*, and a list of them made. _{Hire of Committee Rooms.}

In places where there are no ward or district associations, or permanent political clubs, the local committee should be directed to seek out a suitable room, or rooms, and these should be as near to the polling stations as they can be got. _{To be near polling stations.}

Very often friends will lend an unoccupied room, or house, and others will provide some rough furniture, or the room can be hired and the furniture lent, or *vice versa*, and in either case a saving will be effected. If neither can be done then the election agent will have no alternative but to hire both.

There is no limit put to the number of committee rooms which may be used *gratuitously*, but no *payment* can be made or *expenses* incurred. _{No limit to use of committee rooms lent gratuitously.}

IN A BOROUGH:—

For more than *one* committee room, unless the number of electors on the Register exceeds 500, and then the same number of committee rooms are allowed as paid clerks. _{Number allowed to be hired for payment.}

IN A COUNTY:—

For *more than one central* committee room and *one* committee room for every clerk legally employed for payment in each polling district,

No committee room *whatever* must be on premises: _{Where committee rooms must *not* be used.}

1. Where the sale of *intoxicating liquor* is authorized by a license, whether wholesale or retail, or for consumption on or off the premises.[1]
2. Where *intoxicating liquor* is sold or supplied to members of a club, society, or association, other than a permanent political club.

1 C. P. Act, 1883, sec 20.

3. Where *refreshment* of any kind, whether *food* or *drink*, is *ordinarily* sold for consumption *on* the premises,[1] or

4. Within any public elementary school in receipt of an annual Parliamentary grant.

Objects of Act.

The object of the first three sub-sections is to prevent treating, and of the last to prevent Church and other schools under the Education Act being used for party purposes. If a school is a private venture school, or an endowed, or other school not receiving the annual Parliamentary grant, it may be used as a committee room, and either paid for or not, as can be arranged.

What are "premises."

It will be noticed that no committee room can be used on the "*premises*" of any of these establishments. A proviso to the above section, however, permits any part of such premises which is *ordinarily* let for the purpose of chambers, or offices, or the holding of public meetings, or of arbitrations, to be used, if such part has a *separate* entrance and no *direct communication* with *any part of the premises* on which intoxicating liquor or refreshment is sold or supplied.[1]

It will thus be seen that not only are rooms at inns, beerhouses, and refreshment houses (including eating houses) prohibited from being used as committee rooms, but chambers and offices are prohibited if access to them is through or over any part of the premises mentioned in the sub-section. An assembly room, therefore, to an hotel could not be used if access was through the yard of the hotel and the entrance to the room was direct from the yard.

Permanent political clubs.

A "permanent" political club is a club not originated for the purpose of the particular election, but a club founded with the *bonâ fide* object of being continued for

[1] C. P. Act, 1883, sec. 20.

an indefinite period. If such a club meets, however, at an hotel, or other place where food or drink is sold, its rooms cannot be used as committee rooms.

The expression "committee room" does not include any house or room occupied by a candidate at an election *as a dwelling*, by reason only of the *candidate* there transacting business with his *agents* in relation to such election.[1] Thus a candidate staying at an hotel may see and transact business with his agents in his rooms there, but he must be careful not to see electors generally, or to allow any other election business to be transacted there. *What meant by "committee room."*

No room or building is to be deemed a committee room within the Act by reason only of the *candidate* or any *agent* of the candidate addressing therein electors, committeemen, or others.[1] Thus, public and other meetings to address the electors, meetings of committeemen to receive instructions from the candidate or election agent may be held and deputations of electors and non-electors may be received in hotels, clubs, &c.; but as there is much danger of thoughtless acts being done in such places, by persons who may compromise the candidate, it is much better to have all meetings of committeemen and receptions of deputations at the central committee room. Where it is possible, even public meetings should not be held on licensed premises.

A committee "room" does not necessarily mean a single room, but if more than one room is used they ought to be adjoining rooms, and *must* be in the same house or building.

Every committee room *hired* on behalf of the candidate must be so hired by the election agent, personally, in boroughs; and by the election agent or sub-agents, personally, in counties. The agreements for hire should, in *Must be hired by election agent or sub-agent.*

---

[1] C. P. Act, 1883, sec. 64.

Agreements should be in writing.

every case, be in writing, and should include all charges for fires, lighting, cleaning, attendance, &c., so that the agent will know the precise amount he will have to pay, and not have his calculations upset by claims being made upon him for matters he had not anticipated.

The following form may be used :—

FORM No. 9.
AGREEMENT FOR HIRE OF COMMITTEE ROOM.
..........................Parliamentary Election, 188...

I   being Election Agent (or Sub-Agent) for a Candidate at the above election, do hereby agree to hire, and I   of   do hereby agree to let, in consideration of the sum of   paid to me the said   the premises at   to be used, until the close of the poll, as a committee room for the said Candidate at the above election.

The above sum includes the cost of fire, lighting, and cleaning, and all other charges.

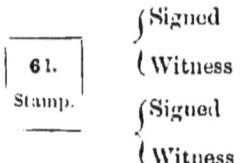

{ Signed
{ Witness

6d. Stamp.

{ Signed
{ Witness

In cases where a committee room is held in a permenent political club it ought to be clearly and distinctly understood that the room or rooms, to be used are, during the election, to be under the exclusive control of the election agent, and that, under no circumstances whatever, is food or drink to be introduced therein. If the authorities of the club grant the free use of the room it ought to be by a formal resolution at a meeting duly convened, a copy of which resolution should be sent to the election agent, and acknowledged by him, subject to the above named conditions.

If payment is to be made to the club either for the use of the room, or for fire, lighting, &c., such payment should be unexceptionally reasonable in amount, and such as might be fairly made to any person for similar accommodation. It would be prudent also to have such agreement in writing, and the following form may be used or adapted as circumstances require:—

FORM No. 10.

..........................Parliamentary Election, 188...

AGREEMENT FOR COMMITTEE ROOMS IN CLUBS.

I   the Election Agent (or Sub-Agent) for Mr.   a Candidate at the present election, do hereby agree to hire a room within the   Club in   the description and position of such room is known and described as   the said room to be used as a committee room for the said Candidate at this election until the close of the poll. And I   acting on behalf of the Committee of the Club, do hereby agree to let the above-mentioned room for the time stated, in consideration of the payment of the sum of   this amount includes every charge for coal, gas, water, and cleaning; and the said   and his agents and committee shall have the entire use and control of the said room; and the members of the Club shall not in any way interfere with the use thereof.

As witness the hands of the parties, this   day of   188

Name of Witness

    Signed

              Election Agent.

    Signed

         On behalf of the Committee
     of the   Club.

The number of public meetings which it is thought desirable to hold should be carefully considered, and, as far as possible, arrangements made as to where they are to be held. They may be held *anywhere*, but where they are held on licensed premises a notice to the following effect should be given to the landlord:— Expenses of public meetings.

Form No. 11.

..........................Parliamentary Election, 188...

NOTICE TO LICENSED VICTUALLERS.

(When Licensed Premises are used for Public Meetings.)

I, the undersigned, being the Election Agent, for a Candidate at the above election, hereby give you notice that the said Candidate will not be answerable or accountable to you for the cost of any meat, drink, entertainment or provision supplied by you to any person acting, or claiming, or pretending to act, on behalf of the said Candidate in connection with the said election, nor for any expense other than the sum agreed upon (viz., £ : :) for the hire of the room used by the said Candidate for the purpose of addressing a public meeting of the electors at your house.

Dated 188
                Signed
To Mr.

The following provisions of the new Elections Act apply to offences committed in regard to licensed houses:—

TREATING.

Sec. 1. Whereas under section four of the Corrupt Practices Act, 1854, persons other than candidates at Parliamentary elections are not liable to any punishment for treating, and it is expedient to make such persons liable; be it therefore enacted in substitution for the said section four as follows:—

(1.) Any person who corruptly by himself or by any other person, either before, during, or after an election, directly or indirectly *gives or provides*, or pays wholly or in part the expense of giving or providing, any meat, *drink*, entertainment, or provision to or for any person, for the purpose of corruptly influencing that person or any other person to give or refrain from giving his vote at the election, or on account of such person or any other person having voted or refrained from voting, or being about to vote or refrain from voting at such election, shall be guilty of *treating*.

(2) And every elector who corruptly accepts or takes any such meat, *drink*, entertainment, or provision shall also be guilty of *treating*.

COMMITTEE ROOMS.

Sec. 20 (*a*.) Any premises on which the sale by wholesale or retail of any intoxicating liquor is authorised by a license (whether the license be for consumption on or off the premises), or (*b.*) Any premises where any intoxicating liquor is sold, or is supplied to members of a club, society, or association other than a permanent political club, or

(*c.*) Any premises whereon refreshment of any kind, whether food or drink, is ordinarily sold for consumption on the premises, shall not be used as a *committee room* for the purpose of promoting or procuring the election of a candidate at an election, and if any person hires or uses any such premises or any part thereof for a committee room he shall be guilty of *illegal hiring*, and the person *letting* such premises, or part, if he knew it was intended to use the same as a committee room, shall also be guilty of *illegal hiring*.

Sec. 21. (1.) A person guilty of an offence of illegal payment, employing *or hiring* shall, on summary conviction, be liable to a fine not exceeding one hundred pounds.

OFFENCES BY HOLDERS OF LICENSES.

Sec. 38. With respect to a person holding a license or certificate under the Licensing Acts (in this section referred to as a licensed person) the following provision shall have effect:—

(*a.*) If it appears to the court by which any licensed person is convicted of the offence of bribery or treating that such offence was committed on his licensed premises, the court shall direct such conviction to be entered in the proper register of licenses.

(*b.*) If it appears to an election court or election commissioners that a licensed person has knowingly suffered any *bribery* or *treating* in reference to any election to take place upon his licensed premises, such court or commissioners (subject to the provisions of this Act as to a person having an opportunity of being heard by himself and producing evidence before being reported) shall report the same; and whether such person obtained a certificate of indemnity or not it shall be the duty of the Director of Public Prosecutions to bring such report before the licensing justices from whom or on whose certificate the licensed person obtained his license, and such licensing justices shall cause such report to be entered in the proper register of licenses.

(*c.*) Where an entry is made in the register of licenses of any such conviction of, or report respecting, any licensed person as above in this section mentioned, it shall be taken into consideration by the licensing justices in determining whether they will or will not grant to such person the renewal of his license or certificate, and may be a ground, if the justices think fit, for refusing such renewal.

D

(9.) Where the evidence showing any corrupt practice to have been committed by *any licensed person* is given before election commissioners, those commissioners shall report the case to the Director of Public Prosecutions, with such information as is necessary or proper for enabling him to act under this section.

(10.) This section shall apply to an election court under this Act, or under Part IV. of the *Municipal Corporations Act*, 1882, and the expression " election" shall be construed accordingly.

If payment is to be made for the use of the room, the sum to be paid should be agreed on beforehand.

MISCELLANEOUS payments.

The sum limited for miscellaneous matters is £200 for every constituency, whatever the size of it may be, unless there are joint candidates, when this sum is proportionately increased. In small constituencies the allowance is a large one, but in large constituencies, like those of the Metropolitan Boroughs, it is a very small sum indeed. It is intended to cover small charges, such as travelling expenses, cab hire, parcels, &c. Refreshments to clerks and others, *bona fide* engaged in carrying on the election, are not prohibited[1] and might be paid out of this sum, but as the providing of such might lead to abuse, it will be better to pay a slightly increased rate of wages, and allow the clerks to provide their own refreshments.

Refreshments.

Election Expenses Book.

Having arrived at the amounts to be approximately allowed under each head of expenditure, the election agent should prepare a book ruled and headed, as follows:—

---

[1] Westminster, 1 O. and H. Case, 91. Bradford Case, *Ibid*, 39.

Form No. 12.

............Parliamentary Election, 18......

MESSRS. SMITH AND JONES.

ELECTION EXPENSES BOOK.

Date.	Name of Creditor.	Clerks' and Messengers' Wages.	Printing and Stationery.	Bill Posting.	Advertising.	Postage and Telegrams.	Hire, &c., of Committee Rooms.	Expenses of Public Meetings.	Miscellaneous.

At the top of the first page, the election agent should enter, under the various heads, the sums he has apportioned to each, and then rule a broad line underneath the entries.

An invoice of everything ordered by him should *invariably* be delivered with the goods, or rendered once or twice a week, and the charges therein entered into the expenses book *daily*. These expenses should also be added up in pencil and carefully scrutinized by the election agent, *personally*, every day. He will, of course, compare them with the apportioned amounts, to see that he is keeping within the expenditure. It may be he will find he has allowed too much under one head and too little under another, but as all the items except that of " miscellaneous " are discretionary and interchangeable, he can regulate his outlay accordingly.

To be entered up daily.

A similar account must, in counties, be provided for the central committee room *and* for each polling district.

In counties.

It will be seen that the above account only contains the *growing* expenditure, which it is necessary the election agent, and sub-agents in counties, should keep constantly under supervision. The agents, sub-agents, and polling agents' fees will generally be *fixed* sums and must, of course, be taken into account in apportioning the maximum amount allowed for election expenses, but beyond this, they need not be entered in the expenses book. A margin of (say) 5 per cent. should also be allowed for unforeseen items.

A margin for unforeseen expenses.

A cash book must, of course, be kept, in which all *payments* should be entered as made, and these should be totalled up each night, and any item not entered in the expenses book, must be entered therein.

Cash book.

All orders, whether for goods, for the insertion of advertisements, or for any other disbursements, should

All orders to be in writing.

be in writing and signed by the election agent or sub-agent.

The following form may be used:—

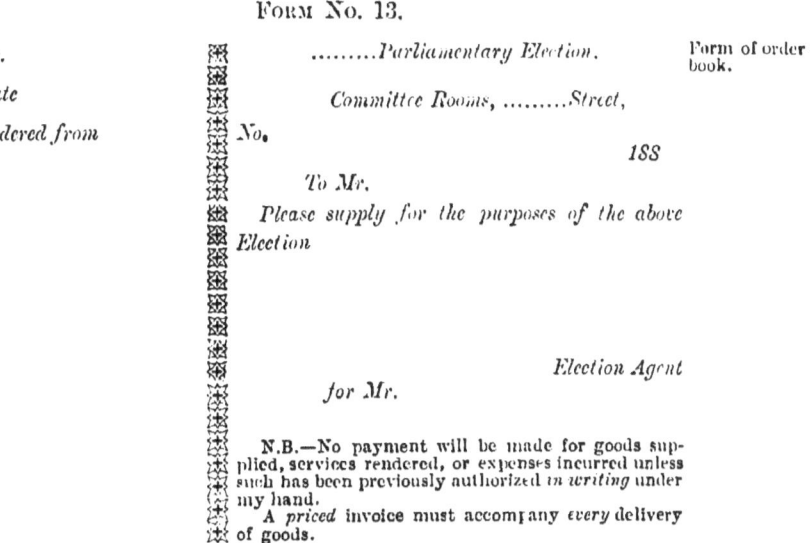

FORM No. 13.

No.
Date
Ordered from

..........Parliamentary Election.

Committee Rooms, ...Street,

No.

188

To Mr.

Please supply for the purposes of the above Election

for Mr.

Election Agent

Form of order book.

N.B.—No payment will be made for goods supplied, services rendered, or expenses incurred unless such has been previously authorized *in writing* under my hand.

A *priced* invoice must accompany *every* delivery of goods.

The order book should be compared *daily* with the expenses book, to see what orders have been completed, and that proper prices have been charged. The uncompleted orders and contracts should also be taken into the account of expenditure from day to day, but not entered in the expenses book until completed. *Election expenses book to be checked by order book.*

The election agent may authorize any person to pay any necessary expenses for stationery, postage, telegrams, and other petty expenses to a *total amount* not exceeding that *named* in the authority, but *any excess* above the amount so named, must be paid by the election agent. This authority *must* be in *writing*, and it need scarcely be mentioned that the greatest care must be taken that it is only granted to thoroughly reliable and trustworthy persons.[1] *Election agent may give authority for payment of petty expenses.*

[1] C. P. Act, 1883, sec. 31.

The following form may be used:—

FORM No. 14.

..................Parliamentary Election, 188......

AUTHORITY FOR PETTY DISBURSEMENTS.

Form.   I, the undersigned, being Election Agent for
a Candidate at the above Election, do hereby authorize Mr.
                        of   to incur and
pay any necessary and legal charges for stationery, postage, telegrams, or other petty expenses in respect of the conduct or management of the above election, to an amount not exceeding
pounds   shillings, particulars of which payment are to be rendered to me by him within FOURTEEN days after the election, and to be vouched for by a receipt, in accordance with the provisions of the Act 46 and 47 Vic., Cap. 51, section 31.
                        Signed
Date   188

(N.B.—No other expense must be incurred without the election agent's *written* sanction, nor must the authority given above be delegated to anyone else.)

Weekly accounts of wages.   Weekly accounts should be sent in to the election agent of the wages due to every person employed in and about the election, those from the ward or district committees verified by the respective chairmen of those committees.

Visiting clerk.   In a borough, a trustworthy clerk should *daily* visit each committee room to inquire what things are required; should make a memorandum of what is wanted, and supply the same under the directions of the election agent. If anything is wanted on an emergency the person entrusted with the above authority should pay for it.

Actual cost of Borough elections per head.   It may be useful to state that at the York and Ipswich elections, which have both taken place since the Act of 1883 was passed, the expenses per head have ranged somewhat as follows. At York, with an electorate of 11,395, and the election extending over three weeks, the expenses (exclusive of the returning officer's fees and the candidate's personal expenses) were for—

Election agent's fees	about 2d.	per voter.
Clerks	,, 2d.	,,
Messengers	,, ½d.	,,
Printing and advertising	,, 3d.	,,
Postages	,, 1¾d.	,,
Rooms for public meetings	,, 1d.	,,
Committee rooms	,, 1½d.	,,
Miscellaneous	,, 1d.	,,

At Ipswich, with a constituency of 7,914, and the election lasting about the same time, the cost per head was for—

Election agent's fees	about 3d.	per voter.
Clerks	from 2d. to 3d.	,,
Messengers	about ½d.	,,
Printing and advertising	,, 5d.	,,
Postage and telegrams	,, 1½d.	,,
Rooms for public meetings, &c.,	,, 2d.	,,
Committee rooms	from ½d. to 1¼d.	,,
Miscellaneous	about ½d.	,,

ELECTION EXPENSES.

Part II.—WHAT ARE.

By the 28th section of the Corrupt Practices Act, 1883, no *payment* and no *advance* or *deposit* can be legally made by any *person* at any *time*, whether *before*, *during*, or *after* an election in respect of any *expenses* incurred *on account of* or *in respect of* the *conduct* or *management* of such election, otherwise than by or through the election agent of the candidate, whether acting in person or by sub-agent.[1]

By the above section of the statute it appears clear, therefore, that no expense can be legally incurred by anyone in respect of what are really *election* expenses,

---

[1] C. P. Act, 1883, sec. 28.

unless such are incurred by the election agent, or his sub-agents, or by their *written* authority, and are included in the maximum amount allowed for the election.

"Person" includes clubs and associations.

The word "person" in the foregoing section includes a club or association;[1] therefore no club, or political, or other association can legally *expend money* in preparing for a particular contest, though there seems to be no objection to the expenditure of money in furtherance of the general organization of the party, irrespective of an election, if the work done is not such as is *necessarily* required to be done in an election. Thus, the cost of a survey of a borough or district made during the existence of a Parliament, and with the view of placing voters on or removing them from the register, would not be considered part of the election expenses, though made in anticipation of an election, but the cost of a canvass of a borough or district in the interest of a particular person who had consented to become a candidate might be, though no election was then imminent or likely to become so. It is submitted,

Requisition.

moreover, that the cost of a requisition to a person to become a candidate, who afterwards accepts the position, would form no part of the election expenses, any more than the expense of holding meetings to select a candidate would. In fact, the prohibition of payment seems to extend merely to those matters and things which a *candidate* would *ordinarily* have to pay after he had become such, either expressly or by implication.

Expenses may be incurred if paid by candidate or agent.

It would appear also that any person might *incur expenses* in preparing for an election if there was no candidate selected or election agent appointed, provided such expenses were afterwards *paid* by the candidate or his election agent, and included in the maximum expenses allowed. This would meet the case of a sudden vacancy

1 C. P. Act, 1883, sec. 64.

where no candidate having been selected, it was considered desirable, in order to save time, to proceed with the preparation of canvass books, &c.

It will be observed that the words of the above section, coupled with those of the 8th section, are directed against the payment of *money* and the incurring of *expenses* on account of or in respect of the conduct or management of the election. If persons, therefore, are willing to *give* their time and labour gratuitously they may do so, and may be employed to do anything in connection with the election. Thus, volunteers may be employed in the preparation of canvass books, ward books, &c., if the books themselves are included in the election expenses. On the same principle the registration survey books, ward books, registers, street lists, &c., of a club or association may be placed at the disposal of a candidate either gratuitously or for payment. If they are lent or given gratuitously, a formal resolution to that effect should be passed by the committee of the club or association, and duly entered in their books. If they are sold or hired to the candidate, it should be for a fair and reasonable sum, and not for a nominal or colourable one. It may be observed that if registration survey books are lent to a candidate, they ought to be carefully returned after use as canvass books, as the information obtained on the canvass will be most valuable for registration purposes. These books should be labelled "*Registration* survey book," "Registration ward book," &c., &c., and spaces should be left in them in which columns can be ruled for the marking of pledges. Of course the expense of ruling the books would, if *paid* for, be an election expense.

[margin: Gratuitous aid may be given for any purpose.]
[margin: Registration, survey, and other books.]
[margin: Lent, should be returned.]

It need scarcely be mentioned, after what has been stated above, that a candidate's subscription to a club, or registration, or other association, if reasonable in amount

[margin: Candidate's subscriptions.]

and given *bonâ fide* and without any intention of corruptly influencing voters, would not only be legal but would form no part of the election expenses.

Meetings, &c.

In like manner the expenses of meetings held during the time a seat is filled, for the purpose of hearing the member or the intended candidate, would not be considered election expenses, the latter, as before mentioned, extending only to expenses which naturally arise from the *conduct* and *management* of the election itself.

THE CANVASS.

Very much of the success of an election (especially since the passing of the Ballot Act) depends upon a well-organized canvass thoroughly carried out. It is, therefore, important that the *object* of the canvass should be constantly borne in mind, not only by the election agent but by the committee and canvassers.

Object of canvass.

The object of the canvass is to ascertain (1) how those electors whose minds are made up intend to vote, (2) how those electors whose minds are not made up may be *legitimately* influenced. The manner in which this object is to be carried out, and the bearing it has on the election we will now endeavour to explain.

Books, papers, &c., for canvass.

In the first place the agent will have to provide himself with the following books and forms, viz. :—

1. Register of voters.
2. Ward or district books.
3. Out voters list.
4. Non-resident voters' list.
5. Canvasser's canvass book.
6. Canvasser's return sheets.
7. Removals list.
8. Ward or district return sheets.

9. Central committee's canvass ledger.
10. Canvass cards.
11. Circulars, &c.
12. Instructions to sub-agents.

The use of each of these will be explained in detail.

1.—REGISTERS OF VOTERS.

These will be obtained from the town clerk or clerk of the peace, or other person who has charge of the Parliamentary roll. They are charged for at the following rate [1]:— *Use of Registers of Voters.*

	s.	d.
Not exceeding 1,000 names	1	0
Exceeding 1,000 and not exceeding 3,000	2	6
Exceeding 3,000 and not exceeding 6,000	5	0
Exceeding 6,000 and not exceeding 9,000	7	6
Exceeding 9,000	10	0

A few copies only will be required at first, viz., two or three for the central committee room and one for each ward or district committee room. One of the former and the *part* relating to each ward or district of the latter, should be ruled in the margin with as many columns as there were candidates at the last election, and headed with the names of the then candidates thus—

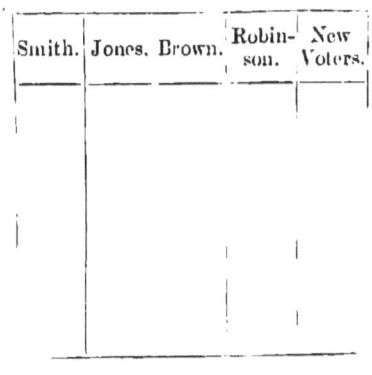

Smith.	Jones.	Brown.	Robinson.	New Voters.

[1] 6 Vic., c. 18, Sched. D.

and a mark thus (/) should be placed *against* the name of the voter and *under* the name of the candidate for whom he then voted, if known, or pledged himself. Should the voter not have voted or pledged at the last election, or if it is not known how he voted, then his politics, if known should be described by the letter *C, R, D,* &c., to indicate that his leanings are Conservative, Radical, or doubtful, as the case may be.

<small>Object of marked Register.</small>

The *object* of the marked register is to give the various committees some indication of the manner in which each voter should be approached when being canvassed, as that he is a known friend or opponent; that he is favourable or otherwise, or that nothing is known of him. Now that the Ballot is in force, it may be difficult to note precisely how each voter votes under it. A practised election agent will, however, be able to make a tolerably correct return from the way in which a voter has hitherto been accustomed to vote; from the pledges he has given, and from his associates, expressed opinions, &c., &c. It will therefore be very necessary to retain this form, bearing in mind the *object* for which it is intended.

2.—THE WARD OR DISTRICT BOOK.

<small>Use of ward or district books.</small>

The ward or district book is a list of all the voters entitled to vote in that *particular* ward or district. It should be made out according to the order of the streets, &c., and can generally be conveniently compiled from the rate book. It should be made foolscap size, two sides to a page, paged throughout; the name of the street placed at the top of each page with the No. of the canvasser's book containing the names on that page noted at the top thus—

BRIDGE STREET.

CANVASSER'S BOOK, No. ———.

Page 180.   Page 180.

Progressive No.	Voted or Pledged, 18				Politics of new Voters.	No. on Register.	Name.	No. of House.	Pledges.				Remarks.
	Smith.	Jones.	Green.	Brown.	Robinson.					Smith.	Jones.	White.	Thompson.

The spaces between each name should be wide and distinct, and, where a street ends, two or three lines should be left before the name of the new street is written. An index of the street should then be made and written at the beginning of the book, with references to the pages where each street, or parts of it, appears.

In some boroughs the provisions of the 41 and 42 Vic. Cap. 26, sec. 21, have been adopted, and the registers are made out as the names of the voters appear in the rate book *i.e.*, in the order of streets. This is a most convenient arrangement, as by interleaving the register and ruling in the margins, a ward or district book can be quickly made. In such case the progressive number will also be the register number and the former column can be dispensed with.

3.—OUT VOTERS LIST.

In counties.

In counties this is a list of voters who appear on the register for the county or division where the election takes place, but who *reside* elsewhere.

In order to have them canvassed, it is necessary to extract their names from the register and arrange them under those of the nearest towns to their residences, from whence they can be canvassed by the party agents.

It may be mentioned here that *paid* canvassing is not permitted, and therefore it is highly necessary that party agents should undertake this work for each other gratuitously. They should remember, moreover, that the success of their party in other places is at least only secondary to their own; in some cases it may even be of greater importance. The work, therefore, should be done in a thorough manner, and not in the perfunctory way in which it often

Out voters committee.

is done. It is a good plan to appoint a small committee, with a clerk, to attend exclusively to their own out-voters, as well as to those received from other places, and they act, in fact, just as if they were in charge of the canvass of a polling district.

It is very desirable that this list should be made out and the out-voters' names sent to the other districts as early as possible, *especially* during a general election, so that the latter, or the out-voters' committee, may arrange for the canvass of the whole of the out-voters of the different counties or districts being done at the same time.

A good registration agent will have these lists prepared for registration purposes and corrected every year. If a loan of these can be obtained they can be verified and copied, and much time gained in doing so.

If, however, they have to be made out from the register, it is the best plan to extract them on loose sheets, headed separately with the name of the town, &c., they are intended to be sent to, and three or four different towns being taken at one time, to thus go through the register until the names of the out-voters are exhausted.

The following form may be used:—

FORM No. 15.

....................Parliamentary Election, 18......

Messrs. SMITH & JONES.

OUT VOTERS.

To be Canvassed from........................

Polling District.	No. on Register.	Supposed Politics.	Voter's Name.	Address	Pledges.	Remarks

N.B.—This list to be returned to [*name and address of Election Agent*].

In boroughs. In boroughs a somewhat similar list must be prepared of those voters who have removed from the borough, as they are entitled to vote so long as their names appear on the register, whether they possess the qualification or not.[1] A copy of the lists sent out, with the dates when sent, should be kept, and the election agent or committee should go over it from time to time to see that returns are being duly made.

4.—NON-RESIDENT VOTERS LIST.

In counties and boroughs This list is applicable both to counties and boroughs, and is a list of voters who have *qualifications* in one ward or district but whose *residences* are in another ward or district of the *same* county, division, or borough. If they reside altogether out of the electoral boundary, their names are placed in the out-voters' list.

Object. The *object* of this list is that the voter shall be canvassed at the place where he is most likely to be found; hence though a voter may happen to reside out of the ward or district, or even out of the county or borough, he may have works, an office, shop, &c., within the ward or district, and may easily be seen there, in which case his name should be omitted from both the out-voters' list and this list, and he should be canvassed in the ward or district in which he polls.

It is a fundamental rule that the committee of each ward or district must see to each voter whose name appears in their part of the register of voters being properly canvassed. With regard to out-voters, they must make enquiries from time to time at the central committee room, where the out-voters' lists are usually dealt with, as to the progress which is being made in their canvass, and as to non-resident voters, they must themselves see to the

1 35 and 36 Vic., cap. 33, sec. 7.

making out of the following list and to the sending of the same to the chairmen or clerks in charge of the various wards or districts where their voters can best be canvassed. A list of the ward or district committee rooms and the places where they are situate, together with the names of the chairman and clerk in charge of each, should be posted up in every committee room. *(List of committee rooms, and names of chairmen and clerks.)*

The non-resident voters list may be in the following form:—

FORM No. 16.

.....................Parliamentary Election, 18......

Messrs. SMITH & JONES.

NON-RESIDENT VOTERS.

On Register for.................Ward [*or District*] to be Canvassed in.................Ward [*or District*].

Register No.	Supposed Politics.	Name.	Address.	Pledges.		Remarks.

N.B.—To be returned without delay to Mr........................... the Chairman of.................Ward [*or District*].

The chairman or clerk in charge of the ward or district *to* whom the list is sent, will make a copy of it, with the result of the canvass upon it, as the voters will have to be seen to by this committee on the day of the poll.

5.—CANVASSERS' CANVASS BOOK.

These are small books for the use of individual canvassers, and are usually made of such a size as will enable them to be carried about conveniently in the pocket. *(Use of canvass books.)*

They should not contain more than four leaves, and the following instructions should be printed in the inside of the cover:—

INSTRUCTIONS TO CANVASSERS.

1. You are requested to call upon each of the voters named herein and to use your best endeavours to induce him to promise his vote and support to Messrs. Smith and Jones.

2. If the voter is not at home a card should invariably be left, and further visits paid until you succeed in seeing him.

3. Great care must be used in noting the *precise* reply of a voter as nearly as possible in his own words; mere expressions of friendly feeling should not be registered *as a promise*, but entered in the "Remarks" column.

4. Call at the Ward [or district] Election Committee Room *daily* to report the result of your canvass, whether it has been completed or not. If the distance is too great, *send a daily report* of the progress of the canvass, on the sheets provided for the purpose.

5. If a voter is found to have removed you should endeavour to obtain his new address or where he is employed, and having carefully noted it in the canvass book, report it to the Committee Room *at once*. It will be better to do this than to go yourself to the new address, if the latter should be out of your neighbourhood.

6. Voters ascertained to be dead, to have gone abroad, or to be very unlikely to vote on account of illness, &c., should also be carefully noted and reported so that steps may be taken to guard against their being personated on the election day. If the voter is a policeman, note the fact in the canvass book, as he is prohibited from voting.

7. Any loss of, alteration in, or misdescription of the qualification of voters, should be carefully noted for use at the next registration.

8. *No gift or promise of money, refreshment, or favour of any kind must on any account be made, directly or indirectly, to an elector as an inducement to vote. Treating voters is also strictly prohibited, and both bribery and treating make the offender liable to 12 months' imprisonment or a fine of £200. The* VOTER *who accepts a bribe or who is treated is also liable to the same punishment.*

9. *No payment for conveyance of voters is allowed to be made by anyone*, but in case a voter unable to walk to the poll, the fact should be reported to the Ward or District Committee who may be able to provide a loaned conveyance.

10. It is understood that all canvassers work voluntarily, without payment or reward. No expense must be incurred by them without the *written* sanction of the Election Agent.

The inside should be ruled as follows:-

Blank canvass book.

Progressive No.	Voted or Pledged in 18 .			Politics of new Voters.	No. on Register.	VOTER'S NAME.	No. of House.	Pledges.			Remarks
	Smith. Jones. Brown	Robinson.						Smith. Jones. White.	Thompson.	

Ward (or District) _____

Page _____

The cover of the book should be of stiff paper, and should be endorsed as follows:—

———————— PARLIAMENTARY ELECTION.

18

WARD [OR DISTRICT].

No.

How prepared. The books must be prepared for the canvassers and copied from the ward or district canvass book, beginning at page 1 of the latter and so on to the end.

No canvasser's book should contain more than a dozen voters' names. If from the class of persons to be canvassed, or for any other reason, a canvasser thinks he can undertake to canvass a greater number of voters, it will be easy for him to take two or more books, but as a rule the fewer persons a canvasser has in his charge the better.

In preparing the canvassers' books, the number of the page of the ward or district canvass book from which the names, &c., are extracted should be placed at the left hand top corner of each book, for facility of reference. The name of the ward or district should also be written in, and the name of the voter and the street where he resides, and the number of the house (if any), with the information as to his known or probable politics, in fact, a precise copy, so far as it goes, of the ward or district canvass book should be made.

The residence of each voter need not be separately stated, but the name of the street or place may be written on the top of a page, and the number of all the voters' residences in that street inserted in the column provided for that purpose.

Canvass books as prepared. The canvasser's book as prepared for the canvasser will then be as follows:—

NORTH WARD [or DISTRICT.]   Page 8.

Progressive No.	Voted or Pledged in 18			Politics of New Voters.	No. on Register.	Name.	No. of House.	Pledges.				Remarks.
	Smith.	Jones.	Brown.	Robinson.					Smith.	Jones.	White.	Thompson.	
						Knowsley Street.						
61					C	897	John Rostron	1					
62	1	1				955	Robert Smith	3					
63			1	1		1048	E. Spratt	5					
64					D	189	A. Carter	7					
						Back Knowsley St.						
65					R	52	John Banks	2					

If the Registration Survey books are made use of for the purpose of canvass books, they will be ruled and made up as near as possible, to the form given above, and a copy of the instructions pasted within the cover.

Some election agents prefer a strong card, folding in the middle, and prepared to contain about a dozen names, but this is, of course, a matter of individual taste.

How used. In this book the canvasser will note the result of his canvass. It will be observed that columns are provided only for absolute pledges. Some agents prefer to have columns for those voters who are "favourable," "doubtful," "won't vote," &c., &c., but we prefer that these answers should be inserted in the "Remarks" column, as a number of columns tends to confuse the canvasser, and voters are liable to be overlooked or considered finally canvassed who ought to be visited again and again, whilst the information is of little real utility.

List to be made. A list of the canvassers' books should be kept in the ward or district book, and opposite each numbered canvasser's book should be the name and address of the person to whose charge it has been entrusted, and the dates when each book is given out, and returns made thus:—

No. of Book.	Name.	Given Out.	Returns.			
			1	2	3	4
1.	John Smith, 3, North Street.	Aug. 10	13th	15th	16th	
2.	William Jones, 17, South Parade.	Aug. 11	15th	16th	17th	18th

6.—CANVASSERS' RETURN SHEETS.

These are intended to contain the canvassers' report to his Ward or District Committee of the progress of his canvass from day to day. They are best in the following form, printed upon paper about the size of letter paper:— *Use of return sheets.*

FORM No. 17.

..................Parliamentary Election, 18......

Return of canvass..................day of..........................18......, Form...................Ward. No...............Book.

No. on Register.	Name.	Smith.	Jones.	White.	Thompson.	Remarks.

Some agents prefer a fuller form giving the progressive number in the canvass book, and the residence of the voter. We strongly, however, advise the use of this form, as it is not desirable to give canvassers *any* unnecessary labour, and the voter's name can easily be found in the Ward book by reference to the number of the canvasser's book at the right hand corner of the return.

7.—REMOVALS LIST.

As the register revised one year does not come into operation until the 1st of January of the succeeding year, and remains in force during the whole of the latter year, it will be found, as the canvass proceeds, that a considerable number of electors have either removed from the county, division, or borough altogether, or have gone to reside in other polling districts or wards therein.

The canvassers will, as before mentioned, report every such removal they meet with in the course of their canvass, and will, if possible, obtain the voter's new address or place of business or trade, or any other information which will enable him to be traced.

For this purpose each ward or district committee must be furnished with a book ruled as follows:—

FORM No. 18.

..........................Parliamentary Election, 18......

MESSRS. SMITH AND JONES.

LIST OF REMOVALS.

From...................Ward (or District).

Register No.	Voter's Name.	Address as on Register.	Supposed Politics.	New Address.	Ward or District.	Pledges.			Remarks.

The fact of the removal and the new address of the voter must be entered in the "Remarks" column of the ward or district book, and from thence transferred to the Removals list, a mark being placed against it in the former book to show that it has been so transferred. The ward or district in which the new address is situate must then be filled in, and lists of these removals must be sent, as they are reported by the canvassers, to the chairman or clerk in charge of such wards or districts, with a request that the voters be immediately canvassed, and the result reported back. The committee of the ward or district *to* which the lists are sent should have a book provided for them, to be called the " Removals to be Canvassed List," and in this book, ruled similar to the above, must be copied the names of the voters sent to them, with the names of the wards or districts *from* whence sent. These names must be given to the canvassers of the district where the voters reside, in a separate canvass book labelled as above, and the canvasser will call upon them and report the result in the same manner as if they were voters originally given to him to canvass. When the report of the latter is received the clerk in charge of his district will enter the result in his " Removals to be Canvassed book," and send a copy to the chairman or clerk of the district from which he received the name. Removals to be canvassed book.

In a large constituency it is a good plan to have a small committee, who will deal exclusively with the " Removals," as very frequently the success or non-success of a candidate depends on the manner in which removals are traced, and the voters canvassed and sent to the poll. "Removals" committee.

8.—WARD OR DISTRICT RETURN SHEETS.

Each ward or district committee will have to make daily returns to the executive committee of the position and progress of the canvass in its ward or district, so that a general return can be prepared of the whole constituency. It should here be pointed out that the *ward* or *district* committees must *alone* deal with *individuals;* the *executive* committee with *numbers only.* Use of daily ward or district return sheets.

The ward or district return sheets will contain *numbers* only, thus—

FORM No. 19.

...................Parliamentary Election, 18......

Messrs. SMITH AND JONES.

Return of Canvass for.............................Ward [or District].
No............   ....day of...............18......

Total Number on Register in this Ward [or District].	Pledges.				Duplicates.	Dead.	Cannot vote, ill, abroad, &c.	Not Canvassed.	Remarks.
	Smith	Jones.	White.	Thompson.					

Signed.................................
CHAIRMAN.

NOTE.—These returns must be sent in under seal to the Executive Committee every morning at 10 a.m. It must state the *total* result of the Canvass up to the date named, irrespective of any returns *previously* sent.

9. CENTRAL COMMITTEE'S CANVASS LEDGER.

Use of central committee's canvass ledger. This, as its name implies, is a book in which a ledger account is opened with each ward or district, as well as a general account with the whole constituency. It should be kept carefully under lock and key by the election agent, and the position of matters should only be known to himself and the principal leaders of his party.

A page will be ruled for each ward or district as follows:—

FORM No. 20.

...................................Ward [or District].

No. of Electors.....................

Date.	No. of Return.	Smith.	Jones.	White.	Thompson.	Total Pledges.	Duplicates.	Dead.	Cannot Vote, Ill, Abroad, &c.	Not Canvassed.	Remarks.

A general account of the whole constituency will be made out in the same way, and entered up daily. It will thus be seen how the canvass is progressing, and the returns from each ward or district will show whether due exertions are being used by each ward or district committee.

10.—CANVASS CARDS.

These are intended to be used by the canvassers when calling upon voters, and are ordinary cards, printed as follows:— *Use of canvass cards.*

FORM No. 21.

.......................Parliamentary Election.

188......

Mr. ....'s vote and interest are respectfully solicited for Messrs. Smith and Jones.

....
Chairman of Committee.

Special cards.

Special cards intended to be used when the canvasser is personally known to, or can influence the voter, should also be provided, thus:—

FORM No. 22.
...............Parliamentary Election.
188......

Mr. ....begs most respectfully to solicit your vote and interest on behalf of Messrs. Smith and Jones.

11.—CIRCULARS, &c.

Blank forms of circulars for the use of the ward or district secretaries, in calling together their committees, &c. They may be in the following form:—

FORM No. 23.
...............Parliamentary Election.
188......

MESSRS. SMITH AND JONES,
    North Ward Committee Room,
        No. 2, John-street,
            ....188......

Dear Sir,

A meeting of the North Ward Committee will be held in the COMMITTEE ROOM as above on..........................at..................o'clock.........m., when the favour of your attendance is requested.

Yours truly,
...............................Chairman.
...............................Vice-Chairman.

Special circulars.

Circulars also in the following form will be found highly useful where a voter can be *legitimately* influenced by some friend who is a known supporter of the candidate. But great care should be used *not* to send such circular to any person who has not influence with the voter apart from his position as a mere employer, landlord, overlooker, &c. :—

FORM No. 24.

..................Parliamentary Election.
188......
Committee Rooms,
No. 2, John-street,
..........................188......

Dear Sir,

You will greatly oblige Messrs. Smith and Jones's Committee by using your friendly influence on their behalf to secure the vote of Mr. ....of...........................

Yours most respectfully,
....

To................................

An answer at your earliest convenience informing me of the result of your canvass of Mr. ....will be considered a favour.

Copies of the candidates' addresses on thin paper and in a portable form for distribution by the canvassers should be provided in proportion to the number of voters. *Candidates' addresses.*

The above will also be found useful, if it is considered desirable, to send out the address to each voter by post, and whether a return circular, asking the voter to pledge, is enclosed with it or not. *Canvassing circulars.*

Many voters are undoubtedly influenced by the mere fact of a candidate being the first in the field, and more are influenced in favour of the candidate who first pays them the compliment, as they regard it, of asking for their votes.

We, therefore, strongly advise that in every case the candidate's address, with a short note, signed by the chairman and other officers of the election committee, requesting the voter's support and influence enclosed, should be sent *by post* to every voter as early as possible.

In constituencies where the registration is well attended to, a set of envelopes or book post wrappers, addressed to *Addressed envelopes, &c.*

the voters, are made out in wards or districts, and kept in the order in which the voters' names appear in the register.

These are corrected after each revision, and are then available on an emergency. These envelopes or post wrappers might be made use of in sending out the candidate's address, but in such case they ought to be *bonâ fide purchased* from the registration association at a full and fair price.

A halfpenny stamp will cover the postage, but it is much better to use a penny stamp, as in the event of the voter having died, removed, &c., the circular will be returned to the committee, and much valuable information thus obtained.

The following is a form which may be used:—

FORM No. 25.
...............Parliamentary Election, 18......
Central Committee Room,
......................Street,
......................188......

Sir,

The committee for securing the election of Messrs. Smith & Jones beg to enclose you copies of their addresses, and most respectfully to solicit the favour of your vote and influence in their behalf.

The committee will also esteem it a favour, should you be so disposed, if you will kindly intimate to them, by filling up and returning the annexed form, whether they may count upon your support.

In making this request the committee have no desire to infringe the secrecy of the ballot, but it will materially assist the committee in the conduct of the election if they can know, as soon as possible, the amount of support upon which they may rely.

Full particulars of the time and place of polling will be notified in due course.

We are, sir,
Your obedient Servants,
......................Chairman.
......................Vice-chairman.

NOTE.—The Elections Act of 1883 forbids, under serious penalties, any candidate or agent *making payment* for the conveyance of voters to or from the poll.

The above circular should be signed, not only by the chairman and vice-chairman of the election committee, but by any other officer thereof, if he is a person of weight and influence in the constituency. It is a good plan also to have, with the same object, a list of the executive committee at the head, or on the fly-leaf, of the circular.

If it is not intended to enclose a circular for reply, the two paragraphs above printed in italics will, of course, be omitted. If a reply circular is enclosed it may be in the following form :—

FORM No. 26.

....................Parliamentary Election, 18......

Messrs. SMITH and JONES.

Sir,—

It is............my intention to vote for Messrs. Smith and Jones at the above Election.

Name ....

Address ....

To the Chairman of the Central Committee.

Register No...........................

Ward or District ....

The register number and the name of the ward or district must, of course, be filled in before the circular is sent to the voter, as they will be required for entering up, in the ward or district register, the replies which are sent back.

An envelope, addressed to the chairman at the central committee room, and bearing a *penny* stamp, must also be enclosed. In large constituencies and in most counties it is a great convenience to have the return envelopes addressed to the ward or district committee in whose register the voter's name appears. A deal of trouble and some time are thus saved, as the replies then go direct to the committees who are responsible for the canvass of the individuals, and are entered up at once in the proper books.

It should be mentioned that the pledges given by circular should be entered in blue or red ink, to distinguish them from those obtained by personal canvass. If the voter subsequently promises to a canvasser, a tick, thus √, in black ink should be placed against the blue or red mark.

Circulars to Out Voters or Voters Removed.

Whether the candidate's address is sent to the voters generally by post, or not, it should certainly be sent to every out-voter at the *earliest* moment, and to those voters who have removed from the county, division, or borough, so soon as their new addresses are ascertained. The circulars, of which the forms are given above, may or may not be used, as may be deemed advisable, or they may be added to, by the expression of a hope that the voter will not deem the time and money expended in recording his vote too great a sacrifice to make.

If the return circular is enclosed, and no reply is received from the voter in the course of a few days, his name should be sent to the agent of the nearest town for canvass, as mentioned *ante* p. 46.

The following form may be useful on forwarding the same:—

FORM No. 27.

.....................Parliamentary Election, 18......

Messrs. SMITH and JONES.

Dear Sir,

I beg to enclose the names and addresses of some voters who have qualifications in this county (*division, borough*), but whose places of residence appear to be near your town.

We are most anxious to secure their support at the poll, and we would, therefore, ask you, in the interest of the cause, to lend your aid in arranging for the canvass of these voters by means of such *voluntary* assistance as you can procure, as you are aware that under the Act of 1883 no payment can be made for this service.

If the voters, or any of them, do not reside within your district, but live nearer to some other agent of our party, will you kindly send on the list, or names, to him, and inform us what you have done.

We shall be glad to receive the result of the canvass as early as convenient, and to afford you similar assistance, as far as possible, should any of your voters reside in this district.

Copies of Messrs. Smith and Jones' addresses have already been sent by post to the voters named.

The polling will *(or is expected to)* take place on the .... inst.

..................Chairman of Committee.

..................Election Agent.

12.—INSTRUCTIONS TO SUB-AGENTS.

It will, of course, be expected that every sub-agent will [In Counties.] make himself fully acquainted with the various Acts of Parliament bearing on elections, and in large districts he will require to know almost as much as the election agent himself. In the latter case, therefore, no mere "Instructions" could be given him which would embrace everything he ought to know, unless they attained a bulk equal to that of a fair-sized book.

In some districts, however, the duties of the sub-agent will be much less, and he will have to act more under the direct control of the election agent. In such cases the following "Instructions" may be of service, as they can be altered or modified to suit any particular set of circumstances :—

FORM No. 28.

..................Parliamentary Election, 18......

Messrs. SMITH and JONES.

PRIVATE INSTRUCTIONS TO SUB-AGENTS.

N.B.—*The following instructions do not profess to contain a complete exposition of the Elections Act of 1883, but should be read in conjunction with it.*

Dear Sir,

You are hereby appointed sub-agent for the above election on behalf of Messrs. Smith and Jones, to act as such within the district of..................................

F

The maximum number of employés and committee rooms which are permitted at the election is shewn in the table below, and that number must on no account be exceeded.

Districts.	No. of Voters.	Sub-Agent.	Employés authorized.				No. of Committee Rooms.
			Clerks.	Messengers.	Polling Agents.		

You are authorized to incur on behalf of the candidate such expenditure, in the conduct and management of the election, as may be legal and necessary, to an amount not exceeding............pounds (£   ). It is advised that this sum should be distributed as follows:—

MAXIMUM EXPENDITURE.

Sub-Agent's Fees.	Clerks.	Messengers.	Polling Agents.	Printing and Stationery.	Bill Posting.	Advertising.	Postage and Telegrams.	Hire of Committee Rooms.	Expenses of Public Meetings.	Miscellaneous.

The remuneration of the election staff should not exceed the following rates:—

Polling Agent - - £1 1s. 0d. (one day).
Clerks - - - - £2 2s. 0d. per week.
Messengers - - - £1 10s. 0d. per week.

Of the above items, all except that for "Miscellaneous" expenditure, are discretionary *and interchangeable*, but the amount allowed for the latter must not in any case be exceeded.

Your fee as sub-agent will be   pounds (£   ), subject to the conditions hereinafter named.

You will receive herewith the following forms and papers:—

A Register of Voters.
Parish or other Lists for the District.   No. of Copies.

Form No. 3. Notice as to Election Expenses. ....
„ 4. List of Volunteer Clerks and Messengers. ....
„ 5. List of Paid   „   „   ....
„ 9. Agreement for Hire of Committee Room. ....
„ 10.   „   „   „   in Clubs. ....
„ 11.   „   „   of Room on Licensed Premises for Public Meetings. ....
„ 12. Election Expenses Book. ....
„ 13.   „   „   Order Book. ....
„ 14. Authority for Petty Disbursements. ....
„ 15. Voters Lists. ....
„ 16. Non-resident Voters Lists. ....
Canvass Books ....
„ 17. Canvassers' Return Sheets. ....
„ 18. Removals List. ....
„ 19. District Return Sheets. ....
„ 21 and 22. Canvassers' Cards. ....
„ 23. Special Canvassing Circulars. ....
„ 30. District Committees' Instructions. ....
„ 31. Clerks in Charge Instructions. ....
„ 32. Canvassers' Instructions. ....

ALL PRINTING, ADVERTISING, AND BILL POSTING WILL BE ORDERED BY ME, AND NO EXPENSE MUST BE INCURRED UNDER THESE HEADS WITHOUT MY WRITTEN AUTHORITY. IN CASES OF EMERGENCY, WHEN COMMUNICATION WITH ME IS IMPOSSIBLE, ANNOUNCEMENTS OF LOCAL MEETINGS MAY BE ADVERTISED BY YOU, THE EXPENSE BEING INCLUDED IN THE AUTHORIZED MAXIMUM AS ABOVE.

The candidate's address will be sent by me to every voter.

Your first step will be to organise an efficient district election committee (if not already done), who should choose an influential chairman. Every parish or township should be represented thereon. Active, and thoroughly reliable supporters only must be placed on the committee, and it should not necessarily consist solely of the existing members of any Conservative Association or Club in the district, but should be a *distinct* body, selected for election purposes alone.

Each sub-agent at the outset of the contest should affix in each election committee room and Conservative club throughout the district a copy of the notice (Form No. 3) limiting and confining his responsibility to those expenses only which he may himself incur.

The election committee of each district should be at once summoned by its chairman. At their first meeting the chairman, or the sub-agent should carefully read over the instructions to district committees, &c., sent herewith, and point out the altered circumstances under which an election has now to be conducted, the *absolute prohibition of any paid employment*, except such as is allowed by the Act; the abolition of *payment for conveyance*, the strict limitation of expenditure, and the severe penalties which will follow a breach of the law.

He should impress upon all present the fact that success can alone result from the well directed efforts of enthusiastic *volunteers*, and he should point out the serious personal responsibility which attaches to all who take part in the election, and the absolute necessity, in their own interests as well as those of the candidate, that each should carry out faithfully the work allotted to him, and that all should adhere rigidly to the provisions of the law.

He should request each member in his own district to exercise a strict supervision over the acts of those working under him, and to discourage, by every means in his power, any resort to improper practices, stating at the same time that the candidate would not hesitate to repudiate, publicly, if necessary, any departure from the requirements of the law.

The arrangements for working the various parishes or districts should be settled at the meeting.

The canvass books or cards should also be allotted at the meeting, care being taken to entrust a canvass book to none but responsible and reliable volunteers, whose authority should be limited to canvass only those voters whose names appear in the canvass book, the possession of a canvass book having sometimes been brought forward at election petitions as a proof of "agency," and the names of all persons to whom they are given should be recorded.

In selecting a committee room in which the business of the district can be carried on, it should be borne in mind that the premises of a permanent political club can be made available for the purpose. In that case it should be agreed with the authorities of the same that the room shall be under the *exclusive* control of the candidate's agent. In case a committee room is hired elsewhere, the agreement should be in writing, and it should be made clear that the payment.

for hiring includes fire and lighting, and any other incidental charges of the same kind, or the sub-agent's calculation may be upset by additional demands on account of these services. A committee room cannot be held in a public-house, refreshment house, or public elementary school, *without vitiating the election*. Hotels, restaurants, and certain grocers' shops are, therefore, not available, and the rooms of a political club, if held on licensed premises, would also, it is believed, be within this prohibition. The voluntary loan of *private* premises, except such as are prohibited by Sec. 20, may be accepted, but a similar understanding to that mentioned above should be arrived at.

The committee room should be carefully locked at night, and all books and papers kept in safe custody.

The number of clerks and messengers allowed by law is one clerk and one messenger for each polling district, or in large districts one clerk and one messenger for every 500 electors, with one each additional for every fractional number beyond. They should be selected in each case from persons having a knowledge of the district, and, if possible, *should not be electors*, as paid employés are debarred from voting. Their appointments should be delivered to them in writing, and in every case it should be understood that they will provide their own meals and refreshments during the contest, and that no charge against the candidate can be admitted on this account.

Every bill, placard, or poster having reference to the election, which may be exhibited, must bear the name and address of the printer and publisher ("Printed and published by_____ "of_____"), and should any reach you, from any source, not bearing this imprint, they must on no account be circulated or exhibited. If, in case of emergency, any bills, &c., are printed locally, the printer must be instructed to affix his imprint as above; *neglect of this precaution may be fatal to the election.*

Stationery for use in the district committee room may be procured according to actual requirements, care being taken that it is not wasted.

Arrangements must be made for any public meetings that may be held during the contest, and a fixed sum should be agreed upon for the hire of the room in each case. If held at a licensed house, a notice should be given to the landlord or manager that the candidate will not be liable for any expense other than for the hire of the room.

When the work of the canvass is begun, a daily return should be called for from each district, which should be carefully examined, and if from any cause it is incomplete, irregular, or unsatisfactory, inquiry should be at once made into the reasons. If the delay arises from an insufficiency of workers, an endeavour should be made to supply the want, or obtain assistance from other places. A summary of the returns must be sent each day to the election agent.

All payments for railway passes, and for the conveyance of voters to or from the poll being now prohibited, reliance must be placed exclusively upon such vehicles *(not being hackney carriages)* as can be obtained voluntarily from active supporters of the party in the various districts or elsewhere. A list of conveyances which can be so procured must be obtained from each district, and if more than are wanted are lent in any district, the sub-agent should allot them, as far as possible, to places where they will be most needed. The lenders should receive a letter of thanks for their promise of gratuitous assistance.

Private conveyances lent voluntarily can alone be employed; the gift or loan of hackney carriages, or of vehicles and animals usually let for hire, cannot be accepted in any case.

You will receive a list of "removals," and of voters (termed "non-resident voters") residing in your district, and registered to vote in other districts. Please include such names in the canvass books for your district, and use your best endeavours to induce them to poll.

As soon as the returning officer's arrangements for the polling day are settled, copies of the notices giving the situation of the various polling stations will be sent to each district.

You will be good enough to select the authorized number of polling agents for the district from persons having an intimate knowledge of the electors. The name and address of each polling agent must be sent to me as soon as he is appointed, in order that the returning officer may be informed. Volunteers should be obtained if possible.

Polling agents must make a declaration of secrecy before a magistrate prior to entering upon their duties. Your polling agent should be instructed as to this, and furnished with the requisite particulars.

Unless they are distributed from a central committee room (in which case you will be informed), polling cards for the district will be sent you as soon as the arrangements are made, and you must arrange for their distribution not later than the day preceding the poll.

One or two days before the poll, the district election committee should be called together, and the arrangements for the election day should be settled. The voters who will require specially visiting should be carefully allotted at this meeting. *You should take particular care to reiterate the necessity for strictly observing the law in every particular.*

The "instructions for the polling day," which will be sent you later on, should be carefully distributed at this meeting.

AS REGARDS EXPENDITURE, THE AMOUNT NAMED ABOVE MUST NOT UPON ANY CONSIDERATION BE EXCEEDED, OR, IF SO, THE EXCESS MUST BE DEDUCTED FROM THE SUB-AGENT'S FEE. AS THE TOTAL EXPENDITURE OF EACH CANDIDATE IS RIGIDLY FIXED BY LAW, AND AN EXCESS WOULD VITIATE THE ELECTION, THE NECESSITY FOR THIS PROVISION IS ABSOLUTE.

Any contributions which may be offered towards the expenses of the election must, according to the Act, be paid to the candidate or the election agent direct, and cannot, under any circumstances, be accepted or disbursed by a sub-agent without imperilling the election.

It will be necessary to utilise voluntary work to the fullest possible extent throughout the contest, and to engage paid assistance only when absolutely necessary and the pressure of work is urgent.

A minute and particular account must be kept of every payment, which must be sent to me, with the voucher, for everything *above forty shillings*, immediately after the close of the poll.

The provisions of the Act as regards corrupt and illegal practices, illegal payment, employment, or hiring, must be carefully studied, and the utmost care must be taken not to infringe them.

The appointments of sub-agents will cease and determine at the close of the poll, unless previously revoked.

I should be obliged by an acknowledgment of receipt of this, and of the forms, &c., by return.

Yours faithfully,

———

Election Agent for Messrs. Smith & Jones.

Whilst the various books and papers mentioned are in course of preparation, the election agent should, if arrangements have not previously been made, take steps for securing

COMMITTEE ROOMS.

The number of these and the places where they can and where they cannot be held are set forth at pp. 27-31 *ante*.

The central committee room for the county or borough should be in the most central and convenient place, and should be under the immediate care and supervision of the principal election agent, who should be there constantly to

<small>Central committee rooms.</small>

give advice and directions. As already mentioned, no provision is made for a central committee room in boroughs, but it can be easily arranged to have the central room in the central ward; or if a committee room is not required for every 500 voters, or if a few committee rooms are lent gratuitously, a separate central committee room may be provided and paid for.

The election agent should have a private room, set apart for his use and the use of the central committee, and no other person should be admitted to that room without the express permission of the agent.

Ward or district committee rooms. Each ward or district committee room should, in like manner, be in the most central and accessible part of the ward or district. It will be under the immediate care and control of the ward or district chairman, and a paid clerk should be constantly there for the purpose of attending to the books, giving information, taking charge of messages, &c. There should also be a private room for the meetings of the district committee, separate from the general enquiry room.

List of. When and as the various committee rooms are selected, a list of them should be made, with the names of the chairmen, sub-agents or hon. secretaries, and clerks in charge, and a copy of the list sent to each ward or district committee, so that they may communicate direct with each other.

The following is the form:—

FORM NO. 29.

..........................PARLIAMENTARY ELECTION, 18......

Messrs. SMITH and JONES.

LIST OF COMMITTEE ROOMS.

CENTRAL. No...............street.

Ward or District.	Where situate.	Chairman.	Sub-agents or Hon. Secretaries.	Clerk in charge.	Hours of Attendance.

..........................Chairman.
..........................Election Agent.

No refreshment of any kind must be allowed in the committee room. If any such are required by the staff (upon pressing occasions) they should be obtained and served elsewhere. *No refreshments in committee rooms.*

On the day of election it will be found convenient to have a committee room as near to each polling booth as possible. *Committee rooms on day of poll.*

Whilst the agent is selecting the committee rooms, he must be taking steps for the formation of the

ELECTION COMMITTEES.

In most, if not all, constituencies, the *nucleus* of the election committee will be found in some political club or association.

<small>Inadvisable to adopt Club or Association Committees.</small>

We use the word "nucleus" advisedly, because it would be in the highest degree dangerous to the candidate if he constituted the whole of the committee of an association *his* election committee, or if he employed its members *generally* as voluntary canvassers.

He may and *must* accept the services of some of the officers and members, as they are the most qualified persons in the constituency to act as committee men and canvassers, but he is not obliged to take them *en bloc*, but is entitled to select those in whom he has *implicit* confidence.

A meeting, therefore, of the principal supporters of the candidate should be called, either by the election agent or the chairman, if there is one, of the party, and to this meeting all those persons who are likely to help in the election should be summoned.

The election agent should attend the meeting, and either he or the chairman should point out the altered circumstances under which an election has now to be conducted, viz., the strict *limitation* of expenditure, the absolute prohibition of any *paid* employment, except such as is allowed by the Act; the abolition of *payment* for railway fares or for other modes of conveyance, &c., &c., and the severe penalties which follow a breach of the law. He should impress upon those present that success can alone result from the well-directed efforts of enthusiastic *volunteers*, while he should point out the serious responsibility which is now imposed upon all who take part in the election, and the absolute necessity in their own interests as well as those of the candidate, that each should carry out faithfully the work allotted to him, and that all should adhere rigidly to the provisions of the law. He should request each member in his own district to exercise a strict supervision over the acts of those working under him, and to discourage by every means in his power any resort to improper practices, stating at the same time that the candidate would not hesitate to repudiate, publicly if necessary, any departure from the requirements of the law.

An election committee should then be formed of those influential and energetic supporters who can be *implicitly* relied upon to assist in conducting the election in strict conformity to law. The names of these should be previously carefully prepared by the chairman or election agent, in consultation with the most influential leaders of the party supporting the candidate. *Election Committees: how formed.*

As previously pointed out, they should not be simply the committee of some club or association, but should include a few outsiders, if possible, or at any rate a selection of the members of various clubs or associations. In short, the election committee should be a special and independent body, and separated, as far as possible, from any club or association. *Should be a special body.*

The names of the members of the election committee should be taken down by the election agent, and they should have power, by resolution, to add to their number.

A meeting of the election committee should be held immediately after their appointment, when a chairman, vice-chairman, and honorary secretary should be elected, and arrangements made for calling meetings to form the

WARD OR DISTRICT COMMITTEES.

To do this, it will be necessary to consider what will be the most convenient arrangement for canvassing and polling the voters, and to divide the county, division, and borough into wards or districts accordingly. In most cases this will have been already done, and it will not be desirable to alter old arrangements unless for very good cause. *How formed.*

The condition of the organization in each district should

then be enquired into. If there is a suitable chairman in the district, he should be requested to call a meeting of friends and supporters, but it is not desirable that he should call the meeting in his official capacity, but should get two or three other influential leaders of the party to sign the circular along with himself. This circular should be sent to all those friends who are likely to come forward and assist in the election, whatever their rank or position may be. They will be required as canvassers, and the more numerous they are, the more the work can be subdivided and attended to.

First meeting of ward or district committee.

At the meeting the names and addresses of the persons present should be taken by the chairman. This is very desirable for several reasons, as, that it prevents spies getting into the committee room, or obtaining possession of canvass books; it shews who are zealous in the cause, &c., &c. It should, of course, be done before the commencement of business. A ward or district committee should then be appointed, the same care and precautions being taken in selecting the names as have been taken in forming the central election committee. They should also have power to add to their number, and should at once proceed to business.

Chairman, &c.

If there is no regular chairman of the ward or district a man of standing with influence in the particular ward or district should, if possible, be got to take that position, and his name should be attached to all letters, circulars, &c., emanating from his committee, so that his influence may be most widely felt. If it is thought fit, a vice-chairman can also be appointed, and it will be necessary

Clerk in charge.

to have an intelligent paid clerk in charge. The latter can, of course, be appointed by the election agent only, but the Ward or District Committee should recommend him for appointment.

In boroughs, where no provision is made for sub-agents, the clerk should, if possible, be the secretary or registration agent usually acting or employed in that particular ward. In counties, one sub-agent may be appointed to each polling district in addition to the clerks, and, therefore, the secretaries or registration agents in counties may be appointed either as sub-agents or clerks in charge or as may be deemed most desirable.

The ward or district meeting should, if possible, be attended by the election agent, who should be careful to see that everybody clearly understands his duty, and that the work of the committee is fairly and properly begun. He should shortly state that the object of the meeting is to organize a committee for canvassing the ward or district and for conducting the election. He should explain that it is necessary to have a staff of canvassers who will be supplied with books containing the names of about a dozen voters residing or carrying on business near to each other, and he will be glad if the gentlemen present will volunteer their services. Ward or District Meeting to be attended by Election Agent.

Great care, however, must be exercised as to whom the canvass books are entrusted, and their authority should be limited to canvassing such voters as are included in the canvass book, as the possession of a canvass book has frequently been brought forward at the hearing of election petitions as a proof of "Agency." The number of the book and the name and address of the person to whom it is given must be carefully recorded. The election agent should then read over and carefully explain to the canvassers the instructions set out further on. If considered necessary, copies might be printed at a small expense, and one copy given to each canvasser, who could then study it at his leisure. Great care to whom Canvass Books entrusted

As a rule a canvasser should only take charge of one Limited number of Voters in a book.

canvass book, for though he may be able to call upon more than a dozen voters to *ask* for their votes, yet on the day of polling he may find great difficulty in getting a greater number to the poll. There may, however, be exceptionable circumstances which will justify a canvasser in taking two or more books, as that the voters are well-known friends or of a class that may be depended upon to poll, or the canvasser may undertake to get the assistance of his friends, &c.

Very frequently there are active friends who cannot, or do not attend the first committee meeting. Sometimes other friends will suggest their names and undertake to see them with a canvass book. In such cases the number of the book and the name of the person undertaking to deliver it, and the name and address of the proposed canvasser should be carefully taken down, and enquiry should be made in a day or two afterwards to ascertain if such book has been accepted by the proposed canvasser. If all the canvass books are not taken out the chairman or vice-chairman should personally see other friends, and urge them to give their assistance.

The chairmen of the various ward or district committees should be furnished by the agent with written or printed instructions, which may be as follows:—

Form No. 30.

......................Parliamentary Election, 18......
Messrs. SMITH and JONES.

INSTRUCTIONS TO WARD OR DISTRICT COMMITTEES.

1. The names and addresses of the chairmen, vice-chairmen, and clerk in charge of each ward or district committee must be sent to Mr.   , the election agent, at the central committee rooms,   street, immediately they are appointed.

2. Each ward or district committee will be held responsible for the immediate and efficient canvass of its ward or district, and must make all arrangements necessary for the purpose.

3. No *paid* canvasser can be appointed. *Paid canvassers &c.*

4. The only paid officers attached to the ward or district committee will be   clerks and   messengers. These may be nominated by the ward or district committee, but their names and addresses must be at once sent in to the election agent, who is the only person who can legally appoint them. They should not be voters, as any elector employed for REWARD by or on behalf of a candidate six months before or during an election is disqualified from voting.

5. The chairman of the ward or district committee, or in his absence the vice-chairman, must *daily* inspect the ward or district book to see that every canvasser is doing his duty and that every part of the ward or district is being canvassed. Wherever, from the absence of returns or otherwise, a canvasser appears not to be progressing with his part of the canvass, enquiry must be at once made into the cause of the delay, and if it is not satisfactorily explained, another canvasser who can be depended upon must be associated with the old canvasser, or if absolutely necessary, the book must be called in, or another one made and placed in the hands of another canvasser. *Ward or district book to be daily examined.*

6. The chairman must see that the canvassers thoroughly understand their instructions.

7. A return of the state of the canvass must be made, upon the forms supplied, to Mr.   , the election agent, *every* morning at ten o'clock. The return must be of the *gross* canvass, and must be signed by the chairman of the ward or district, and must be sent under seal. A copy should be kept by the chairman in his own custody, but should not be seen by anyone beyond the executive committee. These returns must be compared with each other from day to day, and the progress made in the canvass noted. *Return of canvass.*

8. If any voter is returned by a canvasser as having removed into another ward or district, his name must be entered in the book called the " Removals List," under the head of the ward or district *into* which he has removed. His name, *new* address, and register number must also be sent to the chairman of the *latter* ward or district, with a request that the voter may be canvassed and a return made of the result. This return must be noted in the " Removals List," and also in the ward or district book, and the pledge (if given) must be counted as a pledge obtained in the ward or district where the voter's name appears. The chairman of the ward or *Removals list.*

district must daily examine the "Removals List," and if due diligence is not being shown in canvassing the voters therein, he must write to the chairmen of the wards or districts to whom the names of the voters have been sent urging them to make a return of the canvass. It is a fundamental rule that the committee of each ward or district must see to each voter whose name appears in their part of the register of voters being properly *canvassed*.

Removals to be canvassed list.   9. When the chairman of a ward or district receives the name of a voter, resident in his ward or district, for canvass, he must see that the clerk duly enters the name, new address, and register number of the voter in the book called the "Removals to be Canvassed List," under the head of the ward or district *from* which the name is received. He must also see that each name is transferred to the canvass book of the canvasser of the street, &c., where the voter resides, and that the canvasser is instructed to see him. He must daily examine this list in the same manner and for the same purpose as he examines the ward or district book; and when the voter has been canvassed he must cause the result to be entered in the "Removals to be Canvassed List," and must send a copy thereof to the chairman of the ward or district from whom the name was received. In making his return of pledges, the chairman will *not* count the pledges in the "Removals to be Canvassed List," as they will be counted in the ward or district where the voter's name appears. Upon the day of polling, however, the committee of the ward or district where the voter *resides* will be considered to have charge of him, and must arrange for his polling.

Non-resident voters list.   10. In like manner, if a voter *appears* by the ward or district register to *live* in another ward or district to that where his qualification is situate, *and it would be more convenient to canvass him where he resides*, his name and address must be inserted in the "non-resident voters list" and sent to the chairman of the latter ward or district, who will enter his name in the "non-resident to be canvassed list," and cause him to be canvassed and the result reported as in the case of the "removals to the canvassed list."

Voters left town, &c.   11. If any voter is returned by a canvasser as having left the town, &c., his name and register number, and all the information possible about him must be entered in a like list entitled "out voters," and must be sent to the central committee room. The fact of his having left town must also be carefully noted in the ward or district book.

Double qualifications of voters.   12. If a voter's name appears more than once upon the register (whether in the same or different wards or polling districts), information of the fact with the register number, and the name of the list must be sent to the central committee, and also marked in the ward or district canvass book.

13. No payment or promise of payment must, under any circumstances, be made to a voter for loss of time or travelling expenses, nor must refreshments be provided for, or money for refreshments paid to him. *Voters' travelling expenses.*

14. If a voter will not pledge to the canvasser calling upon him and some friend is supposed to have *legitimate* influence with him, the chairman may, in his discretion, fill up and send to such friend the circular letter provided. Great care must, however, be exercised in sending such circular (which ought to be sent to *known* friends only), to send it such friends alone as have influence with a voter, *apart from their positions* as master, overlooker, &c. *Special canvassing circular.*

15. The committee rooms are under the entire control of the chairman or vice-chairman for the time being presiding, who has power to exclude any person therefrom. No refreshments of any kind must be allowed in them, *under any pretence whatever*, and all treating must be *rigidly discountenanced* by every member of the committee and every person engaged for the candidates, whether gratuitously or otherwise. *Control of Committee room.*

16. The clerks and messengers of each ward or district are under the orders of the chairman or vice-chairman for the time being presiding. *Clerks, &c.*

17. The names of all persons attending the committee rooms or meetings should be taken down by the clerk under the directions of the chairman or vice-chairman before any business is discussed. This will show who are the most zealous and earnest supporters, and also be a means of detecting spies if any such should get into the room.

18. The chairman must see that the clerk in charge is attentive to his duties, that he keeps the ward or district book duly posted up, and that all books and papers are kept in a safe place, so that nobody except authorised persons can obtain access to them. *Clerk in charge.*

19. As it is now illegal to hire cabs or carriages for the conveyance of voters to the poll, the ward or district committees should ascertain what friends are willing *gratuitously* to lend vehicles, horses and drivers on the day of election, and send in a list to the central committee. It is not necessary that the conveyance be one for which *duty* is paid, as any conveyance may be used, as farmers' carts, &c., without being liable to licence or duty. The committee should seize every opportunity also of obtaining the gratuitous services of all friends to the cause. If such services are offered they should be thankfully accepted, if from persons upon whom reliance can be placed not to infringe the law. *Cabs, &c.*

G

20. Further instructions will be supplied as to the course to be adopted on the day of polling.

21. The ward or district committees should meet as often as necessary (daily, on the near approach of the election), and the chairman and vice-chairman should attend such meetings as often as they possibly can.

22. The chairman and vice-chairman of each ward or district committee are members of the central committee, and must regularly attend its meetings.

23. Anything required by a ward or district committee involving money expenditure should be reported to Mr.   the election agent, and it will be at once attended to, as it is *illegal* to incur any expenditure except through or with the previous sanction of Mr.

24. The candidates urgently desire and request that the provisions of the Acts now in force for regulating elections may be strictly and rigidly adhered to by their friends and supporters before and during the election, as they will not hesitate to disavow, publicly if necessary, any departure from the requirements of the law; and they hereby expressly declare that they will not sanction or be responsible for any cost, charge, payment, or liability whatever which may be illegally made or incurred.

25. These instructions are to be kept perfectly private and confidential, and must be *returned* to Mr.   immediately after the election.

The clerk in charge in each ward or polling district should also be furnished with the following:—

FORM No. 31.

........................Parliamentary Election, 18......

Messrs. SMITH and JONES.

INSTRUCTIONS TO WARD [OR DISTRICT] CLERKS IN CHARGE.

Clerks in charge   1. Each clerk in charge must attend at his own committee room daily from   a.m. to   p.m., and must at all times be ready to give his advice and assistance to canvassers and voters requiring it.

2. He will be furnished with a register of voters in his [*District*] ward, called the [*District*] "Ward Book," in which he will enter daily the reports of the canvassers. He will be held personally

responsible for its safe custody, and must not on any account allow it to be inspected but by the members of his own committee.

3. A return of the *gross* canvass must be made upon the forms supplied to Mr.   , the election agent, *every* morning at 10 o'clock. This return must be made out by the clerk in charge and signed by the chairman of the ward or district, and must be sent under seal by a trustworthy messenger.

4. If any voter is returned by a canvasser as having removed into another ward or district, the fact must be carefully noted in the ward or district canvass book, and his name must be entered in the book called the "Removals List," under the head of the ward or district into which he has removed. This must be done in the "removals list" supplied you, in which you will open an account, as it were, with each ward or district in which you have voters; all the voters in each foreign ward thus appearing together. The name of the voter, his new address, his supposed politics and his register number must then be sent to the chairman of the ward or district into which the voter has removed, with a request that the latter may be canvassed and a return made of the result. This return must be noted in the "Removals List," and also in the ward or district canvass book where the voter's name appears. If a pledge is given it must be counted as a pledge obtained in *your* ward or district. Removals list.

5. When the name of a voter *resident* in your ward is sent to you by the chairman of another ward to be canvassed, his name, new address, and register number must be entered in a book to be called "Out-voters to be Canvassed List," under the head of the ward or district from which the name is received. It is then your duty to transfer the name, &c., of the voter to the canvass book of the canvasser of the street, &c., where the voter resides, and to instruct the canvasser to see him. You must then make a memorandum in the "Removals to be Canvassed List" of the name or number of the canvasser to whom the canvass of the voter is entrusted. When the voter has been canvassed you must enter the result in the "Removals to be Canvassed List," and must send a copy thereof to the chairman of the ward or district from whom the name was received. In making the return of pledges, the pledges in this list must *not* be counted. Removals to be canvassed.

6. In like manner, if a voter appears by *your* register to *live* in another ward or district, and *it will be more convenient to canvass him where he resides*, you must enter his name in the book or list called the "Non-resident Voters List," and send a copy to the chairman of the ward or district where he is to be canvassed, who is to deal with him in precisely the same manner as if he had *removed* from your ward. Non-resident voters list.

Voters left town, &c.

7. If a voter is returned as having left the town, &c., his name, register number, and every other information respecting him must be entered in a like list entitled "Out Voters," and must be sent to the central committee room. The same information must also be carefully noted in the ward or district book opposite his name.

8. You must keep a list of voters who are returned as "will not pledge," "won't vote," &c., and must submit the same to your committee and chairman day by day for instructions respecting them.

9. You will keep a general supervision over the progress of the canvass, and if you find the progress of the canvass unsatisfactory, or that any particular canvasser is negligent or remiss in his duty, you will report the matter in confidence to your chairman, who will take such action thereon as he deems necessary.

10. In the absence of the chairman and committee you will have charge of the committee rooms, and must take care that no improper persons are allowed in them. You will in the like absence have the control of the messengers, &c., attached to the room.

Account of wages, &c.

11. You must make out an account every Thursday night of the wages due to yourself and the clerks (if any) and messengers employed in your ward or district. This account must be signed by the chairman of the ward and transmitted to Mr.
the election agent, with the Friday's return of the canvass.

12. The clerks and messengers in each ward or district are under the entire control of the chairman or vice-chairman of the ward or district to which they are attached, and must give him implicit obedience.

13. Further instructions with books and papers will be supplied prior to the day of polling.

FORM No. 32.

......................Parliamentary Election, 18......

Messrs. SMITH and JONES.

INSTRUCTIONS TO CANVASSERS.

1. The canvasser will receive with these instructions—
    1. A Canvass Book.
    2. Canvass Return Sheets.
    3. A number of Canvassing Cards.

2. He is urgently requested to read the instructions at the beginning of the canvass book.

3. He must call *immediately* upon each of the voters whose name

appears in the canvass book, and solicit his vote and interest on behalf of Messrs. SMITH and JONES.

4. If the voter is not at home when called upon, the canvasser must leave a canvassing card, and call again as soon as the voter is likely to be at home, and so until he succeeds in seeing him.

5. If the canvasser is personally known to the voter, the former can use the smaller card, inserting his own name in the space provided. If the canvasser is *not* known to the voter the larger card must be used, and the *voter's* name placed at the top.

6. Great care must be used in noting the *precise* reply of a voter.

7. A return of the voters seen should be made as soon as possible to the clerk in charge of the ward or district on the canvass return sheets provided, or the canvasser may call at the ward or district committee room, and get the clerk in charge to enter up the result of his canvass. The canvasser should not wait till he has completed his canvass before doing this, but a return should be made daily.

8. If a voter is found to have removed, the canvasser should use the greatest exertions to ascertain his new address, and failing that, all the information he can get about him, or his trade or business, where he last worked, &c. If the house is again tenanted, he should get the name of the new tenant and where he came from, as a great many removals may thus be traced. The canvasser should carefully note all this information in his canvass book, and report it to the ward or district committee.

9. Voters found to be dead or gone abroad, or not likely to vote, on account of illness, &c., should also be carefully reported, and as far as possible the age and appearance of the voter should be ascertained to prevent personation. If a voter says he "won't pledge," "won't vote," or declines to say what he will do, the canvasser must enquire as to who is likely to have any influence over him, from friendship, business, &c., and must report all the information he can get about him to the ward or district committee.

10. No canvasser will, under any pretence whatever, be allowed to incur *any* expenses, and no promise of payment for loss of time or refreshments or travelling expenses must on any account be made to a voter.

11. The canvasser is requested to ascertain, if possible, the names and addresses of any friends who are willing to place *gratuitously* their *own* conveyances at the disposal of the committee on the day of poll.

12. If the canvasser requires further instructions he must apply to the chairman or clerk in charge of his ward or district, who will give him every assistance.

Canvass in progress.

It may be assumed that the canvass is now in progress, during which time it will be the duty of the principal election agent to receive the daily ward or district canvass returns, and enter them into his "Central Committee's Canvass Ledger."

Very little information will be derived from this for the first two or three days, but it will afford the agent an opportunity of testing his machinery, and of removing incompetent or careless clerks, &c., whose stupidity or inattention might be disastrous later on. He should, therefore, exercise a rigid supervision over the whole of his staff, and if he finds that the progress of the canvass is not equal in all the wards or districts, he should at once institute enquiries into the cause, and adopt measures to remedy the fault. Later on the returns must be most carefully scanned, and pressure must be brought to bear, or more assistance given to the wards or districts where the canvass is not progressing as rapidly as is desirable.

Preparations for poll.

The election agent (if his candidate has made up his mind to go to the poll) should also be making preparations for the day of election, so as not to be hurried at the last moment.

Chances of success.

Most candidates, however, wish to reckon up their chances of success before making up their minds to incur the risk and expense of a poll: and though no certain rule can be propounded which can be absolutely relied upon, so much depending upon local circumstances, yet an approximation may be made of the chances of success or failure.

Of course, if a canvass has been an honest one, and the pledges for a candidate are equal to, or greater than, one-half the number of voters on the register, the candidate's success is all but certain.

It is not always, however, that the candidate finds himself in this satisfactory position. Most frequently the candidate who manages to poll much less than one-half the constituency wins the election.

The first thing, therefore, to be considered in estimating a candidate's chances of success is, how many voters are likely to vote. This will very much depend upon circumstances; whether it is a general election or an extraordinary one; whether there is any important question before the country, or there is apathy in the constituency, &c.; and all these circumstances will have to be weighed in forming an opinion. Some data will be found, however, in the average percentage of votes to voters on previous elections; and if the state of public feeling can be estimated in relation to some former election, the proportion of votes to voters at that election will not be a very unreliable guide to the votes likely to be given at the coming election.

Having arrived at an estimate of the number of voters likely to vote, it will next be necessary to consider the result of the canvass. If this shows a majority of the number likely to vote absolutely pledged to the candidate, his chances of success, assuming the canvass to be a faithful one, will be very good. It is usual, however, to make a deduction from the pledges, generally of ten per cent., though this will vary in different localities, on account of those voters who, from different causes, fail to keep their pledges. If the candidate should still have a majority of the number likely to vote, his election, if properly managed, may be considered pretty certain; but if he finds that he has not pledges equal to one-half of that number, his election will be more or less doubtful, according as the pledges approach near to, or away from, a moiety.

Of course, many disturbing influences may arise or be in operation which will modify the conclusions to be drawn from the above considerations; some influential body, which usually acts together, may not have decided to which candidate it will give its support; some independent candidate may be in the field, whose determination to withdraw or go to the poll may seriously affect one or other of the remaining candidates, &c., &c. In such cases an opinion as to the probable success of a particular candidate must be formed not only upon the data supplied by the canvass, &c., but upon the weight to be attached to these further influences.

It should be borne in mind, however, that where the contest is a purely political one, the **only safe plan to be pursued** in estimating the chances of a candidate is to reckon only upon his *absolute pledges*, giving the opposing candidate credit for the *balance* of the number *likely* to vote. Some election agents adopt the plan of dividing the unpledged electors into thirds, adding one-third of the number to their candidate's pledges, and the other two-thirds to his opponent, but we consider this mode of proceeding a very unsafe one.

Second canvass. It is a very good plan, if time will permit, to institute a *second* canvass of the constituency. This should not be made by the same persons taking the same canvass book, but each canvasser should take a different book to the one held by him on the first canvass. Any errors or false returns in the first canvass are thus easily detected.

Part II.

PREPARATIONS FOR THE ELECTION.

So soon as the candidate has determined to go to the poll, the election agent should proceed to make his arrangements for the day of election. <small>Arrangements for Election.</small>

For this purpose he will require to know—
1. What books, papers, forms, &c., must be provided.
2. What clerks, messengers, inspectors, &c., must be engaged.

The books, papers, forms, &c., will be—
1. Voters' instruction cards, with circulars and envelopes.
2. Canvassers' instructions.
3. Wall sheets.
4.[1] Polls return books, &c.
5. Polling agents' appointments.
6. Polling agents' registers.
7. Polling agents' instructions.
8. Counting agents' appointments.
9. Declarations of secrecy.
10. Ward or district committees' instructions.
11. Inspector of refreshments instructions.
12. *Unpolled* voters cards.
13. Red and blue pencils.

[1] Unnecessary unless it is desired to have an approximate state of the poll.

The staff of clerks, messengers, agents, &c., will be—
For each Polling Station—
 1. One or more polling agents.
 2.[1] Two voters polled counting clerks.
 3.[1] Two messengers to ditto.

For each Committee Room—
 1. Two wall sheet clerks.
 2.[1] Polls return clerk and slip clerk.
 3. Messengers.
 4. Inspector of refreshments.
 5. Carriage superintendent.

General—
 1. Out-door superintendent.
 2. Detective committee.
 3. Central committee clerk.
 4. Ditto messengers.

1.—THE VOTER'S INSTRUCTION CARD, &C.

The card and circular are intended to be sent, or delivered by the canvassers, to every voter *pledged* to the candidate, a day or two before the election.

The *circular* is for the purpose of reminding the voter of his pledge, to urge him to vote early, to instruct him how to fill up his ballot paper, and what to do with his card.

The *card* is to be taken by the voter to *the polling station* to assist him in filling up his ballot paper, and is then to be *given* in at the ward or district committee room (which for this purpose should be immediately adjacent to the door of exit of the polling booth), for the purpose of showing he has voted.

[1] Unnecessary unless it is desired to have an approximate state of the poll.

The circular may be in the following form :— *Voter's circular.*

FORM No. 33.

.... PARLIAMENTARY ELECTION, 188......

SIR,

The committee for securing the return of Messrs. Smith and Jones beg to thank you for your kind promise of support, and would respectfully draw your earnest attention to the following

INSTRUCTIONS TO VOTERS.

1. Vote *early*, to prevent any person voting in your name.
2. The enclosed card will show you WHERE you must vote.
3. You can only vote for two candidates.
4. On going into the polling station you will be asked your name, and where you live. A ballot paper will then be given to you, and you will have to go into a private box, where you will find a pencil. You must then place a X on the *right* hand side of the ballot paper, opposite the name of Messrs. Smith and Jones, which is the *(top, bottom, second, longest, shortest, etc., as the case may be)*, name on the paper. (See the card.)
5. You must on no account make any *other* mark on the ballot paper. If you do your vote will not be counted for Messrs. Smith and Jones.
6. Fold up the ballot paper and put it into the ballot box.
7. If you should accidentally *spoil* a ballot paper, you must give it to the presiding officer, and he will give you another.
8. Take the enclosed CARD with you when you go to vote, and it will remind you what to do.
9. AFTER you have voted kindly take the CARD to the committee room, No.   Street, which is *(just opposite the polling station)* and drop it into the letter box you will find there. It will thus show you HAVE voted, and will prevent canvassers troubling you. If, from any reason, you do not wish to be seen at the committee room, send your card by a friend if possible, or give it to any member of the committee.

Though not absolutely necessary, it is MOST IMPORTANT that the card should be left at the committee room AFTER VOTING, and the committee earnestly hope that you will do what will so very materially assist them in winning the election.

We are, Sir,
Your obedient servants,
.... Chairman.
.... Vice-Chairman.
.... Election Agent.

Voter's card.

The CARD may be in the following form :—

FORM No. 34.

..................PARLIAMENTARY ELECTION, 188......

Prog. No._____   No. on Register_____

Name........................

Day of polling :—

..............................188......

from   a.m., to   p.m.,[1]
                at
        ....

On the other side—

Fill up the ballot paper thus :—

1	Jones.	X
2	Smith.	X
3	Thompson.	
4	White.	

AFTER voting please deliver this card at the committee rooms, No.   Street, or to any member of the committee.

A card, with the canvassing circular, Form No. 25, should also be sent to every voter not known to be pledged to the other side.

Of course, the order of the candidates' names should be *as published*, and as they will appear on the ballot papers, and the X should be placed only against those names the voter is desired to vote for.

If the voter takes the card with him into the polling station, he can hardly fail to fill up his ballot paper correctly.

[1] Hours of Polling Act, 1884. See Appendix.

The card should bear a private mark, or have a line of some peculiar type upon it, not easily imitated, so that the arrangements may not be thrown into confusion by the other side sending in cards falsely purporting to come from voters who have voted. The colour, size, shape, and appearance of the card should be kept secret until the last moment. *Private mark on card.*

The cards and circulars may be prepared so soon as the day of polling and the places for taking the poll are fixed. The envelopes may be addressed previously even to that, and tied up in bundles ready for use.

2.—CANVASSER'S INSTRUCTIONS FOR DAY OF POLLING.

FORM No. 35.

................PARLIAMENTARY ELECTION, 188......

Messrs. SMITH and JONES.

CANVASSER'S INSTRUCTIONS FOR DAY OF POLLING.

1. The committee implicitly *rely* upon you to make such arrangements as will insure the bringing up of the voters favourable to Messrs. Smith and Jones, and whose names are in your canvass book, to the poll.

If you cannot *personally* attend to each voter, you are urgently requested to get some friends (as your sons, brothers, &c.), to assist you, and give to each two or three voters to attend to. You will, however, keep a personal supervision over your assistants.

It is a good plan to arrange for as many of your voters as you can, to meet you at a central point at the opening of the poll, and to proceed at once and vote. It saves you a great deal of time in running after individual voters, and also prevents their being personated.

2. Impress upon each voter the necessity of taking his voting card with him to the poll (to assist him in filling up his ballot paper correctly), and of leaving it at or sending it to the committee room AFTER he has polled. Explain to him the object of this—viz., that it shews who *has* voted, and will prevent half-a-dozen canvassers troubling him to vote *after* he has voted. If you find that he has

some objection to being seen at the committee room (as that he is afraid of his employer, landlord, &c.), arrange for him to send his card (under cover if necessary), by some friend of his or your own.

3. Read over the instructions to voters sent you herewith, so that you can explain them clearly to each voter.

4. When a voter leaves his card at the committee room to indicate that he has polled, the *progressive* number on his card is struck off a large wall sheet in the committee room. Thus, you can at once find which of the voters in your charge have actually voted, by looking at the *progressive* numbers in your canvass book, and the corresponding numbers on the wall sheet, or by asking the clerk in charge of the latter. But it should be *distinctly* understood that the wall sheets are only to *assist* you, and that your main reliance must be upon a personal visit of yourself or assistants to the voter at his house or place of business. Of course, if you have yourself *seen* one of your voters go into the polling station you will be satisfied he has voted, and you can then strike out his name from your book, and instruct the wall sheet clerk to cross out his number. But this must only be done in the case of *your own voters*.

5. If, upon examining the wall sheets from time to time during the day, you find any of the voters in your charge not crossed off, and you do not yourself know whether they have voted or not, you must immediately go to the residence or place of business of the voter and ascertain if he has polled. If he has not, you must use every effort to get him to the poll. If he has voted you will, of course, have his progressive number struck off on the wall sheet, to prevent other persons being sent after him.

6. You must, *on no account whatever*, make any promise of reward to a voter as an inducement for his vote. Such a promise would void the election, and you would incur serious penalties.

7. The committee desire to impress upon you, in the *strongest manner possible*, the duty of exerting yourself without ceasing, until every one of the voters in your charge favourable to Messrs. Smith and Jones has voted. When you have accomplished this you can give valuable assistance at the committee room in looking after chance voters, whose names and addresses will be given you there.

3.—WALL SHEETS.

FORM No. 36.

Use of wall sheet.

The object of these sheets is to afford a ready means of ascertaining which voters have voted.

They consist of large sheets of cardboard, upon which numbers are printed progressively in squares as below. The size of each square should be about an inch or an inch and a quarter, and the figures should be large and distinct. It will be observed that the figures follow progressively in the horizontal direction, and in twenties in the perpendicular, an arrangement very convenient for reference.

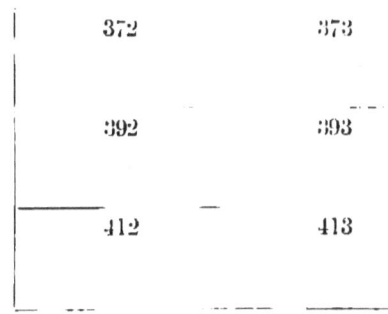

A set of these cards will be required for *each* ward or district.

Each set will begin with the number 1, and will go up to the highest *progressive* number in the ward or district committee register. It will, in fact, be a copy of the *progressive* numbers in that book.

If the *whole* of the voters in any particular ward or district are assigned to poll at *one* station, all the wall sheets may, on the day of election, be placed together; if, on the other hand, a portion of the ward votes at one station and another portion at another station, and so on, the wall sheets must be divided, and those representing each polling station must be placed separate from the others, and under the charge of separate clerks. Over each set of wall sheets must be placed in large letters and figures the number of the station they refer to.

[sidenote: How arranged on day of election.]

It may be mentioned here that where a ward or district has to be divided for the purpose of polling, the agent should endeavour to prevail upon the returning officer to assign that the voters in a particular district (*i.e.* in particular streets according to his ward committee register) should vote at a particular polling booth. This is generally done, and is the most convenient arrangement for all parties.

If the register itself is made out in street order, then it can be made use of as a wall sheet, by merely adding the particulars as hereafter mentioned.

If, however, the returning officer *should* assign that certain numbers should vote at certain polling stations irrespective of residence or place of qualification, and thus render useless for the purpose of polling the street list in the ward or district register, the wall sheets must be prepared according to the *register* number polling at each station.

Their subsequent use will be the same in both cases.

How prepared.
A few days before the election the clerk in charge or a confidential clerk in each ward must begin to fill into the squares of the wall sheets under each voter's progressive or register number as the case may be the name and address of every voter pledged to his candidate, thus—

372	373
John Smith.	
7, Garden Street.	
392	393
	Thomas Styles,
	3, Todd Street.
412	413
Jas. Wood,	
41, Todd Street.	

These names and addresses should be entered in *blue* ink. If it is known that any voter is pledged *against*, a *red* line may be made under his number, and no further notice taken of him. If a voter is known to be *dead*, or has left the country, his name and address should be written in black ink, and a black line drawn transversely across his square, beginning at the left-hand top corner. If a voter has not pledged, his name and address may be left out until the night prior to the election, when a careful revision of the wall sheets with the ward or district committee register (from which the information is obtained) should be made. If a voter is then found to be unpledged, but is known to be favourable, his name and address may be entered in *black* ink, and a *blue* pencil line drawn under it. If nothing is known of him, his name ought to be put down on a separate list, and special canvassers despatched the following morning to make careful enquiries as to his intentions.

When the wall sheets are thus completed, there will be in each committee room, ready for the day of election, a tabulated list of all voters in charge of that committee, with their names and addresses, and the manner in which they are pledged to vote or otherwise. Where voters residing in certain districts are assigned to vote at particular stations, their names will follow according to their order in streets, &c., and it will be seen at a glance on the day of polling what voters in any particular street, &c., have or have not voted, and whether the canvassers in charge are or are not doing their duty.

4.—POLLS RETURN BOOKS,[1] &c.

FORM No. 37.

Viz., Outside and Inside Book.
Slip Book.
Central Committee's Returns.
Ditto   ditto   Polls Return Book.

[1] Unnecessary, unless it is desired to have an approximate state of the poll.

H

These books are only required where an approximate state of the poll during the day is wanted.

<small>Polls return (outside) book.</small>

The polls return (outside) book is given into the charge of one or two men and a messenger, who station themselves in such a position (as at a room window, &c.), as will give them command of the place of *exit* from the polling station. Their duty is to count the number of voters coming *out* of the station, making a tick against each number as a voter comes out, and forwarding the leaves of the book which have been filled or partly filled, every half hour to the station committee room.

The book may be a small one, so as to be easily held in the hand; it should be paged consecutively, and each leaf numbered alike, thus

FORM No. 38.

No..........

Station, No.

1	10
2	11
3	12
4	13
5	14
&c.	&c.

Each leaf should be perforated at the top, so as easily to be torn off.

No person ought to be admitted into a polling station except the officials of the station and voters.[1] The former ought not to leave the station during the time of polling,

---

[1] The Ballot Act, 1872, schedule 1, part 1, rule 21.

so that if this rule is carried out, the person in charge of the polls return book will find no difficulty in correctly noting the number of voters who have polled.

THE POLLS RETURN BOOK (INSIDE)[1]

is a record kept in each ward or district committee room of the numbers who have voted in each station, as sent in by the outside agents every half hour, and of the number of voting cards which have been left by voters AFTER *polling.*

Polls return (inside) book.

If there are only *two* candidates an *approximate* state of the poll may easily be arrived at by deducting the total number of *bona fide* cards left by voters after polling, from the gross number of voters who have polled. The former may be fairly taken to represent supporters, and the balance of the latter opponents.

Where two candidates.

If there are *more* than two candidates, and it is wished to know *approximately* how many votes have been given for each candidate, then it will be necessary to have some method of shewing on the wall sheets how each voter has pledged: thus, if there are two candidates on each side, the names, &c., of those voters who give party votes may be all in *blue* or *red* as the case may be; those who give split votes may have their names *or* addresses marked in blue or red, according as they support the first or second candidate on each side, the *name* in all cases representing the first candidate on each side, and the *address* the second. Thus, if a voter is pledged to vote for the two first candidates on each side, his name will be written in blue with a red line underneath it; if he is pledged to vote for the first candidate on one side and the second on the other, his name will be one colour and his address another; if he intends to vote for *both* second candidates, then his

Where more than two candidates.

---

[1] Unnecessary, unless an approximate state of the poll is required.

address will be blue with a red line underneath it. If he intends to plump, a blue or red line underneath his name *or address* will shew whether he intends to plump either the first or second candidate, and on which side.

Slip book.

It will then be necessary to have a slip clerk, with an ordinary slip book, at each wall sheet, and as the voting cards come in, the wall sheet clerk, when striking off the numbers of those who have voted, will call them out and state how the voter was pledged, and the slip clerk will note it down in his book, thus:—

FORM No. 39.

Slip book.

Slip No.   Station No.

Voters' Progressive Number.	How Pledged.			
	Smith.	Jones.	Brown.	Robinson.
354	1		1	
258	1	1		
167	1			

As each slip is filled, he will send it to the clerk in charge of the polls return book (inside), who will add up the numbers who have voted and the numbers polled for each candidate, and then enter the results in his book.

The totals of the first two columns will give the numbers polled for each friendly candidate *(so far as the cards have come in)*, as it may fairly be assumed that the vast majority of voters will vote as pledged. The other two columns will not, of course, shew the number of votes given to the opposition candidates, but they will shew many of the splits, and if, after the gross number of cards brought in has been deducted from the gross number of voters polled and the balance divided by two, the splits given to each opposition candidate are added, the numbers will shew, *as near as they can be made to shew*—which, after all, will only be approximately—the votes given to each *opponent*.

The form of the polls return book (inside) will be as follows:—

FORM No. 40.

Time.		Name or Number of Station.	No. of Outside Slip.	Voted.	No. of Inside Slip.	Number of Cards.	How Voted.
Hours.	Min.						

This book may be made of a number of sheets of paper, foolscap size.

The clerk in charge of it should be particular in seeing that he gets the slips, both outside and inside, in regular order, and should carefully examine every slip to see that its consecutive number follows the preceding one. If a slip is missing, he should instantly despatch a messenger to enquire into the irregularity. Every half hour he will rule off the books and add up the numbers, making it each time a *gross* state of the polling. He ought then to despatch to the central committee a copy of the totals in his book, thus:—

FORM No. 41.

Return to central committee.

.....................ELECTION, 18......

..................and..................

MESSRS. SMITH AND JONES.

Return of Polling in the

.........................Ward or Polling District.

No.......... ....Time.

Total Number Voted.	Total Number of Cards sent in.	How Voted.		

Signed

.........................Chairman.

To be sent every half-hour to central committee room, No. Street.

These returns should be upon half sheets of paper, large note size, and as they must be sent under cover, a number of envelopes should be addressed to the central committee ready for use.

At the central committee room another polls return book should be kept to show the gross state of the poll through- out the borough or division. It may be made thus: — *Central committee polls return book.*

FORM No. 42.

Time.	Name of Ward or Polling District.	No. of Return.	Total Number Voted.	Total Number of Cards.	How Voted.

Every half hour this will be ruled off, and the *gross*

totals added up, care being taken to see that the returns have first been sent from every ward committee.

The books and forms under this head are, as stated, only required when an *approximate* state of the poll is wanted; as the value of the latter is very doubtful, and as its attainment, where there are more than two candidates, involves a considerable amount of extra labour on the day of polling, when every effort should be used to get up favourable voters to the poll, it may be wise to dispense with it.

5.—POLLING AGENT'S APPOINTMENT.

Appointment of polling agents.

Each *candidate* may appoint one or more agent or agents to attend at each or any of the polling stations on the day of election to detect personation. Notice must however be given in writing to the returning officer or his deputy *previous* to the opening of the poll, of the names and addresses of the persons so appointed.[1]

None of these agents can now be paid.

If it is necessary to *pay* a polling agent, he must be appointed by the *election agent*.[2] The form can be easily adapted.

The following form may be used:—

FORM No. 43.

Form of.

...................PARLIAMENTARY ELECTION, 18......

To......................Esquire, Returning Officer of the ....of......................

I, A.B., of &c., Esquire, a candidate at the above election, do hereby give you notice that I have appointed the undermentioned persons to be agents on my behalf, in the several polling stations

---

[1] 6 & 7 Vic., c. 16, sec. 85, and Ballot Act, 1872, sec. 24, and 3rd schedule thereto.
[2] C. P. Act, 1883, sec. 27.

set opposite their respective names, for the purpose of detecting personation, pursuant to the statute in such case made and provided—

Name.	Address.	Ward or District.	No. of Station.

Dated this..................day of....................A.D. 18......

Signed..

Each personation agent should also be provided with a separate appointment, to be delivered as his credentials, to the deputy returning officer of his station, immediately *before* the opening of the poll.

FORM No. 44.

........................PARLIAMENTARY ELECTION, 18......

I, A.B , of &c., Esquire, a candidate at the now approaching election of members to serve in Parliament for the   of   , do hereby nominate and appoint (name) of (address) an agent on my behalf, to attend at the polling station, No.   in   ward (or district), appointed for taking the poll at such election, for the purpose of detecting personation, pursuant to the statute in such case made and provided.

Dated this..................day of....................A.D. 18......

Signed..

6.—POLLING AGENT'S REGISTER.

This is a copy of the register or of the part of it containing the names of all the voters polling at each polling station.

It should be interleaved, if necessary, and ruled with columns like a canvasser's book, and with wide spaces for remarks.

Object of register.

As its object is to give such information to the personation agent as will enable him to detect any attempt at personation, and prevent voters with double qualifications from voting twice, the way in which each voter is pledged must be carefully marked from the ward or district committee book, and each double qualification correctly noted. Every "remark," too, in the ward or district committee's register referring to voters who are dead, or on the day of election will be away from home, or who "won't vote," or are "too ill to vote," &c., &c., must also be transferred to the name of the voter in the polling agent's register, which must be revised and corrected up to the last moment on the eve of the election.

7.—POLLING AGENT'S INSTRUCTIONS.

A copy of the following instructions should be supplied to each polling agent, who should be requested to read them over carefully:—

FORM No. 45.

.....................PARLIAMENTARY ELECTION, 18......

Messrs. SMITH and JONES.

INSTRUCTIONS TO POLLING AGENTS.

1. The agent to be at the polling station at a quarter before eight o'clock precisely, and *immediately before* the poll opens to deliver his appointment to the deputy returning officer.

2. The poll opens at eight o'clock a.m., and closes at four (five) o'clock p.m.

3. If the agent has not previously ma le the statutory declaration of secrecy, he must make it before the returning officer or a justice of the peace.[1]

4. The presiding officer at every polling station is bound,[2] just before the commencement of the poll, to shew the ballot box, so that it may be seen that it is empty, and then to lock it up, and place his seal upon it in such manner that it cannot be opened without breaking the seal. He should then place it in full view, and keep it locked and sealed until it is opened in the presence of the returning officer. The agent should see that this is done.

5. The agent, if not paid for his services, is urgently and particularly requested, if a voter, to give his own vote immediately the poll is opened. If *paid*, he cannot vote.

6. The agent will be furnished with a copy of the register, containing the names of the voters polling at his station. No other person can poll at his station.

7. This register will be marked with pledges for Messrs. Smith and Jones, and the pledges given to the other candidates, and any other information that is necessary.

8. As a voter comes to the poll and gives his name, the agent will turn to his name in the register, and observe if there be anything *shewing that the voter is to be objected to*. If there is, he will at once request the presiding officer or his clerk to put the questions, and, if necessary, to administer the oath. The only questions the returning officer can put to a voter[3] are:—

1. Are you the same person whose name appears as A.B. in the register of voters now in force for the   of   ?

2. Have you already voted, either here or elsewhere, at this election for the   of   ?

Questions.

The oath is to the same effect, but is sworn to by the voter.

9. The attention of the agent is particularly requested to the fact that no other questions can be put to a voter than the two above quoted, and that *no question* must be put, except on the request of *an agent appointed in writing*, and whose appointment has been given to the returning officer *previous* to the opening of the poll, and who has duly made a declaration of secrecy. The agent should, therefore, be satisfied that this has been done by the other side as to their agent before he allows any questions to be put at his request. The presiding officer has no right to put the questions or tender the oath, unless required by a duly appointed agent.

1 Ballot Act, 1872, schedule 1, part 1, rule 54.
2 Ibid, rule 23.
3 6 and 7 Vic., c. 18, secs. 81, 82, and Ballot Act, 1872, sec. 10.

10. In all cases where the word "dead" is placed opposite a voter's name, and an attempt is made to personate the voter, or where the word "duplicate" is written opposite a voter's name *not pledged* to Messrs. Smith and Jones, the agent is to request the presiding officer to put the questions, and, if necessary, the oath.

11. In all cases where the voter is *not pledged* to Messrs. Smith and Jones the agent should, if he has the slightest reason to suppose an attempt is being made at personation or double voting, require the oath to be put.

12. In case the polling agent is satisfied a voter is being personated, the agent's duty is to declare to the presiding officer that he believes and undertakes to prove that the person voting is not, in fact, the person in whose name he appears to vote, whereupon the presiding officer is bound to order the party to be taken into custody. No clerk of the presiding officer can order a person into custody, or order the removal of any person from the polling booth [1]

13. The ballot paper will consist of a paper containing, on the face of it, the names and description of the candidates, and on the back of it a number. Each paper will have a counterfoil to it, with a number on its *face* corresponding to the number on the back of the ballot paper.

14. When a voter comes up to vote, his number, name, and description, as stated in the copy of the register, will be called out, and his *number* will be marked on the *counterfoil*. *Immediately before the ballot paper is given to him, it must be marked on both sides with the official mark, by being either stamped or perforated*, and then a *mark must be placed by the presiding officer in the register against the number of the voter*, to shew that he has received a ballot paper, but it must *not* shew *which* he has received. The voter must then go into a private compartment *in the station* and mark for whom he votes. He must then fold up the paper, *shew the official mark on the back to the presiding officer*, put it into the ballot box, and quit the station.[2] The agent must see that all these regulations are strictly observed, *particularly* that the official mark is placed on all papers given out to voters pledged to Messrs. Smith and Jones, and if any deviations are made from them he should carefully note down in what cases they occur.

15. As each person receives his ballot paper, the agent will place a mark in *his* register against the voter's number.

16. If a voter accidentally spoils a ballot paper the presiding

[1] Ballot Act, 1872, schedule 1, part 1, rule 50.
[2] Ballot Act, 1872, sec. 2, and schedule 1, part 1, rules 24, 25.

officer must give him another, but the spoiled one must be kept by the presiding officer.

17. If a voter comes up to vote, and it appears that he is pledged to vote for Messrs. Smith and Jones, but that some one has previously voted in his name, he is entitled to mark a ballot paper (of a different colour to the other ballot papers), but instead of putting it into the ballot box he must give it to the presiding officer, who must keep it in a separate packet, and enter it into a list called the "Tendered Votes List."[1] The agent must *insist* upon such votes being taken, and must enter full particulars of them at the end of his register. *Voter personated.*

18. If a voter is blind, or otherwise physically incapable of voting in the manner above mentioned, or if he is a Jew, *and* the polling takes place on the Saturday, and he objects, on religious grounds, to vote in such manner, or if the voter declares he is unable to read, the presiding officer must, *in the presence of the agents of the candidates*, mark the ballot paper as directed by the voter, and place it in the ballot box, and insert the name and register number of the voter in a list to be called "The List of Votes marked by the Returning Officer." The agent need not keep any record of these votes unless something particular arises. *Voter blind, &c.*

19. The agent must see that no persons on the other side are allowed in the polling booth except the *duly appointed* clerks and agents, and if this rule is infringed he must require the presiding officer to exclude them, which he is bound to do.[2] The candidates are entitled to be present.[3] The agent must not communicate, *nor allow anyone else to communicate*, any information as to the names or numbers of the electors who have or have not voted. *Persons allowed in booth.*

20. Immediately after the close of the poll the presiding officer must, *in the presence of the agents of the candidates*, make up into separate packets and seal with his seal, and the agent may, if he thinks fit, also seal with *his* seal— *Close of poll.*
1. The ballot box.
2. The *unused* and *spoilt* ballot papers placed together.
3. The *tendered* ballot papers.
4. The *marked copies of the register* and the *counterfoils*.
5. The *tendered votes* list.
  The list of votes *marked by the presiding officer*.
  A *statement* of the number of voters in the last-named list, under the heads of "physical incapacity," "Jews," and "unable to read," and
  The *declaration of inability to read*.

1 Ballot Act, 1872, schedule 1, part 1, rule 27.
2 Ballot Act, schedule 1, part 1, rule 21.
3 Ibid, rule 51.

These must be delivered forthwith to the returning officer, and the agent must accompany them.

21. If required, the agent must attend at the counting of the votes, to verify his seal on the ballot box and packets.

22. If any irregularity be allowed by the presiding officer, the agent must *forthwith* make a note of the matter for future reference, if necessary.

23. At the close of the poll the agent will collect all the books and papers, and, as soon as convenient, leave them with the election agent.

24. Refreshments will be sent at one p.m.

8.—COUNTING AGENT'S APPOINTMENT.

<small>Candidate to appoint counting agent.</small>

By Rule 31 of the Ballot Act, schedule 1, part 1, the *candidates* may respectively appoint agents to attend the counting of the votes.

By Rule 32 the returning officer shall make arrangements for counting the votes in the presence of the agents of the candidates as soon as practicable after the close of the poll, and shall give notice in writing to the agents appointed to attend the counting of the votes, of the time and place at which he will begin to count the same.

No limit is put to the number of agents who may attend for each candidate, but by the 32nd rule the name and address of every agent " appointed to attend the counting of the votes shall be transmitted to the returning officer *one clear day* at the least *before* the *opening of the poll.*" If this is not done, the returning officer may refuse to admit him to the counting of the votes.

The election agent should therefore send in his own name and the names of all such persons as he desires shall attend the counting of the votes not later than the day but one prior to the election. It may be desirable to include in the list the name of one polling agent from each polling station, who should (where it is thought advisable) be deputed to place a seal upon the ballot box, and afterwards to verify it before the box is opened by the returning officer. A quick, intelligent clerk should also be included, who will check the account of the votes given for each candidate.

The following form of notice to the returning officer may be used:—

FORM No. 46.

Form of Appointment.

.... PARLIAMENTARY ELECTION, 18......

To..Esquire, Returning Officer for the.............................of ....

I, A.B., of &c., Esquire, a candidate at the now approaching election of members to serve in Parliament for the   of   , do hereby appoint the undermentioned persons to be agents on my behalf to attend the counting of the votes.

Name.	Address.

(Signed)

A. B.

This list should be prepared in duplicate, and one sent to the returning officer and one kept.

Every person attending in a polling station, or at the counting of the votes, must make a Declaration of Secrecy, pursuant to the 54th Rule of the Ballot Act. It is a good plan to arrange for the polling and counting agents and others to meet a Justice of the Peace at a certain place, where all the declarations can be taken at once.

Agent dying, &c. If any agent dies or becomes incapable of acting, the candidate may appoint another in his place upon giving notice *forthwith* to the returning officer.[1]

9.—DECLARATION OF SECRECY.

FORM No. 47.

..........................PARLIAMENTARY ELECTION, 18......

MESSRS. SMITH AND JONES.

DECLARATION OF SECRECY.

(NOTICE TO POLLING AGENTS AND COUNTING AGENTS.)

To Mr.

DEAR SIR,

You are requested to attend at on the next at o'clock, in order to make the Declaration of Secrecy required by law to be made by every person who attends on behalf of a Candidate at a Polling Station or at the counting of the votes.

Yours faithfully,

Election Agent.

The Declaration is as follows:—

"I solemnly promise and declare that I will not at this Election for do anything forbidden by Section IV. of the Ballot Act, 1872, which has been read to me."

(Signed)

Made and subscribed this day of 188 before me

A Justice of the Peace for the
of (*or*
Returning Officer for the
of .)

[1] Ballot Act, schedule 1, part 1, rule 53.

10.—WARD OR DISTRICT COMMITTEE'S INSTRUCTIONS.

These instructions are intended to be given to the chairmen of wards or districts two or three days previous to the poll, at a meeting specially convened by the agent for the purpose. The clerk in charge of each ward or district should also be present, and the agent should read over the instructions to the meeting and give such explanations as may be needed. He should also, at the same meeting, detail the *modus operandi* of the whole of the machinery of the election, from the tendering of a vote in the polling station to the record of the voter having voted on the wall sheet, and *if intending to have a state of the poll*, to the final return to the central committee.

FORM No. 48.

.........................PARLIAMENTARY ELECTION, 188......

Messrs. SMITH AND JONES.

INSTRUCTIONS
TO WARD OR DISTRICT COMMITTEES ON
DAY OF POLLING.

1. The chairman and clerk in charge must be at their committee room not later than 7.15 a.m., and must remain there during the whole time of polling.

2. The chairman must see that all wall sheet clerks, messengers, and other officers are in their proper places at 7.45 a.m., and must have one or two persons ready to supply the place of anyone absenting himself.

3. He must see that each person thoroughly understands the duties he has to perform, and must, the day before the election, clearly explain the routine to be gone through at the polling.

4. This election being conducted on the principle of each ward or district managing its own affairs, the committee is particularly requested to use every exertion they possibly can to bring up voters to the poll without instructions from the central committee. The

I

doubtful and *unpledged* voters should *first* be attended to, as strong party men may be relied upon to vote either voluntarily or on being sent for.

5. Arrangements must be made for collecting the cards of friendly voters *after* they have polled. For this purpose they should be urged by the canvassers to deposit their polling cards at the committee room, or to give them to an active member of the committee, *who should be posted outside the polling station to receive them*, as soon as possible *after* polling. It should be *clearly* explained that the object is simply to ascertain whether the voter *has* polled (not *how* he has voted), and to prevent his being visited unnecessarily at a later period of the day. Where the cards are collected outside the polling station, they should be sent as often as possible, by messengers, to the committee room and handed to the wall sheet clerks, who will strike the names off the wall sheets or marked register.

6. The chairman must *frequently* from time to time examine the wall sheets to ascertain who has and who has not voted, and if the voters in charge of any particular canvasser are not polling so rapidly as desirable, he must forthwith despatch a messenger to the canvasser to inquire the reason. If necessary, he must send assistance to the canvasser, and get some active friends to wait upon the voters.

7. It is particularly urged that chairmen, clerks in charge, canvassers, clerks, messengers (who are voters *and unpaid*), should vote at the first convenient opportunity, and that as many friends as possible be got to attend at the polling booth before 8 a.m., so that Messrs. Smith and Jones may head the poll from the first.

8. The chairman should have two canvass books prepared for him, containing the names of *all out-voters*; those *polling* in but *residing* out of his ward or district in one book, and those *residing* in but *polling* out of the ward or district in another. He should constantly during the day refer to the voters in the first book, and see, by reference to the wall sheets, that they are duly polling. As each person is marked off on the wall sheet as having voted, his name should be struck from the canvass book. If any voters remain unpolled after noon, he should send their names upon *a voters unpolled card* to the chairman of the ward or district where they have been canvassed, and if there is any continued delay in their voting, he must send a special messenger to bring them up. When sending to a chairman of another ward or district, each chairman should also send a list of those persons *residing* in the other ward, &c., who have *polled* in his ward, &c. This will enable each chairman to

know that the voters in his second book have polled, and he will mark them off accordingly.

9. *The chairman is personally responsible for the punctual transmission of the state of the poll to the central committee room every half hour upon the forms provided for the purpose.* <small>Only required when a state of poll is wanted.</small>

10. Especial attention should be given to *unpledged* voters, particularly to those who are favourable, and friends of position and weight should see them, if possible, and get them to vote.

11. A small committee or an energetic man should be appointed to take charge of the conveyances gratuitously lent for the day of poll. Infirm, doubtful, and voters pressed for time must be first attended to, and every care must be taken to arrange the routes so as to avoid waste of time.

12. As soon as the voting in their own ward or district is exhausted, the services of as many of the conveyances, committee men and canvassers as possible, should be transferred to any other district where they may be required.

13. The precautions against bribery or treating must be redoubled on the polling day, and every pressure in this direction on the part of voters must be *promptly and resolutely* resisted and their attention called to the consequences *to themselves*, as well as others, which would ensue from any breach of the law.

14. Any instance of improper practices on the part of opponents must be carefully noted in writing, the names of informants, witnesses or others having knowledge of them secured, and the election agent *at once* informed.

15. The chairman will have the custody of the refreshment tickets for canvassers, &c. He will have a card containing the names of the canvassers, clerks, and messengers actively engaged in the election, with a column ruled down one side. Under no circumstances must more than *two* cards be given to a canvasser, &c.; one in the forenoon and the other in the afternoon. When the first card is given the chairman must make a mark thus, 1, opposite the name of the person to whom it is given, and when he gives the second card to the same person he must cross the first mark thus X. It will thus be seen at a glance when a canvasser, &c., has had his two cards. No card is transferable, and *upon no account* must a card be given to a *voter*, either by the chairman or anyone else. The refreshments are intended solely for the use of the officers *necessarily engaged in and actually conducting the election*, and the central committee will hold the chairmen of committees responsible for any departure from this intention.

16. The chairman or clerk in charge of the ward or district must,

at the close of the polling, collect all books, wall sheets, papers, and memoranda whatever relating to the election, and secure them in a safe place.

17. These instructions must be kept by the chairman, and must be returned to Mr.   immediately after the election.

18. In case of any difficulty arising during the polling, application must be made to Mr.   , at the central committee rooms, No.   Street.

11.—INSPECTORS OF REFRESHMENTS. INSTRUCTIONS.

FORM No. 49.

....................PARLIAMENTARY ELECTION, 188......

Messrs. SMITH & JONES.

1. The inspector of refreshments will have sole charge and authority over the refreshment room, and will be responsible to the committee for the strict carrying out of these instructions.

2. No person, *on any pretence whatever*, must be admitted within the refreshment room unless provided with a ticket, a duplicate of which will be given to the inspector on the morning of the day of polling.

3. The refreshments are intended *solely* for the canvassers, clerks, and messengers necessarily carrying on the election, and it is an *imperative* instruction to the inspector not to allow any person (even with a ticket) to enter the room whom he knows does not fill one of these offices.

4. Before a person is admitted into the room his ticket must be carefully scrutinized to ascertain that no forgery is being attempted, and the ticket must be taken from him, and carefully kept by the inspector.

5. No person must be admitted more than *once* in the forenoon and *once* in the afternoon, whether he has more tickets or not.

6. No person must be allowed to remain in the room more than a quarter of an hour, and no refreshments must, *on any account*, be supplied outside the room.

7. The room must be closed punctually at   p.m., and the inspector must then either lock up the room, or have the remainder of the refreshments removed to a place of safety. He must also

seal up the tickets he has received, and return them forthwith to Mr.   , the election agent.

8. The inspector's particular attention is drawn to the Acts of Parliament against bribery and treating, and he is strongly urged not to permit any violation of the law, as such might render the election of Mr.   void. The committee have selected, for inspectors of refreshments, men in whom they have great confidence, and they earnestly hope this confidence will not prove misplaced, but that the inspectors will act up to both the letter and spirit of these instructions, and allow refreshments only

TO PERSONS NECESSARILY ENGAGED IN CARRYING ON THE ELECTION, AND TO THOSE ONLY NEEDFUL REFRESHMENTS.

12.—UNPOLLED VOTERS CARDS.

These are small cards intended for use in the *after* part of the day of polling.

The names and addresses of two or three voters, resident in the same neighbourhood, and who, though *pledged* for the candidate, do not appear from the wall sheets to have *polled*, are written on a card and given into the hands of some active friend in the committee room with instructions to see the voters and get them to poll.

FORM No. 50.

..........................PARLIAMENTARY ELECTION, 18......

The following persons, pledged to Messrs. Smith and Jones, do not appear to have voted. Please see to them immediately, and get them to poll.

Progressive No.	Name.	Address.

The wall sheet clerk and an assistant should employ themselves during the afternoon in extracting from the wall sheets the names, &c., of the unpolled voters and writing them on these cards. The chairman or superintendent of the committee room should then either see the canvasser in whose charge the voters are or some other active friend, and get him to wait upon the voters and see that they vote.

STAFF ON ELECTION DAY.

Staff.

With regard to the staff requisite for conducting the election on the day of polling little need be said, except that each person employed should clearly understand the special work which he is detailed to, so that no confusion may arise as to who is to fill any particular post.

A list should be prepared in each committee room of the persons appointed to each department of work in the committee room and the polling station to which it is attached, and a general list should be prepared for the use of the election agent.

The persons appointed should be sober and intelligent men. They should not be voters—at least those who are *paid* should not be voters, otherwise they are disqualified from voting.[1]

The duties of the various officers may be gathered from the preceding instructions applicable to each, but a few words may be said as to the class of men required for the different positions, and in explanation of matters which might otherwise not be left quite clear.

POLLING AGENTS.

It is no exaggeration to say that the success of a closely-contested election under the Ballot Act will depend mainly

---

[1] Representation of People Act, 1867, sec. 11.

upon a suitable choice being made of men to act as polling or personation agents. They are, under the secret system of voting, the only persons who have the opportunity of watching the proceedings of the returning officers, and as the latter are almost invariably partizans on one side or the other, it will be seen at once how desirable it is that the polling agents should be men of sufficient ability and standing to keep them in check.

It is very desirable, therefore, that the chief polling agent in each polling station should be a lawyer of some standing in his profession, or a man of position and ability, and in selecting the agent for each station regard ought to be had to the standing and capacity of the returning officer of that station, so that the ablest agent should be put with the ablest returning officer, and so on. If the chief agent of a station is one who is well acquainted with the voters polling at that station, so much the better, but if he has little or no knowledge of them, then one or two other agents should be appointed to act with him.

These agents should be men who are well acquainted with the particular voters assigned to poll at that particular station—schoolmasters, collectors of rates or taxes, rent collectors, friendly societies' agents or collectors, &c., are persons very likely to know great numbers of voters, and if friends filling these positions can be got to act as polling agents, they make the most efficient representatives. If such cannot be got, then the best arrangements must be made that are practicable, but it is almost worse than useless to have agents who know nothing about the voters.

The chief agent in each station should have a copy of the instructions to polling agents given to him, and he should be urged to make himself acquainted with them. It should also be strongly impressed upon him that it is his duty to see that every requirement of the Ballot Act is duly and properly carried out by the returning officer, and that a note of any irregularity allowed by the latter should immediately be made for subsequent reference if necessary.

Declaration of secrecy. The polling agents must make the declaration of secrecy.

VOTERS POLLED CLERKS AND MESSENGERS.

The duties of the above are sufficiently shewn by a reference to the description of the " Polls Return Books, &c.," at page 97. These officers are only required when an approximate state of the poll is considered desirable.

WALL SHEET CLERKS.

These should be steady and intelligent men, as bank clerks, schoolmasters, book-keepers, &c. They should have entire control over the wall sheets, which should be nailed upon the wall and within a little barrier made of chairs, tables, &c., behind which no other person must be allowed.

If convenient, the wall sheets may be placed near to a letter box prepared for receiving the voters' cards after polling, and the clerk can then take out the cards as they are dropped into the box. If this arrangement cannot well be carried out, then another clerk must be deputed to attend to the letter box, and to carry the cards from time to time to the wall sheet clerks. When the latter receive the cards they will count them and enter the number in a book provided for the purpose. One of the clerks will then take the cards and call out each *progressive* number and the voter's name, whilst the other, with his red and blue pencil, will strike them out on the wall sheet by a diagonal line from *right* to *left*, as a sign that the voter has voted. As the latter does this, the former will place the card on a file. If the Register itself is used as a wall sheet the *Register* number and name will be called and struck out.

If an approximate state of the poll is required, and there are *more* than two candidates, the clerk striking out the number and name will call out how each is pledged to vote, and a slip clerk (who must in such case be provided with a seat near) will then record it in his slip book.

The wall sheet clerks must from time to time examine their wall sheets, and if they find any particular street or district not voting as rapidly as the general body of voters, they must call the attention of the chairman of the committee to the fact forthwith. As the polling gets slack, they must also extract upon the "unpolled voters cards" the names of voters unpolled and hand them to the chairman, who will instruct friends to fetch them up.

POLLS RETURN CLERKS & SLIP CLERKS.

These clerks will only be necessary where a state of the poll is required, and their duties may be collected from a perusal of the instructions given at pp. 97–104. They ought to be careful and intelligent men, and accustomed to accounts.

INSPECTORS OF REFRESHMENTS.

The inspectors should be steady, sober men, who can be thoroughly relied upon to carry out their instructions. Providing refreshments on the polling day for persons *bonâ fide* engaged in the work of the election is not illegal,[1] but the greatest care should be taken that no mere voter is allowed even inside the refreshment room, let alone to partake of any refreshments. The inspectors should, therefore, be men of good temper, but of firm, unyielding disposition.

It is, of course, desirable that every person engaged in the election should provide his own refreshments; but this cannot be done in every case, and, therefore, it is most necessary, where refreshments have to be provided, that it should be done under stringent regulations.

The inspectors cannot be *paid* for their services.

CARRIAGE SUPERINTENDENT.

Illegal to pay for conveyance of voters to poll.

Any *payment* or *contract* for payment on account of the conveyance of electors *to* or *from* the poll, whether for the hiring of horses or carriages, or for railway fares, or otherwise, is an illegal practice[2] except in a *county*, the nature of which is such that any electors *residing therein* are unable to poll without crossing the sea, or a branch or arm thereof. In the latter case, means of conveyance may be provided, and the cost may be charged over and above the maximum allowed for election expenses.[3]

except where sea or arm thereof to be crossed.

Voters may pay for their own conveyance.

And nothing in the Act is to prevent a carriage, horse, or other animal being let to or hired, employed or used by an elector, or several electors *at their joint cost*, for the purpose of being conveyed *to* or *from* the poll.[4] The joint contribution, however, must be a *bonâ fide* one and not illusory merely, *ex. gr*: If one man paid two shillings and another half a crown, there would be a *bonâ fide* joint

---

[1] Bradford Election Petition, 19, Law Times Reports, N.S., 728. Westminster Election Petition, 20, Law Times Reports, N.S., 238.

[2] C. P. Act, 1883, sec. 7. [3] Ibid. sec. 48. [4] Ibid. sec. 14. sub. sec. 3.

hiring, but if one man paid a sovereign and another a penny, the hiring would be simply an evasion of the Act, and all the parties would be liable to penalties.

It will be observed that the provisions of the Act are directed against the *payment* of travelling expenses, whether by the candidate or his agent, or by any other person voluntarily or otherwise.

There is nothing, therefore, prohibiting the use of vehicles gratuitously lent, even though the object be expressly for the conveyance of voters to and from the poll, indeed the gratuitous use of vehicles for these purposes is so far favoured that it is provided that no person shall be liable to pay any duty or take out a licence for any carriage by reason only of such carriage being used without payment or promise of payment for the conveyance of electors to or from the poll.[1]

Vehicles may be lent gratuitously, and without being liable to pay duty or take out licence.

Not only, therefore, can friends be asked to lend their carriages, for which duty is paid, but friends having carriages, gigs, light carts, &c., which ordinarily are exempted or not chargeable with duty, can lend them for the purpose of conveying voters to and from the poll, if such are lent gratuitously, without being subjected to coach or carriage duties.

As pointed out in the Instructions to Ward and District Committees, enquiries should be made to ascertain what friends have conveyances and whether they are willing to lend them on the day of poll. Many who would object to lend their carriages for general use would be willing to arrange to convey voters from their own neighbourhood, especially those who are known to them, and where an objection is made to placing vehicles at the absolute disposal of the committee, arrangements should be made, as far as possible, for their limited use.

1 C. P. Act, 1883. sec. 14, sub. sec. 4.

Not legal to hire or lend public stage or hackney carriages or horses and carriages kept for hire.

It may be mentioned here that no public stage or hackney carriage, or any horse or other animal kept or used for drawing the same, or any carriage, horse or other animal kept or used for letting out to hire, can be let, *lent*, or *employed* for the conveyance of electors to or from the poll.[1] Hence, no person can lend, gratuitously even, a horse or carriage which he keeps *or uses* for any of the above purposes, and no person can hire such, for the purpose of gratuitously lending the same, without being guilty of an illegal hiring.

Carriages "jobbed."

It is conceived, however, that the above section does not apply to carriages "jobbed" for a term if they are *bonâ fide* hired and intended to be used as private conveyances.

Lists of persons willing to lend conveyances.

Lists should be made of the names and addresses of friends who are willing to place their conveyances at the disposal of the committee, as well as of those who will undertake to bring friends and neighbours from particular districts.

FORM No. 51.

..................PARLIAMENTARY ELECTION, 188......

CONVEYANCES.

..........................Ward (*or District*).

The following friends will lend their vehicles gratuitously on the polling day:—

Name.	Address.	Description of Vehicle.	No. of Seats.	Remarks.

1 C. P. Act, 1883, sec. 11, sub-sec. 1.

Carriages may be hired and paid for by the candidate for the use of messengers and others who are merely desirous of getting quickly from one place to another, but on no account must they be used for bringing up a Voter to or taking him back from the poll, it having been held that it is the intention of the legislature "that persons should go to the poll either by walking or by their own conveyance or the conveyance of some friend."[1] Carriages hired, therefore, on behalf of a candidate should have the following notice posted upon them:— *(Cabs for use of messengers, &c.)*

FORM No. 52.

"This carriage is intended solely for the use of messengers and committee-men, *and must on no account be used for the conveyance of a voter to or from the poll.*

"By order,

———————————————

In boroughs and in every polling district of a county it will be found most convenient to have a carriage superintendent who, either by himself or with the assistance of one or two others, will make all the necessary arrangements for marshalling, placing, and directing the movements of the cabs, &c. *(Carriage superintendent.)*

In boroughs he will solicit the gratuitous loan of conveyances from friends; arrange with chairmen of committees how many cabs for messengers, &c., and carriages for voters respectively are to be sent to each committee room; tell off, the day before the poll, the particular cabs and carriages to attend each committee room; see the notices posted in the candidate's cabs; appoint a deputy to each committee room for the day of polling, and supervise generally the working out of the arrangements. He must have absolute power over the vehicles and drivers, and be *(Duties of in boroughs.)*

---

[1] Martin D.—Salford Election Petition, 30, Law Times Reports, N.S., 122.

empowered to remove them where not wanted to other places where they are wanted. He must be continually going about on the day of election, so as to prevent them being kept idling, and the candidate's cabs being used for conveying voters.

In counties.
In counties it will be the duty of the superintendent to arrange with the various parish or township committees for the conveyances to be at certain fixed points, at certain hours, to meet the voters who will assemble there. He will also arrange the routes which the conveyances must take, so as to pick up single voters on the road, and the places from which and the times at which the conveyances will leave on the return journeys. For these purposes he will require a return to be made to him of the number of voters assembling at each fixed point and the hour at which they will be ready to leave, and it will then be his duty to see that a sufficient number of conveyances are at the appointed places at the appointed times. He cannot, of course, be paid for his services, but the cost of the cabs hired for the messengers must be included in the Election expenses.

OUTDOOR SUPERINTENDENT.

In boroughs it is very desirable to have, on the day of election, a cool-headed and experienced man whose business it will be to visit from time to time the various committee rooms to see that everything is working smoothly and properly. If any difficulty arises, as from the negligence, ignorance, or incapacity of clerks, messengers, &c., he will have the duty of putting it right, and as he will know from frequently visiting the various ward or district committee rooms where assistance is needed and where it is superabundant, he will confer with the chairmen of the respective committees as to obtaining or rendering such assistance. He ought to be provided with a cab specially set apart for his use.

DETECTIVE COMMITTEE.

The use of such a committee has in several instances prevented an election petition.

The committee should be composed of three persons, one of whom should be a lawyer, or otherwise a person well skilled in election law—and the others shrewd sensible men of the class of which the great bulk of electors is composed.

Their duties will be two-fold : first, to prevent illegal practices on their own side ; and secondly, to obtain and *note down at the time*, all the particulars they can get of any illegal practices committed by their opponents. [Duties.]

It will be found during the progress of a canvass that many rumours will be circulated in reference to certain persons having offered or been offered bribes, and as to others having been intimidated or having used intimidation, &c. In most cases these rumours will turn out, upon investigation, to have little or no foundation, but in a few cases they will turn out to be undoubted facts.

If a *rumour* of any illegal practice having been committed by a friend should come to the knowledge of the detective committee, the chairman of the committee should at once seek a private interview with the friend and tell him of the rumour, but should *at once say that he assumes it to be untrue and does not wish for any explanation*, but if the friend thinks that anything he has done is open to misconstruction, he had better take steps to explain. If the rumour should be of illegal practices by the other side, the Chairman should, either himself, or by his two assistants, make every enquiry in the matter, and note down, *in writing*, every particular as to names of informants, parties to transaction, witnesses, dates, &c., he is able to obtain. The enquiries must be quietly and cautiously made, and should not be allowed to become known on the other side. Everything should be put down, whether strictly evidence or not, as in the event of a petition upon the ground of one or two illegal practices, a hint that proof will be forthcoming of illegal practices on the part of the petitioners, which will prevent them claiming the seat, will often deter them from going on.

CENTRAL COMMITTEE CLERKS AND MESSENGERS.

The same class of men will be required in the central committee room for these offices as in the ward or district committee rooms.

Review of staff.
Immediately the agent has received the foregoing books and forms, and has engaged the necessary clerks, &c., he ought to have a general review of his staff, to explain to them their duties. Meetings should therefore be called, first of those persons whose duties will lie in and about the polling stations—viz., the inspectors and polling agents, and (if necessary) the voters polled counting clerks and messengers; and, secondly, of those persons whose duties lie in the committee rooms—viz., wall sheet clerks, inspectors of refreshments, and (if necessary) polls return and slip clerks.

The instructions to each should be carefully gone through and practical illustrations be given of the work each will be called upon to do.

At the meeting of the first-named persons a box to represent the ballot box should be provided and a presiding officer and clerk stationed behind it. Each inspector or polling agent should have his instructions and register before him whilst a person to represent the voter comes in, applies for a ballot paper, is objected to, answers the questions, receives a marked ballot paper, and votes. The manner in which a blind or illiterate voter gives his vote should also be gone through, and the persons present should be encouraged to ask questions as freely as possible. At the meeting of the second-named persons, an enlarged wall sheet should be fixed on the wall, and the mode of reading off the cards, striking off those who have polled, recording numbers, &c., should be acted as if the election was actually proceeding. In like manner every one should be encouraged to ask questions, until every person is thoroughly acquainted with the duty he will be called upon to perform.

The chairmen of committees should attend both meetings, as it is very desirable they should have a general idea of the whole working of the election. The rest of the staff should also be well drilled in their respective duties.

Two days before the election the voters' instructions and cards (in envelopes and addressed) ought to be given to the canvassers, who should, if possible, call upon each voter personally with his card and instructions.

THE NOMINATION.

It is not proposed in this place to set out the duties of a returning officer, on the receipt of a writ for an election, beyond stating that it is incumbent upon him to give public notice by advertisements, placards, &c., of the day, time, and place, on and at which he will proceed to an election, and of the day on which the *poll* will be taken in case the election is contested, and of the time and place at which *forms of nomination papers* may be obtained.[1]

Duty of returning officer.

---

[1] Ballot Act, schedule 1, part 1, rule 1.

Duty of agent. As soon as this notice has been given, the agent should apply for one or more forms of nomination papers, according as he has one or more candidates, inasmuch as each candidate must be separately nominated. The returning officer is bound to supply a form of nomination paper to any *registered* elector during the appointed hours.[1]

Nomination paper—how subscribed. The nomination paper must be subscribed by two *registered* electors of the county or borough, as proposer and seconder, and by eight other *registered* electors of the same county or borough as assenting to the nomination.[2]

The agent should arrange beforehand who are to be the persons to sign the nomination papers, so that no time may be lost in getting the nomination properly made. In deciding who are to sign, great care should be used in getting electors who represent various classes or shades of political opinion, and, as far as possible, the most influential and popular of these.

As stated before, each candidate must be nominated by a separate nomination paper, but the same electors, or any of them, may subscribe as many nomination papers as there are vacancies to be filled, but no more.[3]

If two candidates coalesce, the leading members of each candidate's committee should sign both nominations.

It may be mentioned here that it is not imperative that a nomination paper supplied by the returning officer should be used. If the paper be in the form prescribed by the Act of Parliament it will be sufficient.[4]

The following is the form prescribed:—

[1] Ballot Act, schedule 1.
[2] Ibid., schedule 1, part 1, rule 7.
[3] Ballot Act, schedule 1, part 1, rule 6.
[4] Ibid., rule 7.

FORM No. 53.

Election, 18

We, the undersigned, A. B., of   in the   of   ,
and C.D., of   in   the   of   , being
registered electors of the said borough (or county), do hereby
nominate the following person as a proper person to serve as member
for the said   in Parliament.

Surname.	Other Names.	Abode.	Rank, Profession, or Occupation.

Signed

A. B.
C. D.

In filling up this paper, care must be taken to put the candidate's *surname* first (see form); then his Christian name or names must be stated; then his place of *abode* (not his place of business); and lastly his rank, profession, or calling.[1]

Nomination paper—how filled up.

After the proposer's and seconder's signatures must come the assent of eight other *registered* electors to the nomination. The assent may be in the following form, and must be written on the same paper containing the nomination:—

"We, the undersigned, being registered electors of the (borough or county) of   , do hereby assent to the nomination of the above-mentioned E. F., as a proper person to serve as member for the said   in Parliament.

Signed

G. H., of &c., and by seven others at the least.

[1] Ballot Act, schedule 1, part 1, rule 6.

Who to sign. Of course, more than eight may sign as assenting to the nomination, and where it is desirable to conciliate various interests, an influential man representing each interest should be got to sign, though the number should exceed eight.

How delivered. The nomination paper when duly filled up must be delivered to the returning officer at the place and during the time appointed for the election.[1] It *must* be delivered either by the candidate himself *or* his proposer *or* his seconder.[2] No other person can legally deliver it.

Who entitled to be present. No person except a candidate *and* his proposer *and* seconder, *and* one other person selected by each candidate, is entitled to be present with the returning officer during the time appointed for the election, unless such person is there for the purpose of assisting the returning officer.[3]

How candidate to be described. Each candidate must be described in the nomination paper in such manner as in the opinion of the returning officer is calculated to sufficiently identify such candidate; the description shall include his names, his abode, and his rank, profession, or calling, and his *surname* shall come first in the list of his names. No objection to a nomination paper *on the ground of the description of the candidate therein being insufficient* or *not being in compliance with this rule* shall be allowed or deemed valid unless such objection is made by the returning officer, or by some other person *at* or *immediately after* the time of the delivery of the nomination paper.[4]

Objection to nomination paper—when to be made. If it is intended to object to the sufficiency of the description of the candidate, or that his names, abode, profession, or calling are erroneous, or that his surname is not put first in the list of his names, the objection must be

---

1 Ballot Act, schedule 1, part 1, rule 8.
2 Ibid., sec. 1.
3 Ibid., rule 8.
4 Ballot Act, rule 6.

made before the returning officer publishes the nomination under the rule hereafter mentioned. But before any such objection is made the agent should well consider whether an objection is likely to benefit his candidate or not. If the only effect of an objection would be to more distinctly mark out his opponent, he should not object; but if a correct description of him would tend to confuse the supporters of his opponent, then it would be the agent's duty to object. If there were more serious objections to the opposition candidate, as that he was ineligible for Parliament; had been proposed or seconded by a person not *registered* as an elector, or that his nomination was not duly assented to by eight other *registered* electors, &c., then it would be *most unwise* to object to him until after the expiration of the two hours limited for tendering nominations, as in the latter event, if the objection was a valid one, the duly qualified candidate could claim the seat.

If no objection is made to a nomination paper immediately after it has been handed in, it is the duty of the returning officer *forthwith* to publish a notice of the name of the person nominated as a candidate, and of the names of his proposer and seconder by placarding the same in a conspicuous position outside the building in which the room is situate appointed for the election.[1] The agent should see that this is duly done, both as regards his own candidate and his opponent. If not properly carried out in respect of the latter, he will note the omission as an objection to be made, if necessary, hereafter.

By rule 12 of the Ballot Act, a person shall not be entitled to have his name *inserted in any ballot paper* as a candidate unless he has been nominated in manner provided by that Act, and every person whose nomination

Nomination to be published.

What names to be inserted in nomination paper.

[1] Ballot Act, schedule 1, part 1, rule 11.

paper has been delivered to the returning officer during the time appointed for the election shall be *deemed* to have been *duly nominated* unless objection be made to his nomination paper by the returning officer or some other person before the expiration of the time appointed for the election or *within one hour afterwards.*

<small>Objection to description of candidate— when to be made.</small>

It will thus be seen that an objection to the *description* of a candidate must be made immediately the nomination paper is handed in, but any *other* objection may be made at any time during the election or within an hour afterwards, and if a valid objection is made to a candidate within the last hour his name cannot be inserted in the ballot paper, and if no more candidates stand duly nominated than there are vacancies, the latter can require the returning officer to declare them duly elected.

<small>Returning officer to decide validity of objection.</small>

The returning officer is to decide on the validity of every objection made to a nomination paper; and his decision if *disallowing* the objection shall be final, but if *allowing* it, shall be subject to reversal on petition questioning the election or return.[1]

It will be observed upon reference to the 6th and 12th rules of Schedule 1, part 1 of the Ballot Act, that the returning officer or "some other person" must make objection within the times respectively stated therein. Whether the "some other person" must be some other person *duly authorized to object*, as a registered elector, or a person entitled to attend the election under rule 8, or may be a mere non-elector, does not seem clear.

<small>Who to make objections.</small>

As an objection to the *description* of the candidate must be made "at or immediately after the time of the *delivery* of the nomination paper" nominating him, it would seem that an objection must of necessity be made by some person attending the proceedings, but as an objection to the

---

[1] Ballot Act, schedule 1, part 1, rule 13.

status, &c., of a candidate under rule 12 may be made at any time before the expiration of the time appointed for the election, or within one hour afterwards, it is conceived that such objection may clearly be made by a registered elector, and perhaps by a non-registered elector, the latter being still deemed to take part in the nomination. However, it will be much the safest plan to let both kinds of objections be made by registered electors, and if this is done it is immaterial who they are or of what standing.

By analogy to the old mode of election, if, at the expiration of one hour after the time appointed for the election (the hour being for objections to be made and the returning officer to decide upon them), no more candidates stand nominated, i.e., duly nominated, than there are vacancies to be filled up, the returning officer is forthwith to declare the candidates nominated to be elected, and return their names to the Clerk of the Crown in Chancery. Candidates elected without a poll.

If, on the contrary, at the expiration of the hour more candidates stand nominated than there are vacancies to be filled up, the returning officer must adjourn the election and take a poll.[1] Adjourning to take a poll.

A candidate may, during the time appointed for the election, i.e., between the hours fixed by the returning officer for receiving nominations, *but not afterwards*, withdraw his candidature by giving a notice to that effect *signed by him* to the returning officer. If a candidate has been nominated in his absence out of the United Kingdom, his *proposer* may withdraw him by a like written notice signed by the proposer, *together* with a written declaration of such candidate's absence.[2]

If, after an *adjournment* of an election for the purpose of taking a poll, one of the candidates nominated shall die Candidate dying.

---

[1] Ballot Act, sec. 1, par. 2
[2] Ballot Act, sec. 1, par. 3.

before the poll has commenced, the returning officer shall, upon being satisfied of the fact of such death, countermand the poll, and all proceedings with reference to the election shall be commenced afresh in all respects as if the writ had been received by the returning officer on the day on which proof was given to him of such death—provided that no fresh nomination shall be necessary in the case of a candidate who stood nominated at the time of the countermand of the poll.[1]

If a candidate should be dead at the time he is nominated, or should die during the time appointed for the election, or within the subsequent hour (which might happen unknown to his proposer, &c.), it does not seem very clear what the position of matters would be. It is apprehended the other candidates (if no more than vacancies) would be elected, or (if more than vacancies) would go to the poll.

If the death of the candidate is not known to the returning officer until *after* the commencement of the poll, it seems clear that the latter must go on with the election as if the candidate was alive, and if the dead candidate should be elected, must return him accordingly, as the election will relate back to the day of nomination, and the candidate will be returned as if elected on that day. A new writ must then be issued before a new election can be had.

THE ELECTION.

Very little need be said as to what is necessary to be done on the day of election, as the instructions to the various officers and committees will shew all that is requisite.

Duty of out-door superintendent and election agent. The out-door superintendent and the election agent should meet at the central committee room not later than

[1] Ballot Act, sec. 1, par. 4.

7.30 on the morning of the day of polling. The former should immediately drive round to each polling station to see that the representatives of his candidate are at their posts, whilst the latter visits the various ward or district committee rooms with the like object. After this has been done the agent should return to the central committee rooms, where he should remain during the rest of the day, ready to be consulted by anybody requiring advice and directions.

The leading members of the central committee should also meet at their committee room (if not required in the wards or districts) ready to confer with the agent upon an emergency or to go to any weak place where assistance and encouragement are needed. <small>Duty of central committee.</small>

The out-door superintendent and one or two other committeemen should frequently visit the various ward or district committee rooms, and carefully scrutinize the wall sheets to see that the voters pledged on their side are polling satisfactorily.

The numbers polled should be noted down and reported to the agent, who, having before him a return of the number of pledges in each ward or district, will see at a glance how matters are progressing. If any particular ward or district appears to be behind the rest in the proportion of voters polled to those pledged, he will at once dispatch a committeeman to enquire the reason, and to urge the committee of the ward to greater exertions. <small>Progress of polling.</small>

If it appears that any particular class of voters is standing aloof or voting contrary to their pledges, he will in like manner send off some person to enquire into the cause, and remedy it if possible.

At the close of the poll, the agent will proceed to the place, previously notified to him by the returning officer, for the counting of the votes. He should personally see that <small>Close of poll.</small>

all the requirements of the Ballot Act relating to the sealing up of the ballot box,[1] and the sealing up into separate packets of the—

1. Unused and spoilt ballot papers.
2. The tendered ballot papers.
3. The marked copies of the register of voters, and the counterfoils of the ballot papers; and
4. The tendered votes list, list of votes marked by the presiding officer, and statement of such votes under the heads of "physical incapacity," "Jews," and "unable to read," and the declarations of illiterate voters, have been complied with.[2]

He should also see that the statements made by the presiding officers, accounting for the ballot papers given to each, tally with the numbers in the ballot boxes, and in the separate packets. The returning officer has no power, however, to open the sealed packets of "tendered" ballot papers, but must get the number of tendered votes, from the tendered votes list.[3]

Counting votes

Before proceeding with the counting of the votes, the returning officer must, in the presence of the agents of the candidates, open each ballot box, and taking out the papers, count and record the number, and then mix the contents of all the boxes together.[4] This is to be done to prevent the numbers polled for any particular candidate in any particular ward being known. With a view to prevent the vote of any particular voter becoming known, the returning officer is strictly enjoined to "keep the ballot papers with their faces upwards, and take all proper precautions for preventing any person from seeing the numbers printed on the backs of such papers."[5]

---

1 Ballot Act, sec. 2, par. 3.
2 Ballot Act, schedule 1, part 1, rule 29.
3 Ibid., rule 37.
4 Ibid., rule 34.
5 Ibid., rule 31.

The returning officer may, in addition to any clerks, appoint competent persons to assist him in counting the votes,[1] but with the exception of his staff and the agents of the candidates, no other person may be present when the votes are counted unless with the express permission of the returning officer,[2] which ought not to be given except under very exceptional circumstances. A candidate may be present and may undertake any duties or assist his agent in the performance of any duties the latter might have undertaken.[3] *Persons to be present.*

No person who has been employed by any other person in or about the election must be appointed by the returning officer to assist him in counting or as a clerk or in any manner for the purposes of the election.[4] *Persons not to be employed.*

Every officer, clerk, and agent in attendance at the counting of the votes must (on pain of imprisonment in default) maintain and aid in maintaining the secrecy of the voting, and must not attempt to ascertain the number on the back of any ballot paper, or communicate any information obtained as to the candidate for whom any vote is given in any particular ballot paper.[5] *Secrecy.*

A convenient mode of counting the votes where there are only two candidates is, after the whole of the ballot papers have been mixed together, for each person appointed by the returning officer to assist in the counting, to take a number of the ballot papers and to divide them into two lots, putting all the votes given for each candidate into one lot. This ought to be done under the supervision of an agent of each candidate. If any dispute arises as to the validity of any ballots, the latter may be *Mode of counting.*

---

1 Ballot Act, schedule 1, part 1, rule 18.
2 Ibid., rule 35.
3 Ibid., rule 51.
4 Ibid., rule 49.
5 Ballot Act, sec. 1.

placed apart from the rest to be decided upon by the returning officer. The number of ballot papers for each candidate will then be carefully counted by the returning officer's assistants and entered upon a piece of paper (the agent also taking a note of the number), and then the disputed ballot papers will be counted and entered in like manner. The numbers of the *undisputed* ballot papers counted and admitted by each assistant will then be given to the returning officer, together with the disputed ballot papers, but *before* adding up the former, he ought to decide upon the validity of each of the latter, dividing the latter, as he decides each vote, between the candidates until all are gone through; the additional ballot papers given to each candidate are then counted and added to the number previously given in his favour, and the total of these will give the number polled for each candidate respectively.

Where more candidates than two.
If there are more candidates than two, the process of counting will be more elaborate. The ballot papers will then have to be divided into—1st. Plumpers for each candidate. 2nd. Strictly party votes. 3rd. Cross votes. The great bulk of the papers will, however, be party votes, and after these have been counted and recorded, the cross votes can be gone through *seriatim*, and recorded separately, and then the plumpers added.

The great principle in counting is to first count and dispose of the *undisputed* ballot papers, so that those which are objected to may be brought together and adjudicated upon by the returning officer, whose power in this respect cannot be delegated, and whose decisions are final, and cannot be reversed except upon petition.[1]

Duty of returning officer's assistant.
It should be mentioned that when a number of ballot papers are given to a returning officer's assistant to count,

---

[1] Ballot Act, sec. 2.

he ought, in the presence of an agent for each candidate, first to count and record the gross number given to him, and after he has divided them as before-mentioned, he ought to make out an account showing the numbers polled for each candidate, the number of split votes and the number of votes objected to. The total of the account should, of course, tally with the gross number of papers given to him.

The returning officer must, as far as practicable, proceed *continuously* with the counting of the votes, allowing only time for refreshment. It would seem that he is bound to cease counting from 7 p.m. to 9 a.m. unless he and the agents agree otherwise. During this cessation of counting he must place the ballot papers and other documents relating to the election under his own seal, and the seals of such of the agents of the candidates as desire to affix their seals, and must take proper precautions for the security of such papers and documents.[1]

Votes not to be counted between 7 p.m. and 9 a.m. except by agreement.

The agent should, in the event of an adjournment of the counting, invariably place his seal on the packets or on the safe in which they are placed, and he should request the agent on the other side to do the same. It may be added that the counting should take place in a room newly swept and perfectly clear of papers, so that if any ballot paper is thrown upon the floor, or gets down accidentally, it may be seen immediately.

Adjournment of counting.

As before stated, the returning officer is the only person who can decide as to "any question arising in respect of any ballot paper." The agents on both sides will, therefore, go through the ballot papers objected to with the returning officer, who will hear their arguments for or against each vote and decide between them.

---

1 Ballot Act, schedule 1, part 1, rule 55.

Ballot paper— what are objections to.

It should be particularly remembered that every ballot paper *is void and is not to be counted*—

1. Which has not on its *back* the official mark.
2. On which votes are given to *more* candidates than the voter is entitled to vote for.
3. On which *anything* (except the number on the back) is written or marked by which the *voter* can be *identified*.

Each ballot paper *of a voter on the other side* should therefore be carefully scrutinized by the agents to see if any objection can be made to it on any of these grounds, or if it is so uncertainly marked that it is doubtful which candidate the voter intended to vote for. In all questionable cases the agents will, of course, object, so that the objection may be brought under the notice of the returning officer.

If the returning officer rejects any ballot paper as invalid, he must write across it "rejected," and if his decision is objected to by an agent, add " rejection objected to." He must report to the Clerk of the Crown in Chancery the number of ballot papers rejected and not counted by him under the several heads of—

1. Want of official mark;
2. Voting for more candidates than entitled to;
3. Writing or mark by which voter could be identified;
4. Unmarked or void for uncertainty;

And must, on request, allow any agents of the candidates, before such report is sent, to copy it.[1]

If the agent thinks any decision of the returning officer erroneous, he should not only object to the decision and see his objection endorsed on the ballot paper, but he should take a note of the objection in *general* terms, simply avoiding taking down anything which might lead to the identification of the particular voter—thus "objection

[1] Ballot Act, schedule 1, part 1, rule 36.

No. 1 taken by self [or Mr.   ] vote uncertain, vote rejected," &c., &c. This course is not only legal but proper to be taken, as it would otherwise be all but impossible to know how or upon what grounds to frame a petition where votes had been improperly counted or rejected.[1]

At the conclusion of the counting a statement should be prepared shewing the number of ballot papers and how they have been disposed of, so that any missing ballot papers would be at once detected.

Where there is an equality of votes between any candi- *Equality of votes.* dates, *and the addition of a vote would entitle any of them to be declared elected*, the returning officer, if a *registered* elector of the county or borough, *may* give such additional vote.[2] If he is not a registered elector, or if he does not chose to vote, he must make a double return.

Except in the above case, a returning officer is not to vote at any election for which he is returning officer.[3]

Upon the completion of the counting, the returning *Completion of counting.* officer must seal up in separate packets the counted and rejected ballot papers, and must in the presence of the candidates' agents verify the ballot paper account given by each presiding officer with the number of ballot papers and the unused and spoiled ballot papers, and the tendered votes list, and then re-seal each packet. He must report the result of such verification to the Clerk of the Crown in Chancery, and allow the agents, before such report is sent, to copy it.[4]

Rules 38, 39, 40, 41, 42, and 43 of the Ballot Act,[5] regu- *How papers, &c., to be kept.* late the manner in which the ballot papers and other docu-

---

1 See Ballot Act, sec. 4.
2 Ballot Act, sec. 2, par. 4.
3 Ibid.
4 Ballot Act, schedule 1, part 1, rule 37.
5 See Appendix.

ments relating to the election are to be forwarded to the Clerk of the Crown; how long they are to be kept by him, and how they may be inspected and produced.

<small>How return to be made.</small>

Rule 44 directs how the return of a member or members elected shall be made by the returning officer, and rule 45 provides for public notice being given of the names of the candidates elected, and, in the case of a contested election, of the total number of votes given for each candidate, whether elected or not.

PART III.

PAYMENT OF ELECTION EXPENSES.

The necessary expenses of the election will, if properly incurred, be payable by the candidate, or his friends, but only through the election agent, appointed pursuant to the Corrupt Practices Act, 1883, sec. 24. Expenses only to be paid through agent.

If any part of such expenses is contributed by *any person other than the candidate*, it must be paid *either* to the candidate *or* to his election agent. In the former case, *i.e.*, where subscriptions are sent *direct* to the candidate, it would appear to be unnecessary for him to disclose the names of the subscribers if he handed the same to his election agent in his own name.[1]

All persons who have bills, charges, or claims upon any candidate for or in respect of the election must send them to the election agent within fourteen days from the day of the declaration of the election, otherwise they cannot recover any part thereof.[2] Persons to send in bills, &c., within 14 days of declaration.

It is usual, therefore, to advertise for all claims to be sent in forthwith, with a notification that if not sent in within fourteen days no claim can be paid.

---

1 C. P. Act, 1883, secs. 28 and 33 (*f*), and sub-sec. 3.

2 C. P. Act, 1883, sec. 29.

The following form may be used:—

FORM No. 54.

.................PARLIAMENTARY ELECTION, 188......

Messrs. SMITH and JONES.

BILLS, ETC.

Notice is hereby given, that all bills, charges, and claims against Messrs. Smith and Jones, in respect of the above election, must be sent in immediately to me, their duly appointed election agent, at the address given below.

And take notice that no person having, or claiming to have, any bill, charge, or claim against any candidate at the above election, can be paid the same unless particulars thereof are sent in, as aforesaid, on or before the   day of

Dated this   day of   18
A. B. of &c.
(Address of office as given to returning officer.)

As the bills come in, they should be rigidly examined to see, first, that the work done, or goods supplied, were duly authorized, and, secondly, that the charges made are within the limit agreed upon, or are usual and proper.

<small>Disputed claims.</small>

If the work done, or goods supplied, was done, or supplied, without the authority of the candidate, or of the election agent or his sub-agent, it should be placed aside until the expiration of the fourteen days. If, at that time, the admitted claims do not amount to the sum allowed by law for the election expenses, it can be paid or not, as the election agent in his judgment thinks fit. If it is *not* paid within 28 days from the declaration of the election it becomes a *disputed claim*, and cannot afterwards be paid except by leave of the High Court, or of a court of competent jurisdiction in which an action is brought.[1]

[1] C. P. Act, 1883, sec. 29, sub-secs. 7, 8 and 9.

If the claim is admitted in part, but is incorrect in part, the agent should at once see the person sending it in, and get him to correct and send in a fresh account within the 14 days. If this is not done, or if no settlement can be come to with the claimant, and the *whole* claim is not paid within the 28 days, it will also become a disputed claim, and cannot afterwards be paid except as before mentioned.

In such a case the claimant may bring an action against the candidate, or the election agent, in any competent court, and if the defendant admits his liability, but disputes the amount of the claim, the amount shall, unless the court, on the application of the *plaintiff*, otherwise directs, be forthwith referred for taxation to the master, official referee, registrar, or other proper officer of the court, and the amount he finds to be due is to be the amount recovered in the action.[1] Any sum paid pursuant to such judgment or order of court is to be deemed as paid within the 28 days.[2]

If any claim is *not sent in* within the 14 days, the High Court can *alone* give authority for its payment, the election agent not having *any discretion* in the matter.[3] This provision of the Act should be *most scrupulously* adhered to by the election agent, as any breach of it would be an illegal practice, and subject the candidate to the loss of his seat, if elected, as well as to other penalties, unless he can prove such breach was without his sanction or connivance.[4]

The claims found to be correct must be paid *within* 28 days after the declaration of the poll. If not paid, *from whatever cause*, within that time, they become

Claims not sent in within 14 days.

Admitted claims.

Must be paid within 28 days.

---

1 C. P. Act, 1883, sec. 30.
2 C. P. Act, 1883, sec. 29, sub-sec. 8.
3 C. P. Act, 1883, sec. 29, sub-secs. 2, 9, and 10.
4 C. P. Act, 1883, sec. 29, sub-secs. 4 and 6.

"disputed" claims, for the election agent cannot legally pay them without an order of court.¹

Candidate's personal expenses.

Each candidate may pay any personal expenses incurred by him to an amount not exceeding £100, but if he has incurred personal expenses beyond that sum, the excess must be paid by the election agent.² The candidate, however, must send in to the election agent a *written* statement of the *amount* of personal expenses paid by him, within the 14 days allowed for sending in claims.²

Persons authorized to pay petty expenses.

In like manner, any person who has been authorized in writing, by the election agent, to pay necessary petty expenses to an amount limited in the authority, may pay such expenses to the amount named, but any excess must be paid by the election agent. A statement of the particulars of the payments made by the person so authorized must, however, be sent to the election agent within the 14 days, and must be vouched for by a bill containing the receipt of such person.

Payments of 40s. and upwards to be vouched for by a bill and receipt.

Every payment made, except where *less* than forty shillings, must be vouched for by a bill *stating particulars*, and by a receipt.³

Election agent's remuneration.

The election agent must also treat himself as an ordinary creditor, and must *send* in his claim for remuneration, and must be *paid* within the periods of 14 and 28 days respectively.⁴ It will be advisable to send in the claim to the candidate personally, and to be paid by a separate cheque by him; but if the claim is sent in to the candidate it is submitted the agent might lawfully pay himself out of the moneys provided by the candidate or otherwise.

1 Ibid, sub-secs. 7, 8, 9, and 10.
2 Ibid, sec. 31.
3 C. P. Act, 1883, sec. 29.
4 Ibid, sec. 32.

The returning officer's charges must be sent in to the election agent within 21 days after the return is made of the persons elected.[1] It does not clearly appear within what time they ought to be paid, but it will be the safest plan to pay them within the 28 days. The charges are strictly limited, and are set forth in the Schedule to 38 and 39 Vic., cap. 84. If excessive, they can be taxed in the County Court having jurisdiction at the place of nomination.[2]

Returning officer's charges.

Are limited and can be taxed.

Within 35 days after the declaration of the election, i.e., within a week after the bills can be legally paid, the election agent must transmit to the returning officer a true return, containing a statement of—

Return to be made of election expenses.

    a. All *payments made* by him, with all the bills and receipts;

    b. The *amount* of personal expenses (if any) paid by the candidate;

    c. The sums *paid* to the returning officer for his charges, or, if the amount is in dispute, of the sum claimed and the amount disputed;

    d. All other *disputed claims* of which the agent is aware;

    e. All *unpaid claims* (if any) of which he is aware in respect of which application has been, or is about to be, made to the High Court;

    f. All money securities, and equivalent for money, *received* by the election agent *from* the candidate, or *any other person*, for the purpose of expenses incurred, or to be incurred, on account of or in respect of the conduct or management of the election, with a statement of the name of every person from whom the same may have been received.

1 Ibid, sec. 32.
2 38 & 39 Vic., cap. 84.

Return to be accompanied by a statutory declaration.

This return must be accompanied by a declaration made by the election agent before a justice of the peace, in a form prescribed in a schedule of the Act of 1883.

Candidate his own election agent.

Where a candidate is his own election agent, a statement of all money, securities, and equivalent of money, *paid* by him, must be *substituted* in the return for the like. Statement of money securities and equivalent of money *received* by the election agent *from the candidate*, and the declaration by an election agent respecting election expenses need not be made, and the declaration by the candidate must be modified, as specified in the Schedule to the Act.

Candidate to make statutory declaration.

If the election agent makes the return, the candidate must, nevertheless, make a statutory declaration either then or within seven days afterwards, if he is then within the United Kingdom. If he is not at the time of the return within the United Kingdom he must make the declaration within 14 days after his return thereto, and the declaration must forthwith be sent to the returning officer.[1]

Forms of return and declarations.

The requisite forms are contained in the second Schedule of the Act of 1883 (*see Appendix*), and it is unnecessary to set them out here.

Penalties for breach of Act.

If the return and declarations are not transmitted *before the expiration of the time limited*, the candidate cannot *sit* or vote in the House of Commons, and it will be necessary for him to make an application to the High Court for an authorized excuse, otherwise he will be guilty of an illegal practice.

It will be of the utmost importance, therefore, that the requirements of this section of the Act should be most carefully fulfilled, for though the High Court will, no doubt, exercise its discretion liberally at first, yet it

---

[1] C. P. Act, 1883, sec. 33.

will, in course of time, lay down such rules and principles for its guidance that it will by no means grant an excuse as a matter of course.

Where, after the date of the return, leave is given by the High Court for any claims to be paid, the candidate, or his election agent, must, within seven days after the payment, transmit to the returning officer a return of the sums paid in pursuance of such leave, accompanied by a copy of the order of the Court giving such leave.[1] *Payment of claims after return sent in.*

If the return and declaration have not been transmitted, as required by the Act, or being transmitted contain some error or false statement, the candidate, or election agent, may apply to the High Court, or an election court, which, upon being satisfied by evidence, after notice of the application in the county or borough in which the election has taken place, of the good faith of such application, make such order for allowing an authorized excuse as to the Court seems just.[2] And if such failure to comply with the Act has arisen through the default of the election agent, or any sub-agent, the Court may order him to attend before it, and on his attendance, order him to do what is necessary, under a penalty of £500. *Authorized excuse.*

An order allowing an authorized excuse will relieve the applicant from any liability or consequence under the Act in respect of the matter excused.[3]

If, after the whole expenses of the election have been ascertained, it should be found that the maximum amount of expenses allowed by law has been accidentally exceeded, or that any other illegal practice, payment, employment, or hiring has been inadvertently committed, or made, by either the candidate, the election agent, sub-agent, or *Power of High Court and election court to except innocent act from being an illegal practice, &c.*

---

1 C. P. Act, 1883, sec. 33, sub-sec. 9.

2 C. P. Act, 1883, sec. 34.

3 C. P. Act, 1883, sec. 23.

other person, an application should at once be made to the High Court, or to an election court, for an order allowing such act, or omission, to be an exception from the provisions of the Act, so as not to subject the person doing, or omitting to do, the act to the penal consequences of the statute.[1] The application must be supported by such evidence as the Court deem sufficient, and notice of the application must be given in the county or borough for which the election was held.

Application must be supported by evidence, &c.

As such applications will be of the nature of legal proceedings, and will vary according to the circumstances of each particular case, it is advisable they should be made by and under the direction of an experienced solicitor, who will do what is necessary.

CANDIDATES' ADDRESSES.

Candidates' addresses.

The candidates, whether elected or not, should publish a short address of thanks to those voters who gave them their votes on the day of election. It is also usual to refer to the services of the committeemen, canvassers, &c., acknowledging their value.

It is a graceful act, and not without good results in a future election, for a candidate to send to each of his active supporters a neat card, thanking the latter *by name* for his exertions in the cause. This, of course, is a matter of individual taste, but it very appropriately closes the work of a Parliamentary Election.

---

[1] C. P. Act, 1883, sec. 23.

APPENDIX

OF THE

PRINCIPAL STATUTES RELATING TO

PARLIAMENTARY ELECTIONS.

6 VICT., CHAP. 18.

An Act to amend the Law for the Registration of Persons entitled to vote, and to define certain Rights of voting, and to regulate certain Proceedings in the Election of Members to serve in Parliament for England and Wales.
[31st May, 1843.]

LXXXV. And for the more effectual detection of the personation of voters at elections, be it enacted, that it shall be lawful for any *candidate*, at any election of a member, or members to serve in Parliament for any county, city, or borough, previous to the time fixed for taking the poll at such election, to nominate and appoint an agent or agents on his behalf to attend at each or any of the booths appointed for taking the poll at such election, for the purpose of detecting personation; and such candidate shall give notice in writing to the returning officer, or his respective deputy, of the name and address of the person or persons so appointed by him to act as agents for such purpose, and thereupon it shall be lawful for every such agent to attend during the time of polling at the booth or booths for which he shall have been so appointed. Agents may be appointed by candidates to detect personation at the time of polling.

---

30 & 31 VICT., CHAP. 102.

An Act further to amend the Laws relating to the Representation of the People in England and Wales.
[15th August, 1867.]

11. No elector who within six months before or during any election for any county or borough shall have been retained, hired, or employed for all or any of the purposes of the election for reward No elector who has been employed for Reward within six

months of an election to be entitled to vote.

by or on behalf of any candidate at such election as agent, canvasser, clerk, messenger, or in other like employment, shall be entitled to vote at such election, and if he shall so vote he shall be guilty of a misdemeanor.

---

31 & 32 VICT., CHAP. 125.

An Act for amending the Laws relating to Election Petitions, and providing more effectually for the prevention of corrupt practices at Parliamentary Elections.

[31st *July*, 1868.]

Preliminary.

Short title of Act.

1. This Act may be cited for all purposes as "The Parliamentary Elections Act, 1868."

Definition and Jurisdiction of Court.

2. The expression "the Court" shall, for the purposes of this Act, in its application to *England* mean the Court of Common Pleas at *Westminster*, and in its application to *Ireland* the Court of Common Pleas at *Dublin*, and such court shall, subject to the provisions of this Act, have the same powers, jurisdiction, and authority with reference to an election petition and the proceedings thereon as it would have if such petition were an ordinary cause within their jurisdiction.

Interpretation of terms.

3. The following terms shall in this Act have the meanings herein-after assigned to them, unless there is something in the context repugnant to such construction; (that is to say,)

"Metropolitan District."

"Metropolitan District" shall mean the City of *London* and the liberties thereof, and any parish or place subject to the jurisdiction of the Metropolitan Board of Works:

"Election."

"Election" shall mean an election of a member or members to serve in Parliament:

"County."

"County" shall not include a county of a city or county of a town, but shall mean any county, riding, parts or division of a county returning a member or members to serve in Parliament:

"Borough."

"Borough" shall mean any borough, university, city, place, or combination of places, not being a county as herein-before defined, returning a member or members to serve in Parliament:

"Corrupt Practices."

"Corrupt Practices" or "Corrupt Practice" shall mean bribery, treating, and undue influence, or any of such offences, as defined by Act of Parliament, or recognized by the common law of Parliament:

"Rules of Court" shall mean rules to be made as herein-after mentioned: "Rules of Court."

"Prescribed" shall mean "Prescribed by the Rules of Court." "Prescribed."

Punishment of Corrupt Practices.

44. If on the trial of any election petition under this Act any candidate is proved to have personally engaged at the election to which such petition relates as a canvasser or agent for the management of the election, any person knowing that such person has within seven years previous to such engagement been found guilty of any corrupt practice by any competent legal tribunal, or been reported guilty of any corrupt practice by a committee of the House of Commons, or by the report of the Judge upon an election petition under this Act, or by the report of commissioners appointed in pursuance of the Act of the session of the fifteenth and sixteenth years of the reign of her present Majesty, chapter fifty-seven, the election of such candidate shall be void. *Penalty for employing corrupt agent.*

35 & 36 VICT., CHAP. 33.

An Act to amend the Law relating to Procedure at Parliamentary and Municipal Elections. [18th July, 1872.]

PART I.—PARLIAMENTARY ELECTIONS.

Procedure at Elections.

1. A candidate for election to serve in Parliament for a county or borough shall be nominated in writing. The writing shall be subscribed by two registered electors of such county or borough as proposer and seconder, and by eight other registered electors of the same county or borough as assenting to the nomination, and shall be delivered during the time appointed for the election to the returning officer by the candidate himself, or his proposer or seconder. *Nomination of candidates for parliamentary elections.*

If at the expiration of one hour after the time appointed for the election no more candidates stand nominated than there are vacancies to be filled up, the returning officer shall forthwith declare the candidates who may stand nominated to be elected, and return their names to the Clerk of the Crown in Chancery; but if at the expiration of such hour more candidates stand nominated than there are vacancies to be filled up, the returning officer shall adjourn the election and shall take a poll in manner in this Act mentioned.

A candidate may, during the time appointed for the election, but not afterwards, withdraw from his candidature by giving a notice to that effect signed by him, to the returning officer: Provided, that the proposer of a candidate nominated in his absence out of the United Kingdom may withdraw such candidate by a written notice signed by him and delivered to the returning officer, together with a written declaration of such absence of the candidate.

If after the adjournment of an election by the returning officer for the purpose of taking a poll, one of the candidates nominated shall die before the poll has commenced, the returning officer shall, upon being satisfied of the fact of such death, countermand notice of the poll, and all the proceedings with reference to the election shall be commenced afresh in all respects as if the writ had been received by the returning officer on the day on which proof was given to him of such death; provided that no fresh nomination shall be necessary in the case of a candidate who stood nominated at the time of the countermand of the poll.

Poll at elections.

2. In the case of a poll at an election the votes shall be given by ballot. The ballot of each voter shall consist of a paper (in this Act called a ballot paper) showing the names and the description of the candidates. Each ballot paper shall have a number printed on the back, and shall have attached a counterfoil with the same number printed on the face. At the time of voting, the ballot paper shall be marked on both sides with an official mark, and delivered to the voter within the polling station, and the number of such voter on the register of voters shall be marked on the counterfoil, and the voter having secretly marked his vote on the paper, and folded it up so as to conceal his vote, shall place it in a closed box in the presence of the officer presiding at the polling station (in this Act called "the presiding officer"), after having shown to him the official mark at the back.

Any ballot paper which has not on its back the official mark, or on which votes are given to more candidates than the voter is entitled to vote for, or on which anything, except the said number on the back, is written or marked by which the voter can be identified, shall be void and not counted.

After the close of the poll the ballot boxes shall be sealed up, so as to prevent the introduction of additional ballot papers, and shall be taken charge of by the returning officer, and that officer shall, in the presence of such agents, if any, of the candidates as may be in attendance, open the ballot boxes, and ascertain the result of the poll by counting the votes given to each candidate, and shall forthwith declare to be elected the candidates or candidate to whom the majority of votes have been given, and return their names to the Clerk of the Crown in Chancery. The decision of the returning officer as to any question arising in respect of any ballot paper shall be final, subject to reversal on petition questioning the election or return.

Where an equality of votes is found to exist between any candidates at an election for a county or borough, and the addition of a vote would entitle any of such candidates to be declared elected, the returning officer, if a registered elector of such county or borough, may give such additional vote, but shall not in any other case be entitled to vote at an election for which he is returning officer.

Offences at Elections.

3. Every person who,—

(1.) Forges or fraudulently defaces or fraudulently destroys any nomination paper, or delivers to the returning officer any nomination paper, knowing the same to be forged; or

(2.) Forges or counterfeits or fraudulently defaces or fraudulently destroys any ballot paper or the official mark on any ballot paper; or

(3.) Without the due authority supplies any ballot paper to any person; or

(4.) Fraudulently puts into any ballot box any paper other than the ballot paper which he is authorized by law to put in : or

(5.) Fraudulently takes out of the polling station any ballot paper; or

(6.) Without due authority destroys, takes, opens, or otherwise interferes with any ballot box or packet of ballot papers then in use for the purposes of the election;

shall be guilty of a misdemeanour; and be liable, if he is a returning officer, or an officer or clerk in attendance at a polling station, to imprisonment for any term not exceeding two years, with or without hard labour, and if he is any other person, to imprisonment for any term not exceeding six months, with or without hard labour.

Any attempt to commit any offence specified in this section shall be punishable in the manner in which the offence itself is punishable.

In any indictment or other prosecution for an offence in relation to the nomination papers, ballot boxes, ballot papers, and marking instruments at an election, the property in such papers, boxes, and instruments may be stated to be in the returning officer at such election, as well as the property in the counterfoils.

<small>Infringement of secrecy.</small>

4. Every officer, clerk, and agent in attendance at a polling station shall maintain and aid in maintaining the secrecy of the voting in such station, and shall not communicate, except for some purpose authorized by law, before the poll is closed, to any person any information as to the name or number on the register of voters of any elector who has or who has not applied for a ballot paper or voted at that station, or as to the official mark, and no such officer, clerk, or agent, and no person whosoever shall interfere with or attempt to interfere with a voter when marking his vote, or otherwise attempt to obtain in the polling station information as to the candidate for whom any voter in such station is about to vote or has voted, or as to the number on the back of the ballot paper given to any voter at such station. Every officer, clerk, and agent in attendance at the counting of the votes shall maintain and aid in maintaining the secrecy of the voting, and shall not attempt to ascertain at such counting the number on the back of the ballot paper, or communicate any information obtained at such counting as to the candidate for whom any vote is given in any particular ballot paper. No person shall directly or indirectly induce any voter to display his ballot paper after he shall have marked the same, so as to make known to any person the name of the candidate for or against whom he has so marked his vote.

Every person who acts in contravention of the provisions of this section shall be liable, on summary convictions before two justices of the peace, to imprisonment for any term not exceeding six months, with or without hard labour.

Amendment of Law.

5. The local authority (as hereinafter defined) of every borough shall take into consideration the division of such borough into polling districts, and, if they think it desirable, by order, divide such borough into polling districts in such manner as they may think most convenient for taking votes of the electors at a poll.

The local authority of every county and borough shall, on or before the first day of May, one thousand eight hundred and seventy-three, send to one of Her Majesty's Principal Secretaries of State, to be laid by him before both Houses of Parliament, a copy of any order made by such authority in pursuance of this section, and a report, in such form as he may require, stating how far the provisions of this Act with respect to polling districts have been complied with in their county or borough; and if they make any order after the first day of May one thousand eight hundred and seventy-three, with respect to polling districts or polling places in their county or borough, they shall send a copy of such order to the said Secretary of State, to be laid by him before both Houses of Parliament.

The local authority in a county or borough in this section means the authority having power to divide such county or borough into polling districts under section thirty-four of the Representation of the People Act, 1867, and any enactments amending that section; and such authority shall exercise the powers thereby given to them for the purposes of this section; and the provisions of the said section as to the local authority of a borough constituted by the combination of two or more municipal boroughs shall apply to a borough constituted by the combination of a municipal borough and other places, whether municipal boroughs or not; and in the case of a borough of which a town council is not the local authority, and which is not wholly situate within one petty sessional division, the justices of the peace for the county in which such borough or the larger part thereof in area is situate, assembled at some court of general or quarter sessions, or at some adjournment thereof, shall be the local authority thereof, and shall for this purpose have jurisdiction over the whole of such borough; and in the case of such borough and of a county, a court of general session shall be assembled within twenty-one days after the passing of this Act, and any such court may be assembled and adjourned from time to time for the purpose.

No election shall be questioned by reason of any non-compliance with this section or any informality relative to polling districts or polling places, and any order made by a local authority in relation to polling districts or polling places shall apply only to lists of voters made subsequently to its date and to registers of voters formed out of such lists, and to elections held after the time at which a register of voters so formed has come into force: Provided that where any such order is made between the first day of July and the first day of November in any year, and does not create any new division between two or more polling districts of any parish for which a separate poor rate is or can be made, such order shall apply to the register of voters which comes into force next after such order is made, and to elections held after that register so comes into force; and the clerk of the peace or town clerk, as the case may be, shall copy, print, and arrange the list of voters for the purpose of such register in accordance with such order.

Use of school and public room for poll.

6. The returning officer at a parliamentary election may use, free of charge, for the purpose of taking the poll at such election, any room in a school receiving a grant out of moneys provided by Parliament, and any room the expense of maintaining which is payable out of any local rate, but he shall make good any damage done to such room, and defray any expense incurred by the person or body of persons, corporate or unincorporate, having control over the same on account of its being used for the purpose of taking the poll as aforesaid.

The use of any room in an unoccupied house for the purpose of taking the poll shall not render any person liable to be rated or to pay any rate for such house.

Conclusiveness of register of voter.

7. At any election for a county or borough, a person shall not be entitled to vote unless his name is on the register of voters for the time being in force for such county or borough, and every person whose name is on such register shall be entitled to demand and receive a ballot paper and to vote: Provided that nothing in this section shall entitle any person to vote who is prohibited from voting by any statute, or by the common law of Parliament, or relieve such person from any penalties to which he may be liable for voting.

Duties of Returning and Election Officers.

General powers and duties of returning officer.

8. Subject to the provisions of this Act, every returning officer shall provide such nomination papers, polling stations, ballot boxes, ballot papers, stamping instruments, copies of register of voters, and other things, appoint and pay such officers, and do such other acts and things as may be necessary for effectually conducting an election in manner provided by this Act.

All expenses properly incurred by any returning officer in carrying into effect the provisions of this Act, in the case of any parliamentary election, shall be payable in the same manner as expenses incurred in the erection of polling booths at such election are by law payable.

Where the sheriff is returning officer for more than one county as defined for the purposes of parliamentary elections, he may, without prejudice to any other power, by writing under his hand, appoint a fit person to be his deputy for all or any of the purposes relating to an election in any such county, and may, by himself or such deputy, exercise any powers and do any things which the returning officer is authorised or required to exercise or do in relation to such election. Every such deputy, and also any under sheriff, shall, in so far as he acts as returning officer, be deemed to be included in the term "returning officer" in the provisions of this Act relating to parliamentary elections, and the enactments with which this part of this Act is to be construed as one.

9. If any person misconducts himself in the polling station, or fails to obey the lawful orders of the presiding officer, he may immediately, by order of the presiding officer, be removed from the polling station by any constable in or near that station, or any other person authorized in writing by the returning officer to remove him; and the person so removed shall not, unless with the permission of the presiding officer, again be allowed to enter the polling station during the day. *Keeping of order in station.*

Any person so removed as aforesaid, if charged with the commission in such station of any offence, may be kept in custody until he can be brought before a justice of the peace.

Provided that the powers conferred by this section shall not be exercised so as to prevent any elector who is otherwise entitled to vote at any polling station from having an opportunity of voting at such station.

10. For the purpose of the adjournment of the poll, and of every other enactment relating to the poll, a presiding officer shall have the power by law belonging to a deputy returning officer; and any presiding officer and any clerk appointed by the returning officer to attend at a polling station shall have the power of asking the questions and administering the oath authorized by law to be asked of and administered to voters, and any justice of the peace and any returning officer may take and receive any declaration authorised by this Act to be taken before him. *Powers of presiding officer and administration of oaths, &c.*

11. Every returning officer, presiding officer, and clerk who is guilty of any wilful misfeasance or any wilful act or omission in contravention of this Act shall, in addition to any other penalty or liability to which he may be subject, forfeit to any person aggrieved by such misfeasance, act, or omission a penal sum not exceeding one hundred pounds. *Liability of officers for misconduct.*

Section fifty of the Representation of the People Act, 1867 (which relates to the acting of any returning officer, or his partner or clerk, as agent for a candidate), shall apply to any returning officer or officers appointed by him in pursuance of this Act, and to his partner or clerk. *30 and 31 Vict., c. 102.*

Miscellaneous.

Prohibition of disclosure of vote.

12. No person who has voted at any election shall, in any legal proceeding to question the election or return, be required to state for whom he has voted.

Non-compliance with rules.

13. No election shall be declared invalid by reason of a non-compliance with the rules contained in the First Schedule to this Act, or any mistake in the use of the forms in the Second Schedule to this Act, if it appears to the tribunal having cognizance of the question that the election was conducted in accordance with the principles laid down in the body of this Act, and that such non-compliance or mistake did not affect the result of the election.

Use of municipal ballot boxes, &c., for parliamentary election, and vice versa.

14. Where a parliamentary borough and municipal borough occupy the whole or any part of the same area, any ballot boxes or fittings for polling stations and compartments provided for such parliamentary borough or such municipal borough may be used in any municipal or parliamentary election in such borough free of charge, and any damage other than reasonable wear and tear caused to the same shall be paid as part of the expenses of the election at which they are so used.

Construction of Act.

15. This part of this Act shall, so far as is consistent with the tenor thereof, be construed as one with the enactments for the time being in force relating to the representation of the people, and to the registration of persons entitled to vote at the election of members to serve in Parliament, and with any enactments otherwise relating to the subject matter of this part of this Act, and terms used in this part of this Act shall have the same meaning as in the said enactments; and in construing the said enactments relating to an election or to the poll or taking the votes by poll the mode of election and of taking the poll established by this Act shall for the purposes of the said enactments be deemed to be substituted for the mode of election or poll, or taking the votes by poll, referred to in the said enactments; and any person applying for a ballot paper under this Act shall be deemed "to tender his vote," or "to assume to vote," within the meaning of the said enactments; and any application for a ballot paper under this Act, or expressions relative thereto, shall be equivalent to "voting" in the said enactments and any expressions relative thereto; and the term "polling booth" as used in the said enactments shall be deemed to include a polling station; and the term "proclamation" as used in the said enactments shall be deemed to include a public notice given in pursuance of this Act.

Application of Part of Act to Scotland.

16. This part of this Act shall apply to Scotland, subject to the following provisions:— <small>Alterations for application of Part I. to Scotland.</small>

(1.) The expression "crime and offence" shall be equivalent to the expression "misdemeanor," and shall be substituted therefor:

(2.) All offences under this Act for which any person may be punished on summary conviction shall be prosecuted before the sheriff under the provisions of "The Summary Procedure Act, 1864;" and all jurisdictions, powers, and authorities necessary for that purpose are hereby conferred on sheriffs:

(3.) The expression "sheriff" shall include sheriff substitute:

(4.) The provisions of this Act relating to the division of counties and boroughs into polling districts shall not apply to Scotland:

(5.) The ballot boxes, ballot papers, stamping instruments, and other requisites for a parliamentary election shall be provided and paid for in the same manner as polling rooms or booths under the fortieth section of the Act of the second and third years of the reign of King William the Fourth, chapter sixty-five, intituled "An Act to amend the Representation of the People in Scotland;" and the reasonable remuneration of presiding officers, assistants, and clerks employed by the returning officer at such an election, and all other expenses properly incurred by the returning officer, and by sheriff clerks and town clerks, in carrying into effect the provisions of this Act, shall be paid by the candidates; provided always that, if any person shall be proposed as a candidate without his consent, the person so proposing him shall be liable to defray his share of all those expenses in like manner as if he had been a candidate himself; provided also, that the fee to be paid to each presiding officer shall in no case exceed the sum of three guineas per day, and the fee to be paid to each assistant to the returning officer shall not exceed two guineas per day, and the fee to be paid to each clerk shall not exceed one guinea per day.

Application of Part of Act to Ireland.

Alterations for application of Part I. to Ireland.

17. This part of this Act shall apply to Ireland, subject to the following modifications:—

(1.) The expression "Clerk of the Crown in Chancery" shall mean the Clerk of the Crown and Hanaper in Ireland:

(2.) The preceding provisions of this part of this Act with respect to the division of counties and boroughs into polling districts shall not extend to Ireland:

(3.) In the construction of the preceding provisions of this part of this Act as applying to Ireland, section thirteen of "The Representation of the People (Ireland) Act, 1868," shall be substituted for section fifty of "The Representation of the People Act, 1867," wherever in such provisions the said last-mentioned section occurs. The provision contained in the sixth section of this Act providing for the use of school rooms free of charge, for the purpose of taking the poll at elections, shall not apply to any school adjoining or adjacent to any church or other place of worship, nor to any school connected with a nunnery or other religious establishment:

(4.) No returning officer shall be entitled to claim, or be paid, any sum or sums of money for the erection of polling booths or stations and compartments other than the sum or sums actually and necessarily incurred and paid by him in reference to the same, any statute or statutes to the contrary now in force notwithstanding, nor shall the expenses of providing sufficient polling stations or booths and compartments at every polling place exceed the sum or sums now given and allowed by statute in Ireland.

Provisions as to polling districts and polling places in Ireland.

18. With respect to polling districts and polling places in Ireland, the following regulations shall have effect; that is to say,

(1.) The Lord Lieutenant, by and with the advice of the Privy Council in Ireland, shall appoint special sessions to be held by the chairmen of quarter sessions and justices of the peace having jurisdiction in each county or riding of a county in Ireland, at such places and times before the first day of November next after the passing of this Act as shall seem fit for the purpose of dividing such county or riding into polling districts and appointing polling places for such districts:

(2.) The clerk of the said Privy Council shall cause each such appointment to be notified to the clerk of the peace of the county to which the same relates, and shall cause notice of the same to be published twice in each of two consecutive weeks in one or more newspapers usually circulated in such county, and once in the Dublin Gazette:

(3.) The clerk of the peace of each county in Ireland shall, within five days after the receipt of such notification as aforesaid, send a written or printed notice of the same to the chairman and to every justice of the peace having jurisdiction within the county or riding to which the same relates:

(4.) The chairman of quarter sessions and the justices of the peace having jurisdiction in any county or riding assembled at such special sessions appointed in manner aforesaid, or at any adjournment of the same before the first day of December next after the passing of this Act, shall make an order dividing such county or riding of a county into polling districts, and appointing in each such polling district a place (in this section referred to as a "polling place") for taking the poll at contested elections of members to serve in Parliament for such county:

(5.) Every such division shall be made in such manner so that, as far as practicable, every building or place in such county in which petty sessions are at the time of the passing of this Act held shall be a polling place: Provided always, that where it appears to the chairman and justices assembled at special sessions that, for the purpose of affording full facilities for taking the poll at contested elections, there should be polling places in addition to such buildings or places where petty sessions are held as aforesaid, they shall appoint so many polling places in addition to such buildings or places as they may think necessary, and constitute a polling district for each such polling place:

(6.) Every such order shall specify the barony or baronies, half barony or half baronies, townland or townlands, parish or parishes, and places constituting each such polling district:

(7.) A copy of each such order shall forthwith be sent by the clerk of the peace for such county to the clerk of the said Privy Council, who thereupon shall submit the same for confirmation by the Lord Lieutenant and Privy Council in Ireland, in the manner by this Act provided, and such order shall not be of any validity until the same has been so confirmed:

(8.) Notice of the intended confirmation of any such order shall be given by the clerk of the said Privy Council at least one month before the day fixed for such confirmation by the publication of such notice and order in one or more newspapers circulating within such county or riding to which the order has reference:

(9.) It shall be lawful for the Lord Lieutenant and Privy Council, on the day fixed for the intended confirmation of any such order, to confirm the same as it stands, or with such variation, alteration, or modification as may seem fit: Provided always, that where any person is dissatisfied with any such order it shall be lawful for such person, within fourteen days after the publication of the notice of the intended confirmation of such order, to appeal against the same, and such appeal shall be in writing, stating the grounds thereof, and shall be signed by such person, and shall within such time be lodged with the clerk of the Privy Council; and it shall be lawful for the Lord Lieutenant and Privy Council, previous to the confirmation of any such order, to hear and determine such appeal against the same, and to make such order as to the costs of such appeal as may seem meet:

(10.) When any such order has been confirmed as aforesaid, the clerk of the said Privy Council shall transmit a copy of the same to the clerk of the peace of the county to which the same relates, and shall cause the same to be published once in the Dublin Gazette, and once in the newspaper in which the notice of intended confirmation was published:

(11.) The provisions of the Act of the session of the twenty-seventh and twenty-eighth years of the reign of Her present Majesty, chapter twenty-two, for ascertaining the voters in the new or altered polling districts referred to in the ninth section of the said Act, and for making separate lists of voters, and otherwise in relation thereto, shall extend and apply to every case in which any order in relation to any county has been confirmed under the authority of this section, in like manner as if such sections were herein re-enacted, and the polling districts to which the same refer or apply had been polling districts constituted under the authority of this section; and the register of voters in force in such county at the time of confirming such order as amended by the printed books given into the custody of the sheriff of such county in manner by the said Act provided, and the said printed books shall be the register of persons entitled to vote at any election of a member or members to serve in Parliament which shall take place in and for such county until the first day of January next after the giving of the said books as aforesaid: Provided always, that in the construction of the said provisions, the terms "the passing of this Act" and the "said Act" shall respectively be construed to mean the confirming of any order made under the authority of this section and this Act:

(12.) At any election of a member or members to serve in Parliament, for any county to which any such order relates, held after the confirming of any such order, and before the register of voters to be formed subsequently to the date of the confirming of such order under the provisions of this section shall be in force, the poll shall be taken as if no such order had been made:

(13.) All precepts, notices, and forms relating to the registration of voters shall be framed and expressed in such manner and form as may be necessary for the carrying the provisions of this Act into effect:

(14.) When the chairman of quarter sessions and justices of the peace having jurisdiction in any county or riding in Ireland, assembled at any general or quarter sessions in any division of such county or riding, are of opinion that for the purpose of affording further facilities for polling at contested elections there should be within such district polling places in addition to the places appointed in manner aforesaid, they may by resolution determine that at the next general or quarter sessions in such division of such county the necessity for such additional polling places shall be considered by the chairman and justices assembled at the same:

(15.) The clerk of the peace of such county shall, within five days after the making of such resolution, send a written or printed copy of the same to the chairman and to every justice of the peace having jurisdiction within the county to which the same relates, and shall cause a copy of such resolution to be published twice in each of two consecutive weeks in some newspaper circulated in such county:

(16.) The said chairman and justices assembled at such general or quarter sessions holden next after the making of such resolution shall consider whether additional polling places are necessary, and if they are of such opinion they may, by an order to be made in like manner and subject to the same provisions as to the making, confirming, and taking effect of the same as are in this section contained in relation to orders to be made at special sessions under the authority of the same, appoint such other places to be polling places as they shall think fit, and shall constitute polling districts for such polling places:

(17.) No election shall be questioned by reason of any polling district not having been constituted in conformity with the provisions of this Act, or by reason of any informality relative to any polling district:

(18.) When any day fixed for taking the poll at any election is the day fixed for the holding of the petty sessions court at any polling place, the court shall stand ipso facto adjourned till the next day, which shall in that case be the legal day for holding said court, and if that day be a Sunday or legal holiday, till the next day:

(19.) The term "the Lord Lieutenant" in this section shall mean the Lord Lieutenant of Ireland and the lords justices or other chief governors or governor of Ireland for the time being, and the term "chairman of quarter sessions" in this section shall include any person duly appointed to do the duty of such chairman during his sickness or absence.

Amendment of law as to voting in wards in certain boroughs.

19. Where the name of any person is required to be inserted in any list of voters for any ward of any city, town, or borough under the provisions of section seven of the Act passed in the session of Parliament held in the thirteenth and fourteenth years of the reign of Her present Majesty, chapter sixty-eight, as qualified in respect of any property qualification, or as the occupier of any lands, tenements, or hereditaments situate in whole or in part beyond the limits of such ward, then and in every such case the names so

required to be inserted shall be placed in alphabetical order in a separate part of such list to be styled "the list of rural or out voters of such ward," and the property, lands, tenements, and hereditaments in respect of which such person is qualified as aforesaid shall, for the purposes of the said Act and the Acts amending the same, in relation to the providing of booths and compartments within each ward of any city, town, or borough, and the voting therein of persons entitled to vote in respect of any such qualifications aforesaid, be deemed to constitute a separate ward: Provided always, that the name of any such person shall not be placed in such separate list if such person shall, in writing under his hand, object thereto, and if such objection is delivered to such clerk of the peace on or before the twenty-fifth day of August next preceding the making of such list under the provisions aforesaid, and in such case in relation to such person the provisions of this section shall not apply.

Part II.

MUNICIPAL ELECTIONS.

20. The poll at every contested municipal election shall, so far as circumstances admit, be conducted in the manner in which the poll is by this Act directed to be conducted at a contested parliamentary election, and, subject to the modifications expressed in the schedules annexed hereto, such provisions of this Act and of the said schedules as relate to or are concerned with a poll at a parliamentary election shall apply to a poll at a contested municipal election: Provided as follows: *Application to municipal elections of enactments relating to the poll at parliamentary elections.*

(1.) The term "returning officer" shall mean the mayor or other officer who, under the law relating to municipal elections, presides at such elections:

(2.) The term "petition questioning the election or return" shall mean any proceeding in which a municipal election can be questioned:

(3.) The mayor shall provide everything which in the case of a parliamentary election is required to be provided by the returning officer for the purpose of a poll:

(4.) All expenses shall be defrayed in manner provided by law with respect to the expenses of a municipal election:

(5.) No return shall be made to the Clerk of the Crown in Chancery:

(6.) Nothing in this Act shall be deemed to authorize the appointment of any agents of a candidate in a municipal election, but if in the case of a municipal election any agent of a candidate is appointed, and a notice in writing of such appointment is given to the returning officer, the provisions of this Act with respect to agents of candidates shall, so far as respects such agent, apply in the case of that election:

(7.) The provisions of this Act with respect to—

(a.) The voting of a returning officer; and
(b.) The use of a room for taking a poll; and
(c.) The right to vote of persons whose names are on the register of voters;

shall not apply in the case of a municipal election.

Abolition of ward assessors.

A municipal election shall, except in so far as relates to the taking of the poll in the event of its being contested, be conducted in the manner in which it would have been conducted if this Act had not passed.

21. Assessors shall not be elected in any ward of any municipal borough, and a municipal election need not be held before the assessors or their deputies, but may be held before the mayor, alderman, or other returning officer only.

Application of Part of Act to Scotland.

Alterations for application of Part II. to Scotland.

22. This part of this Act shall apply to Scotland, subject to the following provisions:—

(1.) The term " mayor " shall mean the provost or other chief magistrate of a municipal borough, as defined by this Act:

(2.) All municipal elections shall be conducted in the same manner in all respects in which elections of councillors in the royal burghs contained in Schedule C. to the Act of the session of the third and fourth years of the reign of King William the Fourth, chapter seventy-six, intituled " An Act to alter and amend the laws for the " election of the Magistrates and Councillors of the Royal " Burghs in Scotland," are directed to be conducted by the Acts in force at the time of the passing of this Act as amended by this Act; and all such Acts shall apply to such elections accordingly.

Application of Part of Act to Ireland.

23. This part of this Act shall apply to Ireland, with the following modifications :— Alterations for application of Part II. to Ireland.

(1.) The term "mayor" shall include the chairman of commissioners, chairman of municipal commissioners, chairman of town commissioners, and chairman of township commissioners:

(2.) The provisions of "The Municipal Corporation Act, 1859," 22 Vic. c. 55. following; that is to say, section five and section six, and section seven except so much thereof as relates to the form of nomination papers, and section eight except so much thereof as relates to assessors, shall extend and apply to every municipal borough in Ireland, and shall be substituted for any provisions in force in relation to the nomination at municipal elections : Provided always, that the term "councillor" in these sections shall, for the purposes of this section, include alderman, commissioner, municipal commissioner, town commissioner, township commissioner, or assessor of any municipal borough.

PART III.

PERSONATION.

24. The following enactments shall be made with respect to personation at parliamentary and municipal elections:

A person shall for all purposes of the laws relating to parliamentary and municipal elections be deemed to be guilty of the offence of personation who at an election for a county or borough, or at a municipal election, applies for a ballot paper in the name of some other person, whether that name be that of a person living or dead or of a fictitious person, or who, having voted once at any such election, applies at the same election for a ballot paper in his own name. Definition and punishment of personation.

It shall be the duty of the returning officer to institute a prosecution against any person whom he may believe to have been guilty of personation, or of aiding, abetting, counselling, or procuring the commission of the offence of personation by any person, at the election for which he is returning officer, and the costs and expenses of the prosecutor and the witnesses in such case, together with compensation for their trouble and loss of time, shall be allowed by the court in the same manner in which courts are empowered to allow the same in cases of felony.

The provisions of the Registration Acts, specified in the Third Schedule to this Act, shall in England and Ireland respectively apply to personation under this Act in the same manner as they apply to a person who knowingly personates and falsely assumes to vote in the name of another person as mentioned in the said Acts.

Vote to be struck off for bribery, treating, or undue influence.

25. Where a candidate, on the trial of an election petition claiming the seat for any person, is proved to have been guilty, by himself or by any person on his behalf, of bribery, treating, or undue influence in respect of any person who voted at such election, or where any person retained or employed for reward by or on behalf of such candidate for all or any of the purposes of such election, as agent, clerk, messenger, or in any other employment, is proved on such trial to have voted at such election there shall, on a scrutiny, be struck off from the number of votes appearing to have been given to such candidate one vote for every person who voted at such election and is proved to have been so bribed, treated, or unduly influenced, or so retained or employed for reward as aforesaid.

Alterations in Act as applying to Scotland.

26. This part of this Act shall apply to Scotland, subject to the following provision:—

The offence of personation shall be deemed to be a crime and offence, and the rules of the law of Scotland with respect to apprehension, detention, precognition, commitment, and bail shall apply thereto, and any person accused thereof may be brought to trial in the court of justiciary, whether in Edinburgh or on circuit, at the instance of the Lord Advocate, or before the sheriff court, at the instance of the procurator fiscal.

Construction of part of Act.

27. This part of this Act, so far as regards parliamentary elections, shall be construed as one with "The Parliamentary "Elections Act, 1868," and shall apply to an election for a university or combination of universities.

Part IV.

MISCELLANEOUS.

28. The schedules to this Act, and the notes thereto, and directions therein, shall be construed and have effect as part of this Act. <small>Effect of schedules.</small>

29. In this Act— <small>Definitions.</small>

The expression "municipal borough" means any place for the time being subject to the Municipal Corporation Acts, or any of them: <small>"Municipal borough:"</small>

The expression "Municipal Corporation Acts" means— <small>"Municipal Corporation Acts."</small>

(a.) As regards England, the Act of the session of the fifth and sixth years of the Reign of King William the Fourth, chapter seventy-six, intituled "An Act to provide for "the regulation of municipal corporations in England "and Wales," and the Acts amending the same:

(b.) As regards Scotland, the Act of the session of the third and fourth years of the reign of King William the Fourth, chapter seventy-six, intituled "An Act to alter and " amend the laws for the election of Magistrates and "Councillors of the Royal Burghs in Scotland," and the Act of the same session, chapter seventy-seven, intituled " An Act to provide for the appointment and election of " Magistrates and Councillors for the several Burghs " and Towns of Scotland which now return or contribute " to return members to Parliament, and are not Royal "Burghs," and the Act of the session of the thirteenth and fourteenth years of the reign of Her present Majesty, chapter thirty-three, intituled " An Act to make more " effectual provision for regulating the Police of Towns " and populous Places in Scotland, and for paving, " draining, cleansing, lighting, and improving the same ; " and " The General Police and Improvement (Scotland) " Act, 1862," and any Acts amending the same:

(c.) As regards Ireland, the Act of the session of the third and fourth years of the reign of Her present Majesty, chapter one hundred and eight, intituled " An " Act for the Regulation of Municipal Corporations in " Ireland," the Act of the ninth year of George the Fourth, chapter eighty-two, "The Towns Improvement "(Ireland) Act, 1854," and every local and personal Act providing for the election of commissioners in any towns or places for purposes similar to the purposes of the said Acts.

"Municipal election." The expression "municipal election" means—

(a.) As regards England, an election of any person to serve the office of councillor, auditor, or assessor of any municipal borough, or of councillor for a ward of a municipal borough; and

(b.) As regards Scotland, an election of any person to serve the office of councillor or commissioner of any municipal borough, or of a ward or district of any municipal borough:

(c.) As regards Ireland, an election of any person to serve the office of alderman, councillor, commissioner, municipal commissioner, town commissioner, township commissioner, or assessor of any municipal borough.

Application of Act. 30. This Act shall apply to any parliamentary or municipal election which may be held after the passing thereof.

Saving. 31. Nothing in this Act, except Part III. thereof, shall apply to any election for a university or combination of universities.

Repeal.

Repeal of Acts in schedules. 32. The Acts specified in the fourth, fifth, and sixth schedules to this Act, to the extent specified in the third column of those schedules, and all other enactments inconsistent with this Act, are hereby repealed.

Provided that this repeal shall not affect—

(a.) Anything duly done or suffered under any enactment hereby repealed; or

(b.) Any right or liability acquired, accrued, or incurred under any enactment hereby repealed; or

(c.) Any penalty, forfeiture, or punishment incurred in respect of any offence committed against any enactment hereby repealed; or

(d.) Any investigation, legal proceeding, or remedy in respect of any such right, liability, penalty, forfeiture, or punishment as aforesaid; and any such investigation, legal proceeding, and remedy may be carried on as if this Act had not passed.

33. This Act may be cited as "The Ballot Act, 1872," and shall continue in force till the thirty-first day of December, one thousand eight hundred and eighty, and no longer, unless Parliament shall otherwise determine; and on the said day the Acts in the fourth, fifth, and sixth schedules shall be thereupon revived; provided that such revival shall not affect any act done, any rights acquired, any liability or penalty incurred, or any proceeding pending under this Act, but such proceeding shall be carried on as if this Act had continued in force.

Short title.

SCHEDULES.

FIRST SCHEDULE.

Part I.

RULES FOR PARLIAMENTARY ELECTIONS.

Election.

1. The returning officer shall, in the case of a county election, within two days after the day on which he receives the writ, and in the case of a borough election, on the day on which he receives the writ or the following day, give public notice, between the hours of nine in the morning and four in the afternoon, of the day on which and the place at which he will proceed to an election and of the time appointed for the election, and of the day on which the poll will be taken in case the election is contested, and of the time and place at which forms of nomination papers may be obtained, and in the case of a county election shall send one of such notices by post, under cover, to the postmaster of the principal post office of each polling place in the county, endorsed with the words "Notice of election," and the same shall be forwarded free of charge; and the postmaster receiving the same shall forthwith publish the same in the manner in which post office notices are usually published.

2. The day of election shall be fixed by the returning officer as follows; that is to say, in the case of an election for a county or a district borough not later than the ninth day after the day on which he receives the writ, with an interval of not less than three clear days between the day on which he gives the notice and the day of election; and in the case of an election for any borough other than a district borough not later than the fourth day after the day on which he receives the writ, with an interval of not less than two clear days between the day on which he gives the notice and the day of election.

3. The place of election shall be a convenient room situate in the town in which such election would have been held if this Act had not passed, or where the election would not have been held in a town, then situate in such town in the county as the returning officer may from time to time determine as being in his opinion most convenient for the electors.

4. The time appointed for the election shall be such two hours between the hours of ten in the forenoon and three in the afternoon as may be appointed by the returning officer, and the returning officer shall attend during those two hours and for one hour after.

5. Each candidate shall be nominated by a separate nomination paper, but the same electors or any of them may subscribe as many nomination papers as there are vacancies to be filled, but no more.

6. Each candidate shall be described in the nomination paper in such manner as in the opinion of the returning officer is calculated to sufficiently identify such candidate; the description shall include his names, his abode, and his rank, profession, or calling, and his surname shall come first in the list of his names. No objection to a nomination paper on the ground of the description of the candidate therein being insufficient, or not being in compliance with this rule, shall be allowed or deemed valid, unless such objection is made by the returning officer, or by some other person, at or immediately after the time of the delivery of the nomination paper.

7. The returning officer shall supply a form of nomination paper to any registered elector requiring the same during such two hours as the returning officer may fix, between the hours of ten in the morning and two in the afternoon on each day intervening between the day on which notice of the election was given and the day of election, and during the time appointed for the election; but nothing in this Act shall render obligatory the use of a nomination paper supplied by the returning officer, so, however, that the paper be in the form prescribed by this Act.

8. The nomination papers shall be delivered to the returning officer at the place of election during the time appointed for the election; and the candidate nominated by each nomination paper, and his proposer and seconder, and one other person selected by the candidate, and no person other than aforesaid, shall, except for the purpose of assisting the returning officer, be entitled to attend the proceedings during the time appointed for the election.

9. If the election is contested the returning officer shall, as soon as practicable after adjourning the election, give public notice of

the day on which the poll will be taken, and of the candidates described as in their respective nomination papers, and of the names of the persons who subscribe the nomination paper of each candidate, and of the order in which the names of the candidates will be printed in the ballot paper, and, in the case of an election for a county, deliver to the postmaster of the principal post office of the town in which is situate the place of election a paper, signed by himself, containing the names of the candidates nominated, and stating the day on which the poll is to be taken, and the postmaster shall forward the information contained in such paper by telegraph, free of charge, to the several postal telegraph offices situate in the county for which the election is to be held, and such information shall be published forthwith at each such office in the manner in which post office notices are usually published.

10. If any candidate nominated during the time appointed for the election is withdrawn in pursuance of this Act, the returning officer shall give public notice of the name of such candidate, and the names of the persons who subscribed the nomination paper of such candidate, as well as of the candidates who stood nominated or were elected.

11. The returning officer shall, on the nomination paper being delivered to him, forthwith publish notice of the name of the person nominated as a candidate, and of the names of his proposer and seconder, by placarding or causing to be placarded the names of the candidate and his proposer and seconder in a conspicuous position outside the building in which the room is situate appointed for the election.

12. A person shall not be entitled to have his name inserted in any ballot paper as a candidate unless he has been nominated in manner provided by this Act, and every person whose nomination paper has been delivered to the returning officer during the time appointed for the election shall be deemed to have been nominated in manner provided by this Act, unless objection be made to his nomination paper by the returning officer or some other person before the expiration of the time appointed for the election or within one hour afterwards.

13. The returning officer shall decide on the validity of every objection made to a nomination paper, and his decision, if disallowing the objection, shall be final; but if allowing the same, shall be subject to reversal on petition questioning the election or return.

The Poll.

14. The poll shall take place on such day as the returning officer may appoint, not being in the case of an election for a county or a district borough less than two or more than six clear days, and not being in the case of an election for a borough other than a district borough more than three clear days after the day fixed for the election.

15. At every polling place the returning officer shall provide a sufficient number of polling stations for the accommodation of the electors entitled to vote at such polling place, and shall distribute the polling stations amongst those electors in such manner as he thinks most convenient, provided that in a district borough there shall be at least one polling station at each contributory place of such borough.

16. Each polling station shall be furnished with such number of compartments, in which the voters can mark their votes screened from observation, as the returning officer thinks necessary, so that at least one compartment be provided for every one hundred and fifty electors entitled to vote at such polling station.

17. A separate room or separate booth may contain a separate polling station, or several polling stations may be constructed in the same room or booth.

18. No person shall be admitted to vote at any polling station except the one allotted to him.

19. The returning officer shall give public notice of the situation of polling stations and the description of voters entitled to vote at each station, and of the mode in which electors are to vote.

20. The returning officer shall provide each polling station with materials for voters to mark the ballot papers, with instruments for stamping thereon the official mark, and with copies of the register of voters, or such part thereof as contains the names of the voters, allotted to vote at each station. He shall keep the official mark secret, and an interval of not less than seven years shall intervene between the use of the same official mark at elections for the same county or borough.

21. The returning officer shall appoint a presiding officer to preside at each station, and the officer so appointed shall keep order at his station, shall regulate the number of electors to be admitted at a time, and shall exclude all other persons except the clerk, the agents of the candidates, and the constables on duty.

22. Every ballot paper shall contain a list of the candidates described as in their respective nomination papers, and arranged alphabetically in the order of their surnames, and (if there are two or more candidates with the same surname) of their other names: it shall be in the form set forth in the Second Schedule to this Act or as near thereto as circumstances admit, and shall be capable of being folded up.

23. Every ballot box shall be so constructed that the ballot papers can be introduced therein, but cannot be withdrawn therefrom, without the box being unlocked. The presiding officer at any polling station, just before the commencement of the poll, shall show the ballot box empty to such persons, if any, as may be present in such station, so that they may see that it is empty, and shall then lock it up, and place his seal upon it in such manner as to prevent it being opened without breaking such seal, and shall place it in his view for the receipt of ballot papers, and keep it so locked and sealed.

24. Immediately before a ballot paper is delivered to an elector, it shall be marked on both sides with the official mark, either stamped or perforated, and the number, name, and description of the elector as stated in the copy of the register shall be called out, and the number of such elector shall be marked on the counterfoil, and a mark shall be placed in the register against the number of the elector, to denote that he has received a ballot paper, but without showing the particular ballot paper which he has received.

25. The elector, on receiving the ballot paper, shall forthwith proceed into one of the compartments in the polling station, and there mark his paper, and fold it up so as to conceal his vote, and shall then put his ballot paper, so folded up, into the ballot box; he shall vote without undue delay, and shall quit the polling station as soon as he has put his ballot paper into the ballot box.

26. The presiding officer, on the application of any voter who is incapacitated by blindness or other physical cause from voting in manner prescribed by this Act, or (if the poll be taken on Saturday) of any voter who declares that he is of the Jewish persuasion, and objects on religious grounds to vote in manner prescribed by this Act, or of any voter who makes such a declaration as hereinafter mentioned that he is unable to read, shall, in the presence of the agents of the candidates, cause the vote of such voter to be marked on a ballot paper in manner directed by such voter, and the ballot paper to be placed in the ballot box, and the name and number on the register of voters of every voter whose vote is marked in

pursuance of this rule, and the reason why it is so marked shall be entered on a list in this Act called " the list of votes marked by the presiding officer."

The said declaration, in this Act referred to as "the declaration of inability to read," shall be made by the voter at the time of polling, before the presiding officer, who shall attest it in the form hereinafter mentioned, and no fee, stamp, or other payment shall be charged in respect of such declaration, and the said declaration shall be given to the presiding officer at the time of voting.

27. If a person, representing himself to be a particular elector named on the register, applies for a ballot paper after another person has voted as such elector, the applicant shall, upon duly answering the questions and taking the oath permitted by law to be asked of and to be administered to voters at the time of polling, be entitled to mark a ballot paper in the same manner as any other voter, but the ballot paper (in this Act called a tendered ballot paper) shall be of a colour differing from the other ballot papers, and, instead of being put into the ballot box, shall be given to the presiding officer and endorsed by him with the name of the voter and his number in the register of voters, and set aside in a separate packet, and shall not be counted by the returning officer. And the name of the voter and his number on the register shall be entered on a list, in this Act called the tendered votes list.

28. A voter who has inadvertently dealt with his ballot paper in such manner that it cannot be conveniently used as a ballot paper may, on delivering to the presiding officer the ballot paper so inadvertently dealt with, and proving the fact of the inadvertence to the satisfaction of the presiding officer, obtain another ballot paper in the place of the ballot paper so delivered up (in this Act called a spoilt ballot paper), and the spoilt ballot paper shall be immediately cancelled.

29. The presiding officer of each station, as soon as practicable after the close of the poll, shall, in the presence of the agents of the candidates, make up into separate packets sealed with his own seal and the seals of such agents of the candidates as desire to affix their seals,—

    (1.) Each ballot box in use at his station, unopened but with the key attached; and

    (2.) The unused and spoilt ballot papers, placed together; and

    (3.) The tendered ballot papers; and

    (4.) The marked copies of the register of voters, and the counterfoils of the ballot papers; and

(5.) The tendered votes list, and the list of votes marked by the presiding officer, and a statement of the number of the voters whose votes are so marked by the presiding officer under the heads "physical incapacity," "Jews," and "unable to read," and the declarations of inability to read;

and shall deliver such packets to the returning officer.

30. The packets shall be accompanied by a statement made by such presiding officer, showing the number of ballot papers entrusted to him, and accounting for them under the heads of ballot papers in the ballot box, unused, spoilt, and tendered ballot papers, which statement is in this Act referred to as the ballot paper account.

Counting Votes.

31. The candidates may respectively appoint agents to attend the counting of the votes.

32. The returning officer shall make arrangements for counting the votes in the presence of the agents of the candidates as soon as practicable after the close of the poll, and shall give to the agents of the candidates appointed to attend at the counting of the votes notice in writing of the time and place at which he will begin to count the same.

33. The returning officer, his assistants, and clerks, and the agents of the candidates, and no other person, except with the sanction of the returning officer, may be present at the counting of the votes.

34. Before the returning officer proceeds to count the votes, he shall, in the presence of the agents of the candidates, open each ballot box, and, taking out the papers therein, shall count and record the number thereof, and then mix together the whole of the ballot papers contained in the ballot boxes. The returning officer, while counting and recording the number of ballot papers and counting the votes, shall keep the ballot papers with their faces upwards, and take all proper precautions for preventing any person from seeing the numbers printed on the backs of such papers.

35. The returning officer shall, so far as practicable, proceed continuously with counting the votes, allowing only time for refreshment, and excluding (except so far as he and the agent otherwise agree) the hours between seven o'clock at night and nine o'clock on the succeeding morning. During the excluded time the

returning officer shall place the ballot papers and other documents relating to the election under his own seal and the seals of such of the agents of the candidates as desire to affix their seals, and shall otherwise take proper precautions for the security of such papers and documents.

36. The returning officer shall endorse "rejected" on any ballot paper which he may reject as invalid, and shall add to the endorsement "rejection objected to," if an objection be in fact made by any agent to his decision. The returning officer shall report to the Clerk of the Crown in Chancery the number of ballot papers rejected and not counted by him under the several heads of -

1. Want of official mark;
2. Voting for more candidates than entitled to;
3. Writing or mark by which voter could be identified;
4. Unmarked or void for uncertainty;

and shall on request allow any agents of the candidates, before such report is sent, to copy it.

37. Upon the completion of the counting, the returning officer shall seal up in separate packets the counted and rejected ballot papers. He shall not open the sealed packet of tendered ballot papers or marked copy of the register of voters and counterfoils, but shall proceed, in the presence of the agents of the candidates, to verify the ballot paper account given by each presiding officer by comparing it with the number of ballot papers recorded by him as aforesaid, and the unused and spoiled ballot papers in his possession and the tendered votes list, and shall reseal each sealed packet after examination. The returning officer shall report to the Clerk of the Crown in Chancery the result of such verification, and shall, on request, allow any agents of the candidates, before such report is sent, to copy it.

38. Lastly, the returning officer shall forward to the Clerk of the Crown in Chancery (in manner in which the poll books are by any existing enactment required to be forwarded to such clerk, or as near thereto as circumstances admit) all the packets of ballot papers in his possession, together with the said reports, the ballot paper accounts, tendered votes lists, lists of votes marked by the presiding officer, statements relating thereto, declarations of inability to read, and packets of counterfoils, and marked copies of registers, sent by each presiding officer, endorsing on each packet a description of its contents and the date of the election to which they relate, and the name of the county or borough for which such

election was held; and the term "poll book" in any such enactment shall be construed to include any document forwarded in pursuance of this rule.

39. The Clerk of the Crown shall retain for a year all documents relating to an election forwarded to him in pursuance of this Act by a returning officer, and then, unless otherwise directed by an order of the House of Commons, or of one of Her Majesty's Superior Courts, shall cause them to be destroyed.

40. No person shall be allowed to inspect any rejected ballot papers in the custody of the Clerk of the Crown in Chancery, except under the order of the House of Commons, or under the order of one of Her Majesty's Superior Courts, to be granted by such court on being satisfied by evidence on oath that the inspection or production of such ballot papers is required for the purpose of instituting or maintaining a prosecution for an offence in relation to ballot papers, or for the purpose of a petition questioning an election or return: and any such order for the inspection or production of ballot papers may be made subject to such conditions as to persons, time, place, and mode of inspection or production as the House or Court making the same may think expedient, and shall be obeyed by the Clerk of the Crown in Chancery. Any power given to a court by this rule may be exercised by any judge of such court at chambers.

41. No person shall, except by order of the House of Commons or any tribunal having cognizance of petitions complaining of undue returns or undue elections, open the sealed packet of counterfoils after the same has been once sealed up, or be allowed to inspect any counted ballot papers in the custody of the Clerk of the Crown in Chancery; such order may be made subject to such conditions as to persons, time, place, and mode of opening or inspection as the House or tribunal making the order may think expedient; provided that on making and carrying into effect any such order, care shall be taken that the mode in which any particular elector has voted shall not be discovered until he has been proved to have voted, and his vote has been declared by a competent court to be invalid.

42. All documents forwarded by a returning officer in pursuance of this Act to the Clerk of the Crown in Chancery, other than ballot papers and counterfoils, shall be open to public inspection at such time and under such regulations as may be prescribed by the Clerk of the Crown in Chancery, with the consent of the Speaker of the House of Commons; and the Clerk of the Crown shall supply copies of or extracts from the said documents to any person

demanding the same, on payment of such fees and subject to such regulations as may be sanctioned by the Treasury.

43. Where an order is made for the production by the Clerk of the Crown in Chancery of any document in his possession relating to any specified election, the production by such clerk or his agent of the document ordered, in such manner as may be directed by such order, or by a rule of the court having power to make such order, shall be conclusive evidence that such document relates to the specified election; and any endorsement appearing on any packet of ballot papers produced by such Clerk of the Crown or his agent shall be evidence of such papers being what they are stated to be by the endorsement. The production from proper custody of a ballot paper purporting to have been used at any election, and of a counterfoil marked with the same printed number and having a number marked thereon in writing, shall be primâ facie evidence that the person who voted by such ballot paper was the person who at the time of such election had affixed to his name in the register of voters at such election the same number as the number written on such counterfoil.

General Provisions.

44. The return of a member or members elected to serve in Parliament for any county or borough shall be made by a certificate of the names of such member or members under the hand of the returning officer endorsed on the writ of election for such county or borough, and such certificate shall have effect and be dealt with in like manner as the return under the existing law, and the returning officer may, if he think fit, deliver the writ with such certificate endorsed to the postmaster of the principal post office of the place of election, or his deputy, and in that case he shall take a receipt from the postmaster or his deputy for the same; and such postmaster or his deputy shall then forward the same by the first post, free of charge, under cover, to the Clerk of the Crown, with the words " Election Writ and Return " endorsed thereon.

45. The returning officer shall, as soon as possible, give public notice of the names of the candidates elected, and in the case of a contested election, of the total number of votes given for each candidate, whether elected or not.

46. Where the returning officer is required or authorised by this Act to give any public notice, he shall carry such requirement into effect by advertisements, placards, handbills, or such other means as he thinks best calculated to afford information to the electors.

47. The returning officer may, if he think fit, preside at any polling station, and the provisions of this Act relating to a presiding officer shall apply to such returning officer with the necessary modifications as to things to be done by the returning officer to the presiding officer, or the presiding officer to the returning officer.

48. In the case of a contested election for any county or borough, the returning officer may, in addition to any clerks, appoint competent persons to assist him in counting the votes.

49. No person shall be appointed by a returning officer for the purposes of an election who has been employed by any other person in or about the election.

50. The presiding officer may do, by the clerks appointed to assist him, any act which he is required or authorised to do by this Act at a polling station except ordering the arrest, exclusion, or ejection from the polling station of any person.

51. A candidate may himself undertake the duties which any agent of his, if appointed, might have undertaken, or may assist his agent in the performance of such duties, and may be present at any place at which his agent may, in pursuance of this Act, attend.

52. The name and address of every agent of a candidate appointed to attend the counting of the votes shall be transmitted to the returning officer one clear day at the least before the opening of the poll; and the returning officer may refuse to admit to the place where the votes are counted any agent whose name and address has not been so transmitted, notwithstanding that his appointment may be otherwise valid, and any notice required to be given to any agent by the returning officer may be delivered at or sent by post to such address.

53. If any person appointed an agent by a candidate for the purposes of attending at the polling station or at the counting of the votes dies, or becomes incapable of acting during the time of the election, the candidate may appoint another agent in his place, and shall forthwith give to the returning officer notice in writing of the name and address of the agent so appointed.

54. Every returning officer, and every officer, clerk, or agent authorised to attend at a polling station or at the counting of the votes shall, before the opening of the poll, make a statutory declaration of secrecy, in the presence, if he is the returning officer, of a justice of the peace, and if he is any other officer or an agent, of a justice of the peace or of the returning officer; but no such returning officer, officer, clerk, or agent, as aforesaid shall, save as afore-

said, be required, as such, to make any declaration or take any oath on the occasion of any election.

55. Where in this Act any expressions are used requiring or authorising or inferring that any act or thing is to be done in the presence of the agents of the candidates such expressions shall be deemed to refer to the presence of such agents of the candidates as may be authorised to attend, and as have in fact attended, at the time and place where such act or thing is being done, and the non-attendance of any agents or agent at such time and place shall not, if such act or thing be otherwise duly done, in anywise invalidate the act or thing done.

56. In reckoning time for the purposes of this Act, Sunday, Christmas-day, Good Friday, and any day set apart for a public fast or public thanksgiving, shall be excluded; and when anything is required by this Act to be done on any day which falls on the above-mentioned days such thing may be done on the next day, unless it is one of the days excluded as above mentioned.

57. In this Act—

The expression "district borough" means the borough of Monmouth and any of the boroughs specified in Schedule E. to the Act of the session of the second and third years of the reign of King William the Fourth, chapter forty-five, intituled "An Act to amend the Representation of " the people in England and Wales;" and

The expression "polling place" means, in the case of a borough, such borough or any part thereof in which a separate booth is required or authorized by law to be provided; and

The expression "agents of the candidates," used in relation to a polling station, means agents appointed in pursuance of section eighty-five of the Act of the session of the sixth and seventh years of the reign of Her present Majesty, chapter eighteen.

Modifications in Application of Part One of Schedule to Scotland.

58. In Scotland, the place of election shall be a convenient room situate in the town in which the writ for the election would, if this Act had not passed, have been proclaimed.

59. In Scotland the candidates may respectively appoint agents to attend at the polling stations. The ballot papers and other documents other than the return required to be sent to and kept by

the Clerk of the Crown in Chancery, shall in Scotland be kept by the sheriff clerks of the respective counties in which the returns (including those for burghs) are made, and the provisions of this Schedule relating thereto shall be construed as if the sheriff clerk were substituted for Clerk of the Crown in Chancery.

60. In Scotland, the term "district borough" shall mean the combined burghs and towns specified in Schedule E. of the Act of the session of the second and third years of the reign of King William the Fourth, chapter sixty-five, intituled "An Act to amend the Representation of the People in Scotland;" and in Schedule A. of the Representation of the People (Scotland) Act, 1868.

61. The provisions of the Act of the session of the second and third years of the reign of King William the Fourth, chapter sixty-five, intituled "An Act to amend the Representation of the People in Scotland," in so far as they relate to the fixing and announcement of the day of the election, the interval to elapse between the receipt of the writ and the day of election, the period of adjournment for taking the poll in the case of Orkney and Shetland, and of the district of burghs comprising Kirkwall, Wick, Dornoch, Dingwall, Tain, and Cromarty, and to the keeping open of the poll for two consecutive days in the case of Orkney and Shetland, shall remain in full force and effect, anything in this Act or any other Act of Parliament now in force notwithstanding; but nothing herein contained shall be construed to exclude Orkney and Shetland or Orkney or Shetland, or the said district of burghs, or any of the burghs in the said district, from any of the benefits and obligations of the other portions of this Act.

Modifications in Application of Part One of Schedule to Ireland.

62. The expression "Clerk of the Crown in Chancery" in this schedule shall mean, as regards Ireland, "the Clerk of the Crown and Hanaper in Ireland."

63. A presiding officer at a polling station in a county in Ireland need not be a freeholder of the county.

Part II.

HERE FOLLOW RULES RELATING TO MUNICIPAL ELECTIONS.

SECOND SCHEDULE.

Note.—The forms contained in this schedule, or forms as nearly resembling the same as circumstances will admit, shall be used in all cases to which they refer and are applicable, and when so used shall be sufficient in law.

Writ for a County or Borough at a Parliamentary Election.

* Victoria, by the Grace of God, of the United Kingdom of Great Britain and Ireland, Queen, Defender of the Faith, to the
 † of the county [*or* borough] of
greeting:
‡ Whereas by the advice of our Council we have ordered a Parliament to be holden at Westminster on the   day of   next. We command you that, notice of the time and place of election being first duly given, you do cause election to be made according to law of   members [*or* a member] to serve in Parliament for the said county [*or* the division of the said county [*or* the borough, *or as the case may be*] of   § and that you do cause the names of such members [*or* member] when so elected, whether they [*or* he] be present or absent, to be certified to us, in our Chancery, without delay.

Witness ourself at Wesminster, the   day of
   in the   year of our reign, in the year of
   our Lord 18

Label or direction of Writ.

To the   † of
A writ of a new election of members [*or* member] for the said county [*or* division of a county *or* borough, *or as the case may be*].

Endorsement.

Received the within writ on the   day of   18 .
                                  (Signed)   *A.B.*,
                    High Sheriff [*or* Sheriff, *or* Mayor, *or as the case may be*].

Certificate endorsed on the Writ.

I hereby certify, that the members [*or* member] elected for   in pursuance of the within-written writ, are [*or* is] *A.B.* of   in the county of   and *C.D.* of   in the county of   .

                                  (Signed)   *A.B.*,
                    High Sheriff [*or* Sheriff, *or* Mayor, *or as the case may be*].

Note.—A separate writ will be issued for each county as defined for the purposes of a parliamentary election.

Form of Notice of Parliamentary Election.

The returning officer of the   of   will, on the   day of   now next ensuing, between the hours of   and   , proceed to the nomination, and, if there is no opposition, to the election, of a member [*or* members] for the said county [*or* division of a county *or* borough] at the*   ,

* Note.—Insert description of place and room.   Forms of nomination paper may be obtained at   *, between the hours of   and   on   .

Every nomination paper must be signed by two registered electors as proposer and seconder, and by eight other registered electors as assenting to the nomination.

Every nomination paper must be delivered to the returning officer by the candidate proposed, or by his proposer and seconder, between the said hours of   and   on the said   day of   at the said   *.

Each candidate nominated, and his proposer and seconder, and one other person selected by the candidate, and no other persons, are entitled to be admitted to the room.

In the event of the election being contested, the poll will take place on the   day of

(Signed)   A.B.,

Sheriff [*or* Mayor, *or as the case may be*].

            day of   18 .

Take notice, that all persons who are guilty of bribery, treating, undue influence, personation, or other corrupt practices at the said election will, on conviction of such offence, be liable to the penalties mentioned in that behalf in " The Corrupt Practices Prevention Act, 1854," and the Ballot Act, 1872, and the Acts amending the said Acts.

Form of Nomination Paper in Parliamentary Election.

We, the undersigned A.B. of   in the of   and C.D. of   in the of   , being electors for the   of   , do hereby nominate the following person as a proper person to serve as member for the said   in Parliament:

Surname.	Other Names.	Abode.	Rank, Profession, or Occupation.
BROWN	John - - - -	52, George-street, Bristol	Merchant.
JONES	*or* William David -	High Elms, Wilts.	Esquire.
MERTON	*or* Hon. George Travis, commonly called Viscount	Swanworth, Berks.	Viscount.
SMITH	*or* Henry Sydney -	72, High-street, Bath	Attorney.

(Signed)   A.B.
                    C.D

We the undersigned, being registered electors of the
do hereby assent to the nomination of the above-mentioned *John
Brown* as a proper person to serve as a member for the said
in Parliament.

      (Signed)   E.F. of
           G.H. of
           I.J. of
           K.L. of
           M.N. of
           O.P. of
           Q.R. of
           S.T. of

Note.—Where a candidate is an Irish peer, or is commonly known by some title, he may be described by his title as if it were his surname.

Form of Ballot Paper.

Form of front of Ballot Paper.

Counterfoil
No. 1.

Note:
The counterfoil is to have a number to correspond with that on the back of the Ballot Paper.

1   **BROWN**
(John Brown, of 52, George St., Bristol, Merchant.)

2   **JONES**
(William David Jones, of High Elms, Wilts, Esq.)

3   **MERTON**
(Hon. George Travis, commonly called Viscount Merton, of Swanworth, Berks.)

4   **SMITH**
(Henry Sidney Smith, of 72, High St., Bath, Attorney.)

Form of Back of Ballot Paper.

No.
     Election for   county [*or* borough, *or* ward].
     18

Note.—The number on the ballot paper is to correspond with that in the counterfoil.

Directions as to printing Ballot Paper.

Nothing is to be printed on the ballot paper except in accordance with this schedule.

The surname of each candidate, and if there are two or more candidates of the same surname, also the other names of such candidates, shall be printed in large characters, as shown in the form, and the names, addresses, and descriptions, and the number on the back of the paper, shall be printed in small characters.

Form of Directions for the Guidance of the Voter in voting, which shall be printed in conspicuous Characters, and placarded outside every Polling Station and in every Compartment of every Polling Station.

The voter may vote for   candidate

The voter will go into one of the compartments, and, with the pencil provided in the compartment, place a cross on the right-hand side, opposite the name of each candidate for whom he votes, thus X

The voter will then fold up the ballot paper so as to show the official mark on the back, and leaving the compartment will, without showing the front of the paper to any person, show the official mark on the back to the presiding officer, and then, in the presence of the presiding officer, put the paper into the ballot box, and forthwith quit the polling station.

If the voter inadvertently spoils a ballot paper, he can return it to the officer, who will, if satisfied of such inadvertence, give him another paper.

If the voter vote for more than   candidate, or places any mark on the paper by which he may be afterwards identified, his ballot paper will be void, and will not be counted.

If the voter takes a ballot paper out of the polling station, or deposits in the ballot box any other paper than the one given him by the officer, he will be guilty of a misdemeanour, and be subject to imprisonment for any term not exceeding six months, with or without hard labour.

Note.—These directions shall be illustrated by examples of the ballot paper.

O

Form of Statutory Declaration of Secrecy.

I solemnly promise and declare, That I will not at this election for   do anything forbidden by Section Four of The Ballot Act, 1872, which has been read to me.

Note.—This section must be read to the declarant by the person taking the declaration.

Form of Declaration of inability to read.

I. *A.B.*, of   , being numbered   on the Register of Voters for the county [*or* borough] of   do hereby declare that I am unable to read.

A.B.,   his mark.

day of

I, the undersigned, being the presiding officer for the polling station for the county [*or* borough] of   , do hereby certify, that the above declaration, having been first read to the above-named *A.B.*, was signed by him in my presence with his mark.

Signed, *C.D.*,

Presiding officer for   polling station

for the county [*or* borough] of

day of

ABSTRACT.

An abstract of the principal provisions of the Ballot Act, 1872, for the information of returning officers at parliamentary and municipal elections in England and Wales, has been prepared officially. It is prefaced as follows:—

"The object of the following abstract is to inform returning officers of the alterations that have been made in their duties by the Ballot Act, a copy of which is sent herewith. The abstract does not relate to so much of the previous law as remains unaltered, and will not relieve returning officers from the necessity of making themselves intimately acquainted with the provisions of the Act itself. The abstract cannot in any way override the directions of the Act, and must not be considered as an authoritative interpretation of it. The paragraphs of the abstract are numbered for facility of reference. The sections and rules referred to are the sections of the Ballot Act and the rules contained in the first, schedule to that Act. As this Act is now in force, every election whether parliamentary or municipal, held to supply a casual vacancy must be conducted in accordance with its provisions. The attention of each returning officer is therefore specially directed to paragraphs 7 and 18, in order that he may be prepared for any such election.

"H. A. BRUCE.

"Home Office, Whitehall, 24th July, 1872."

"PRELIMINARY.

"1. All notices required by the Act may be given by advertisements, placards, or in some similar manner (rule 46).

"NOMINATIONS.

"2. In this Act the term 'election' applies to elections which, not being contested, are completed at the time of nomination, as well as to elections which, being contested, are decided by poll.

" 3. A separate writ will be sent for each electoral division of a county, and the sheriff may appoint by writing a deputy to act as returning officer for all or any of the purposes of the election in such electoral division (s. 8).

" 4. A time table, showing the limits of time allowed for the different stages in an election, is appended in a schedule to these instructions.

" 5. The returning officer will, within the time limited by rule 1, give notice between 9 a.m. and 4 p.m. of the several particulars specified in rule 1. For this purpose he must fix the time and place of nomination (rules 2, 3, 4), the time and place at which forms of nomination papers will be supplied (rule 7), and the day of the poll (rule 14). In the case of a county election notices are also to be sent by post. (See rule 1.) The form of the notice is given in the second schedule. The old proclamation and the holding of a county court for the purposes of a county election are abolished.

" 6. The time and place of nomination are to be fixed by the returning officer in accordance with rule 2. It will be observed that the place of nomination is to be a room, and that no hustings will be required.

" 7. In the interval between the day of giving notice and the day of nomination the returning officer is required to supply printed forms of nomination papers to electors during such two hours between 10 a.m. and 2 p.m. on each day as he may fix. He must therefore provide such forms as soon as possible after the receipt of the writ. The form will be found in the second schedule.

" 8. On the day appointed for the nomination the returning officer must attend at the appointed place during the two hours fixed for the nomination, in order to receive nominations, and for one hour afterwards in order to receive objections. No oath is now required to be taken by the returning officer (rule 54).

" 9. The only persons entitled to attend the proceedings at the time of nomination, except for the purpose of assisting the returning officer, are the returning officer and the candidate nominated by each nomination paper, with his proposer and seconder, and one other person selected by the candidate.

" 10. The returning officer will take care that the nomination paper is in the proper form and is properly signed and delivered in accordance with section 1 and rules 5, 6, and 7. The use of a form supplied by the returning officer, however advisable, is not obligatory, provided that the form prescribed in the Act is followed (rule 7).

" 11. The objections which may be made to the validity of a nomination paper are of two kinds :—(1.) Objections under rule 6, which must be made immediately on the delivery of the nomination paper to the returning officer. (2.) Objections under rule 12, which must be made either during the time appointed for the nomination or within one hour afterwards. The returning officer is to determine the validity of any objection (rule 13), but he will bear in mind that the making or allowing trivial objections may lead to the delay and expense of a petition.

" 12. Immediately after each nomination paper has been delivered to the returning officer notice of the nomination is to be placarded outside the building.

" 13. A candidate once nominated, unless nominated in his absence from the United Kingdom, can only withdraw from his candidature by delivering to the returning officer, during the time appointed for the nomination, a notice of withdrawal signed by himself.

" 14. If at the expiration of one hour after the time appointed for the nomination the number of candidates who have been duly nominated and not withdrawn does not exceed the number of vacancies to be filled up, the returning officer is forthwith to declare the candidates so duly nominated to be elected, to give public notice of the names of the candidates elected (rules 45, 46), and to return their names to the Clerk of the Crown in Chancery (s. 1, rule 44). This notice must also state the names of any candidates who may have withdrawn, and the names of the subscribers to their nomination papers (rule 10). The return is to be made by a certificate endorsed on the writ, and may be sent by post (rule 44). The indenture by which the return was formerly made is abolished.

" 15. If at the expiration of one hour after the time appointed for the nomination the number of the candidates who have been duly nominated, and not withdrawn, exceeds the number of vacancies to be filled up, the returning officer is to adjourn the election and to give public notice of the particulars specified in rules 9, 10. In the case of a county election the notice must also be given to the postmaster to be telegraphed (rule 9).

" 16. If a candidate dies in the interval after the adjournment of the election and before the poll has commenced, notice of the poll is to be countermanded, and the proceedings commenced afresh (s. 1).

"THE POLL.

"17. In cases where a poll is required, the returning officer must, immediately after the adjournment of the election, give public notice of the matters specified in rule 19. The form of directions as to the mode in which electors are to vote is given in the second schedule, and must be placarded outside every polling station, and in every compartment of every polling station, and illustrated by examples of the ballot paper.

"18. In the event of a poll being required, the first business of the returning officer will be to provide polling stations, appoint presiding officers and clerks for each polling station, and provide a sufficient supply of ballot boxes, ballot papers, materials for marking ballot papers, stamping instruments, and copies of the register of voters. He must also, as under the previous law (6 Vic., c. 18, s. 90), provide a sufficient number of constables to attend in each polling station.

"19. The office of a presiding officer is equivalent to that of a deputy returning officer under the previous law (s. 10). There is to be one presiding officer for each polling station (rule 21), but the returning officer himself may act as a presiding officer (rule 47), and no doubt will do so when there is only one polling station. The returning officer may appoint clerks to assist the presiding officer at each station (s. 8, rule 48), but he will of course not do so where the number of voters at a station is small. A presiding officer or clerk must not have been employed in or about the election (rule 49), and must not act by himself, his partner or clerk, as an agent for the candidate (s. 11).

"20. The returning officer must provide each polling place with at least one polling station under a separate presiding officer (rule 15), and must furnish each polling station with such number of compartments as allows one compartment to every 150 persons entitled to vote at the station (rule 16). 'Polling place' in the case of a county means some town or village at which the electors of a polling district are to poll; and in the case of a borough means the particular spot in each borough or polling district of a borough which the returning officer under the previous law has power to fix as the place at which the votes are to be taken (rule 57). The term 'district borough' in rule 15 is explained in rule 57. The polling station may be either in a room or a booth, but sec. 37 of 30th and 31st Vict., chap. 102, directs that a room is to be used where practicable. Under sec. 6 any room in a school receiving an annual grant out of moneys provided by Parliament, and any room the expense of maintaining which is payable out of any local rate, may be taken compulsorily, and used free of charge, for the purpose of a polling station, subject to the necessity of making good any damage actually done, and of defraying any expenses actually incurred by the persons having control over the room taken on account of its being so taken. Care will of course be taken to interfere as little as practicable with the ordinary use of the room, and to use all possible speed in erecting and taking away the necessary fitting. More than one polling station may, if necessary, be fitted up in the same room (rule 17).

"21. Care must be taken that the partitions dividing the compartments in the polling stations are sufficient to effectually screen the voter from observation (rule 16). It may be found advantageous that each polling station should contain on one side the seats of the presiding officer and his clerks, and of the personation agents entitled to attend, and on the other side the compartments into which the voters are to retire in order to mark their votes. It will be convenient so to arrange the room that voters who have marked their papers can reach the ballot-box and leave the station without meeting the fresh voters who are entering the station.

"22. The ballot-box must be constructed so that ballot papers can be introduced therein, and not withdrawn without unlocking the box (rule 23). Care should be taken that the ballot-box is of adequate size, so that it will not be choked by papers, and that it is of sufficient strength to enable it to be carried about with safety. Ballot-boxes provided for municipal elections may be used, free of charge, for parliamentary elections, and *vice versâ* (s. 14).

"23. The ballot papers must be printed strictly in accordance with rule 22, and with the form in the second schedule. The names of those candidates only who have been duly nominated and not withdrawn can be printed on the ballot papers (rule 12). Ballot papers of a different colour must be provided for 'tendered votes' (rule 27). Every ballot paper must have a counterfoil, and must be numbered on the back with a number corresponding to that on the face of the counterfoil (s. 2). As the object of the numbering is to make it possible to ascertain how votes have been given in the event of a scrutiny, all the ballot papers in any one election, at whatever station they are used, ought to be numbered in a continuous series. The ballot papers and counterfoils should be bound up in books like ordinary cheque or receipt books. Care must be taken that no ballot paper is supplied to any presiding officer except by the returning officer, or to any other person except by the presiding officer in the station at the time of voting, in accordance with the Act (see penalties in sec. 3). The returning officer must keep accounts of the number of ballot papers supplied to each presiding officer (see paragraph 47).

"24. The official mark to be stamped on the ballot paper is to be kept secret (rule 20). As the mark is to be visible on both sides of the paper (sec. 2, rule 24), a perforating or embossing stamp should be used.

"25. Each compartment in the polling station should be supplied with pencils for voters to mark the ballot papers (rule 20, and see directions in second schedule).

"26. Each polling station must be supplied with a copy of the register of voters or such part thereof as contains the names of the voters allotted to vote at that station (rule 20).

"27. Before the opening of the poll the returning officer and every officer, clerk, and agent authorized to attend at the polling station or at the counting of the votes, must make a declaration of secrecy in the form provided in the second schedule (rule 54). The person administering this declaration must, before it is taken, read over s. 4. of the Act to the declarant. All other oaths are abolished (rule 54).

"28. The only persons entitled to attend at the polling station are the presiding officer, the personation agents, of whose appointment notice has been given in accordance with 6 and 7 Vic., c. 18, s. 85 (see rule 57), or with rule 56, the candidates themselves if they wish (rule 51), and the constables on duty. Check-clerks and the commissioners who might have been appointed to administer oaths under 34 Geo. III., c. 78, and 42 Geo. III., c. 62, are abolished (see repeals in 3rd schedule).

"29. The hours of the poll remain unaltered. Just before the commencement of the poll the presiding officer at each polling station is to show the ballot-box, empty, to such persons as may be present, and then to lock it up and seal it (rule 23). He should then place it near him, and keep it in his view.

"30. The presiding officer has all the powers of a deputy returning officer under the previous law (section 10). He has power to ask the authorized questions and administer the authorized oaths (section 10). The presiding officer may delegate to his clerks any of his powers, except that of ordering the arrest, exclusion, or ejection of any person (rule 50). The attention of each presiding officer will have been particularly directed by his declaration of secrecy to the provisions of section 4, and should be directed to the powers of maintaining order conferred by section 9. It will be his duty to see that secrecy of voting is strictly maintained, to prevent unauthorized persons from entering the station, to direct the constables on duty only to admit a limited number of voters at any one time (rule 21), and to see that each voter votes secretly in accordance with the Act, and without undue delay, and leaves the station immediately after giving his vote (rule 25).

"31. Candidates may appoint agents for the purpose of detecting personation (6 and 7 Vict., c. 18, s. 85), an offence the definition of which is extended by s. 24. These agents are also entitled under rule 26 to be present at the voting of illiterate voters. They are to take the same declaration of secrecy as the presiding officer (rule 54), and are expressly prohibited from interfering with the voters or applicants for ballot papers, from attempting to look at the ballot papers or obtain information as to how any vote is given, and from communicating to any person any information about any vote or the number of any ballot paper (s. 4). It will be the duty of the presiding officer to see that the agents conform to the directions of the Act, and to remove them if they misconduct themselves (s. 9).

"32. The mode of voting in ordinary cases is described in s. 2, in rules 24 and 25, and in the directions contained in the 2nd schedule. The result is as follows:—When the voter comes up to vote, the presiding officer or his clerk (see rule 50) will ascertain that he is entitled to vote at that particular station (rule 18), he will then mark one of the official ballot papers with the official mark, so that it be visible on both sides : call out the number, name, and description of the voter, as stated in the copy of the register; enter such number on the counterfoil of the ballot paper; place against the number of the voter in the register a tick, which will denote that the voter has received a ballot paper, but will not denote the particular ballot paper which he has received; and will then deliver the ballot paper to the voter. The old law as to the questions which may be asked of the voter, and the oath which may be administered to him, remains unaltered. The voter having received his ballot paper is to proceed at once to one of the compartments, is there secretly to mark his ballot paper, and fold it up so as to conceal the mark or marks which he has made and so as to leave the official mark visible on the back, and to take it so folded, without showing the front of the paper to any person, to the presiding officer himself (not to a clerk, see section 2), show him the official mark, place the ballot paper at once in the ballot-box, and immediately leave the station. The presiding officer must take care that no person interferes with the voter while he is giving his votes, puts into the ballot-box any paper which has not the official mark on the back, takes a ballot paper out of the station, or otherwise infringes the provisions of sections 3 and 4. If any person attempt to put into the ballot-box any ballot paper which has not the official mark on the back, or to take any ballot paper out of the station, or in other way to infringe the provisions of sections 3 or 4, the presiding officer should order him to be arrested, or at all events removed (see sections 3 and 9).

" 33. If a voter accidentally spoils a ballot paper he may return it to be cancelled, and may be given another (rule 28).

" 34. In three cases only is the ballot paper allowed to be marked by any person other than the voter himself, and then only by the presiding officer. These are—(1.) Persons incapacitated by blindness or any other physical cause; (2.) Jews, if the polling takes place on a Saturday, and they object on religious grounds to mark their votes; and (3.) Persons unable to read. If a voter declares that he is unable to read he must make before the presiding officer a declaration of inability to read in the form prescribed in the second schedule. This declaration must be read by the presiding officer to the voter, signed by the voter with his mark in the presence of the presiding officer, attested by the presiding officer, and kept by him to be sent to the returning officer (see rule 38). In any of these three cases the presiding officer, or one of his clerks, is, in the presence of the personation agents, if they are in attendance (see rule 55), to mark a ballot paper in the way directed by the voter, place it in the ballot-box, and enter the name and number of the voter on a list headed " the list of votes marked by the presiding officer," mentioning in such list the reason why the vote has been so marked (rule 26). It must be remembered that the declaration of secrecy and the penalties under section 4 apply to votes given under these circumstances.

" 35. The mode of tendering a vote where a person claims to vote after another person has already voted in his name is prescribed by rule 27. The register is now made conclusive by section 7, and therefore no vote can be tendered, except in the case of personation.

" 36. The presiding officer is not allowed to open the ballot-box, which, under section 2, is, at the close of the poll, to be sealed up so as to prevent the introduction of additional ballot papers. As soon as practicable after the close of the poll, the presiding officer is, in the presence of the personation agents, if any are in attendance, to make up into separate packets the ballot-box and the several papers there mentioned, seal the packets with his own seal, and allow the agents, if they wish, to affix their seals, and then, unless he is himself the returning officer, to deliver the several packets, together with the ballot paper account mentioned in rule 30, to the returning officer (rule 29). Care should be taken that the several classes of documents mentioned in the different paragraphs of rule 29 are made up in separate packets, as only some of them are allowed to be subsequently opened by the returning officer.

"COUNTING VOTES.

"37. The returning officer is to count the votes as soon as practicable after the close of the poll (rule 32).

"38. The candidates are allowed to appoint agents to attend at the counting, but they must give the returning officer notice of the name and address of each agent one clear day before the opening of the poll (rules 31, 52).

"39. The returning officer is to give notice to the agents of the time and place of the counting of votes (rules 32, 52).

"40. The returning officer may, in addition to any clerks, appoint competent persons to assist in counting (rule 48).

"41. The persons entitled to be present at the counting are the returning officer, his assistants and clerks, the candidates (rule 50), and the duly appointed agents of the candidates. No one else is entitled to be present, except with the sanction of the returning officer. It is obvious that this sanction ought not to be given except for the purpose of assisting the returning officer in the counting. All officers, clerks, and agents authorised to attend at the counting must take the declaration of secrecy (rule 44).

"42. Before beginning to count the votes the returning officer is to open the ballot-boxes, count and record the number of papers in each box, so as to check any attempt at fraud, and then mix all the ballot papers together in such a way that it may not be known which papers came out of any particular ballot-box (rule 34). Directions as to counting the votes will be found in rule 35. In counting and recording the number of the ballot papers, and also in counting the votes, the returning officer must take care to keep the ballot papers with their faces upwards, and must take all proper precautions to prevent any person from seeing the numbers printed on the backs of the papers (rule 34). Provisions are contained in section 4 as to secrecy at the counting of the votes as well as at the proceedings at the poll.

"43. Any ballot paper which has not the official mark, or on which votes are given to more candidates than the voter is entitled to vote for, or on which anything except the number printed on the back is written or marked by which the voter can be identified, is to be void and not counted (s. 2). The power of deciding on the validity of votes rests with the returning officer alone, and cannot be delegated (s. 2). The returning officer is to mark ' Rejected ' on any ballot paper which he may reject as invalid, and to add ' Rejection objected to ' if an objection be in fact made by any agent to his decision. The rejected votes are to be classified under different heads (rule 36). If a vote is rejected on any other ground than those specified in rule 36, it must be entered under a special head. The returning officer is to make out a report of the rejected papers so classified.

" 44. The returning officer is prohibited from voting except in the case mentioned in section 2. In a case of equality of votes, if he cannot vote he must make a double return.

" 45. As soon as the result of the poll is ascertained, the returning officer is to declare elected the candidate or candidates for whom the majority of votes have been given, and to return their names to the Clerk of the Crown in Chancery (s. 2). The return is to be made by a certificate endorsed on the writ (rule 44), and may be sent by post. The indenture by which the return was formerly made is abolished.

" 46. Public notice of the names of the candidates elected, and of the total number of votes given for each candidate, is to be given as soon as possible (rules 45, 46).

" 47. Upon the completion of the counting, the returning officer is to seal up in separate packets the counted and rejected ballot papers. He is not to open the packets containing tendered ballot papers, marked copy of register of voters, or counterfoils, but he is, in the presence of the agents, to verify the ballot paper account in manner directed by rule 37, so as to see that all the ballot papers are accounted for, and that no wrong papers have been introduced, and to make out a report of the result of such verification. The returning officer will finally forward to the Clerk of the Crown in Chancery, as the poll books used to be forwarded (see 6 Vict., c. 18, s. 93), his reports made up into a packet and the several packets mentioned in rule 38, taking care to endorse on each packet the description of its contents, the date of the election to which they relate, and the name of the county or borough for which such election was held (rule 38).

"EXPENSES OF ELECTION.

"48. The necessary expenses of the election will, if properly incurred, be payable as heretofore by the candidates (s. 8). The enactment (2 & 3 W. 4, c. 45, s. 71) which formerly fixed the amount payable to deputy returning officers and poll clerks has been repealed. The enactments requiring an indenture for the purpose of the return have been repealed, and by 7 and 8 W. 3, c. 25, s. 2, a returning officer is prohibited, under a penalty of £500, from taking any fee or reward for the receipt, return, or execution of any writ.

"TIMES FOR NOMINATION AND POLL.

Counties.

(Say) July 1. Receipt of writ.
,, 2.
,, 3. Last possible day for notice.
,, 4.
,, 5. First possible day for nomination.
,, 6.
,, 7.
,, 8. First possible day for poll.
,, 9.
,, 10. Last possible day for nomination.
,, 11.
,, 12.
,, 13.
,, 14.
,, 15.
,, 16.
,, 17. Last possible day for poll.

Boroughs.

(Say) July 1. Receipt of writ.
,, 2. Last possible day for notice.
,, 3.
,, 4. First possible day for nomination.
,, 5. Last possible day for nomination.
,, 6. First possible day for poll in ordinary boroughs.

(Say) July 7. First possible day for poll in district boroughs.
,, 8.
,, 9. Last possible day for poll in ordinary boroughs.
,, 10.
,, 11.
,, 12. Last possible day for poll in district boroughs.

" N.B.—Sundays, Christmas Day, Good Friday, and any public fast or thanksgiving day are not counted (see rule 56)."

38 & 39 VICT., CHAP. 84.

An Act to regulate the Expenses and to control the Charges of Returning Officers at Parliamentary Elections.

A.D. 1875.

[*13th August, 1875.*]

1. The Ballot Act, 1872, as modified by this Act, and this Act shall be construed as one Act. <small>Construction of Act.</small>

This Act shall apply only to parliamentary elections.

2. The returning officer at an election shall be entitled to his reasonable charges, not exceeding the sums mentioned in the first schedule of this Act, in respect of services and expenses of the several kinds mentioned in the said schedule, which have been properly rendered or incurred by him for the purposes of the election. <small>Payments to returning officers.</small>

The amount of such charges shall be paid by the candidates at the election in equal several shares, or where there is only one candidate, by such candidate. If a candidate is nominated without his consent, the persons by whom his nomination is subscribed shall be jointly and severally liable for the share of the charges for which he would be liable if he were nominated with his consent.

A returning officer shall not be entitled to payment for any other services or expenses, or at any greater rates than as in the said schedule mentioned, any law or usage to the contrary notwithstanding.

3. The returning officer, if he think fit, may, as herein-after provided, require security to be given for the charges which may become payable under the provisions of this Act in respect of any election. <small>Returning officer may require deposit or security.</small>

The total amount of the security which may be required in respect of all the candidates at an election shall not in any case exceed the sums prescribed in the third schedule to this Act.

Where security is required by the returning officer it shall be apportioned and given as follows: viz.,

(1.) At the end of the two hours appointed for the election the returning officer shall forthwith declare the number of the candidates who then stand nominated, and shall, if there be more candidates nominated than there are vacancies to be filled up, apportion equally among them the total amount of the required security:

(2.) Within one hour after the end of the two hours aforesaid, security shall be given, by or in respect of each candidate then standing nominated, for the amount so apportioned to him:

(3.) If in the case of any candidate security is not given or tendered as herein mentioned, he shall be deemed to be withdrawn within the provisions of the Ballot Act, 1872:

(4.) A tender of security in respect of a candidate may be made by any person:

(5.) Security may be given by deposit of any legal tender or of notes of any bank being commonly current in the county or borough for which the election is held, or, with the consent of the returning officer, in any other manner:

(6.) The balance (if any) of a deposit beyond the amount to which the returning officer is entitled in respect of any candidate shall be repaid to the person or persons by whom the deposit was made.

The accounts of a returning officer may be taxed.

4. Within twenty-one days after the day on which the return is made of the persons elected at the election, the returning officer shall transmit to every candidate or other person from whom he claims payment either out of any deposit or otherwise of any charges in respect of the election, or to the agent for election expenses of any such candidate, a detailed account showing the amounts of all the charges claimed by the returning officer in respect of the election, and the share thereof which he claims from the person to whom the account is transmitted. He shall annex to the account a notice of the place where the vouchers relating to the account may be seen, and he shall at all reasonable times and without charge allow the person from whom payment is claimed, or any agent of such person, to inspect and take copies of the vouchers.

The returning officer shall not be entitled to any charges which are not duly included in his account.

If the person from whom payment is claimed objects to any part of the claim, he may, at any time within fourteen days from the time when the account is transmitted to him, apply to the court as defined in this section for a taxation of the account, and the court shall have jurisdiction to tax the account in such manner and at such time and place as the court thinks fit, and finally to determine the amount payable to the returning officer and to give and enforce judgment for the same as if such judgment were a judgment in an action in such court, and with or without costs at the discretion of the court.

The court for the purposes of this Act shall be in the city of London the Lord Mayor's Court, and elsewhere in England the County Court, and in Ireland the Civil Bill Court, having jurisdiction at the place of nomination for the election to which the proceedings relate.

The court may depute any of its powers or duties under this Act to the registrar or other principal officer of the court.

Nothing in this section shall apply to the charge of the returning officer for publication of accounts of election expenses.

5. Every person having any claim against a returning officer for work, labour, materials, services, or expenses in respect of any contract made with him by or on behalf of the returning officer for the purposes of an election, except for publication of accounts of election expenses, shall, within fourteen days after the day on which the return is made of the person or persons elected at the election, transmit to the returning officer the detailed particulars of such claim in writing, and the returning officer shall not be liable in respect of anything which is not duly stated in such particulars. *Claims against a returning officer*

Where application is made for taxation of the accounts of a returning officer, he may apply to the court as defined in this Act to examine any claim transmitted to him by any person in pursuance of this section, and the court after notice given to such person, and after hearing him, and any evidence tendered by him, may allow or disallow, or reduce the claim objected to, with or without costs, and the determination of the court shall be final for all purposes, and as against all persons.

6. In any case to which the fourteenth section of the Ballot Act, 1872, is applicable, it shall be the duty of the returning officer, so far as is practicable, to make use of ballot boxes, fittings, and compartments provided for municipal or school board elections, and *Use of ballot boxes, &c., provided for municipal elections*

P

the court, upon taxation of his accounts, shall have regard to the provisions of this section.

7. There shall be added to every notice of election to be published under the provisions of the Ballot Act, 1872, the notification contained in the second schedule to this Act with respect to claims against returning officers.

8. Nothing in this Act shall apply to an election for any university or combination of universities.

9. This Act shall come into operation on the first day of October one thousand eight hundred and seventy-five, and continue in force until the thirty-first day of December one thousand eight hundred and eighty, and no longer, unless Parliament shall otherwise determine.

10. This Act may be cited for all purposes as the "Parliamentary Elections (Returning Officers) Act, 1875."

11. This Act shall not apply to Scotland.

SCHEDULES.

FIRST SCHEDULE.

CHARGES OF RETURNING OFFICERS.

The following are the maximum charges to be made by the returning officer, but the charges are in no case to exceed the sums actually and necessarily paid or payable:—

PART I.

COUNTIES AND DISTRICT OR CONTRIBUTORY BOROUGHS.

This Part of this Schedule applies to an election for a county, or for either of the boroughs of Aylesbury, Cricklade, Monmouth, East Retford, Stroud, and New Shoreham, or for any borough or burgh consisting of a combination of separate boroughs, burghs, or towns.

	£ s. d.	
For preparing and publishing the notice of election	2 2 0	
For preparing and supplying the nomination papers	1 1 0	
For travelling to and from the place of nomination, or of declaring the poll at a contested election, per mile	0 1 0	
For hire or necessary fitting up of rooms or buildings for polling, or damage or expenses by or for use of such rooms or buildings.		The necessary expenses, not exceeding at any one polling station the charge for constructing and fitting a polling station
For constructing a polling station, with its fittings and compartments, in England	7 7 0	
And in Ireland the sum or sums payable under the provisions of the 13th and 14th Victoria, chap. 68, and 35th and 36th Victoria, chap. 33.		

FIRST SCHEDULE.—PART I.—*continued.*

	£ s. d.
In Ireland the returning officer shall use a court house where one is available as a polling station, and his maximum charge for using and fitting the same shall in no case exceed three pounds three shillings.	
For each ballot box required to be purchased	1 1 0
For the use of each ballot box, when hired	0 5 0
For stationery at each polling station ..	0 10 0
For printing and providing ballot papers, per thousand	1 10 0
For each stamping instrument	0 10 0
For copies of the register	The sums payable by statute for the necessary copies.
For each presiding officer	3 1 0
For one clerk at each polling station where not more than 500 voters are assigned to such station	1 3 0
For an additional clerk at a polling station for every number of 500 voters, or fraction thereof beyond the first 500 assigned to such polling station ..	1 1 0
For every person employed in counting votes, not exceeding six such persons where the number of registered electors does not exceed 3,000, and one for every additional 2,000 electors ..	1 1 0
For making the return to the clerk of the Crown	1 1 0
For the preparation and publication of notices (other than the notice of election).	Not exceeding for the whole of such notices 20*l.*, and 1*l.* for every additional 1,000 electors above 3,000.
For conveyance of ballot boxes from the polling stations to the place where the ballot papers are to be counted, per mile	0 1 0

FIRST SCHEDULE.—Part I.—continued.

	£ s. d.
For professional and other assistance in and about the conduct of the election.	In a contested election not exceeding 25*l.*, and an additional 3*l.* for every 1,000 registered electors or fraction thereof above 3,000 and up to 10,000, and 2*l.* for every 1,000 or fraction thereof above 10,000. In an uncontested election, one fifth of the above sums.
For travelling expenses of presiding officers and clerks, per mile	0 1 0
For services and expenses in relation to receiving and publishing accounts of election expenses, in respect of each candidate	2 2 0
For all other expenses	In a contested election, not exceeding 10*l.*, and an additional 1*l.* for every 1,000 electors or fraction thereof above 1,000. In an uncontested election, nil.

NOTE.—*Travelling expenses are not to be allowed in the case of any person unless for distances exceeding two miles from the place at which he resides.*

PART II.—BOROUGHS.

This Part of the Schedule applies to all boroughs not included in Part I. of this Schedule.

	£ s. d.
For preparing and publishing the notice of election	2 2 0
For preparing and supplying the nomination papers	1 1 0
For hire or necessary fitting up of rooms or buildings for polling, or damage or expenses by or for use of such rooms or buildings.	The necessary expenses, not exceeding at any one polling station, the charge for constructing and fitting a polling station.

FIRST SCHEDULE.—Part II.—*continued.*

	£	s.	d.
In England, for constructing a polling station, with its fittings and compartments, not exceeding two in number	7	7	0
For each compartment required to be constructed, when more than two be used	1	1	0
For the use of each compartment hired, when more than two are used	0	5	0
And in Ireland, in lieu of the charges payable in respect of the foregoing last three services, the sum or sums payable under the provisions of 13th and 14th Victoria, chap. 68, and 35th and 36th Victoria, chap. 33.			
For each ballot box required to be purchased	1	1	0
For the use of each ballot box, when hired	0	5	0
For stationery at each polling station	0	10	0
For printing and providing ballot papers, per thousand	1	10	0
For each stamping instrument	0	10	0
For copies of the register	The sums payable by statute for the necessary copies.		
For each presiding officer	3	3	0
For one clerk at each polling station where not more than 500 voters are assigned to such station	1	1	0
For an additional clerk at a polling station for every number of 500 voters, or fraction thereof beyond the first 500 assigned to such station	1	1	0
For every person employed in counting votes, not exceeding six such persons where the number of registered electors does not exceed 3,000, and one for every additional 2,000 electors	1	1	0
For making the return to the clerk of the Crown	1	1	0
For the preparation and publication of notices (other than the notice of election).	Not exceeding for the whole of such notices 10*l.*, and 1*l.* for every additional 1,000 electors above 1,000.		

FIRST SCHEDULE.—Part II.—*continued*.

	£ s. d.
For professional and other assistance in and about the conduct of the election.	In a contested election, not exceeding 20*l*., an additional 2*l*. for every 1,000 registered electors or fraction thereof above 1,000 and up to 10,000, and 1*l*. additional for every 1,000 or fraction thereof above 10,000. In an uncontested election one fifth of the above sum.
For services and expenses in relation to receiving and publishing accounts of election expenses, in respect of each candidate..	1 1 0
For all other expenses	Not exceeding 10*l*., and an additional 1*l*. for every 1,000 electors above the first 1,000.

NOTE TO PARTS I. AND II. OF SCHEDULE I.

The above sums are the aggregate charges, the amount of which is to be apportioned among the several candidates or other persons liable for the same.

SECOND SCHEDULE.

1.—NOTIFICATION to be added to the NOTICE of ELECTION.

Take notice, that by the Parliamentary Elections (Returning Officers) Act, 1875, it is provided that every person having any claim against a returning officer for work, labour, materials, services, or expenses in respect of any contract made with him by or on behalf of the returning officer, for the purposes of an election (except for publications of account of election expenses), shall, within fourteen days after the day on which the return is made of the person or persons elected at the election, transmit to the returning officer the detailed particulars of such claim in writing, and the returning officer shall not be liable in respect of anything which is not duly stated in such particulars.

THIRD SCHEDULE.

Maximum Amount of Security which may be required by a Returning Officer.

	County or District of Contributory Borough	Borough.
	£	£
Where the registered electors do not exceed 1,000	150	100
Where the registered electors exceed 1,000 but do not exceed 2,000	200	150
Where the registered electors exceed 2,000 but do not exceed 4,000	275	200
Where the registered electors exceed 4,000 but do not exceed 7,000	400	250
Where the registered electors exceed 7,000 but do not exceed 10,000	550	300
Where the registered electors exceed 10,000 but do not exceed 15,000	700	450
Where the registered electors exceed 15,000 but do not exceed 20,000	800	500
Where the registered electors exceed 20,000 but do not exceed 30,000	900	600
Where the registered electors exceed 30,000	1,000	700

If at the end of the two hours appointed for the election, not more candidates stand nominated than there are vacancies to be filled up, the maximum amount which may be required is one-fifth of the maximum according to the above scale.

46 & 47 Vic., Chap. 51.

An Act for the Better Prevention of Corrupt and Illegal Practices at Parliamentary Elections.

[25th August, 1883.]

ARRANGEMENT OF SECTIONS.

Corrupt Practices.

Section.
1. What is treating.
2. What is undue influence.
3. What is corrupt practice.
4. Punishment of candidate found, on election petition, guilty personally of corrupt practices.
5. Punishment of candidate found, on election petition, guilty by agents of corrupt practices.
6. Punishment of person convicted on indictment of corrupt practices.

Illegal Practices.

7. Certain expenditure to be illegal practice.
8. Expense in excess of maximum to be illegal practice.
9. Voting by prohibited persons and publishing of false statement of withdrawal to be illegal.
10. Punishment on conviction of illegal practice.
11. Report of election court respecting illegal practice, and punishment of candidate found guilty by such report.
12. Extension of 15 & 16 Vict., c. 57, respecting election commissioners to illegal practices.

Illegal Payment, Employment, and Hiring.

13. Providing of money for illegal practice or payment to be illegal payment.
14. Employment of hackney carriages, or of carriages and horses kept for hire.
15. Corrupt withdrawal from a candidature.

Section.
16. Certain expenditure to be illegal payment.
17. Certain employment to be illegal.
18. Name and address of printer on placards.
19. Saving for creditors.
20. Use of committee room in house for sale of intoxicating liquor or refreshment, or in elementary school, to be illegal hiring.
21. Punishment of illegal payment, employment, or hiring.

Excuse and Exception for Corrupt or Illegal Practice or Illegal Payment, Employment, or Hiring.

22. Report exonerating candidate in certain cases of corrupt and illegal practice by agents.
23. Power of High Court and election court to except innocent act from being illegal practice, &c.

Election Expenses.

24. Nomination of election agent.
25. Nomination of deputy election agent as sub-agent.
26. Office of election agent and sub-agent.
27. Making of contracts through election agent.
28. Payment of expenses through election agent.
29. Period for sending in claims and making payments for election expenses.
30. Reference to taxation of claim against candidates.
31. Personal expenses of candidate and petty expenses.
32. Remuneration of election agent and returning officer's expenses.
33. Return and declaration respecting election expenses.
34. Authorized excuse for non-compliance with provisions as to return and declaration respecting election expenses.
35. Publication of summary of return of election expenses.

Disqualification of Electors.

36. Prohibition of persons guilty of corrupt or illegal practices, &c., from voting.
37. Prohibition of disqualified persons from voting.
38. Hearing of person before he is reported guilty of corrupt or illegal practice, and incapacity of person reported guilty.
39. List in register of voters of persons incapacitated for voting by corrupt or illegal practices.

Proceedings on Election Petition.

Section.
40. Time for presentation of election petitions alleging illegal practice.
41. Withdrawal of election petition.
42. Continuation of trial of election petition.
43. Attendance of Director of Public Prosecutions on trial of election petition, and prosecution by him of offenders.
44. Power to election court to order payment by county or borough or individual of costs of election petition.

Miscellaneous.

45. Inquiry by Director of Public Prosecutions into alleged corrupt or illegal practices.
46. Removal of incapacity on proof that it was procured by perjury.
47. Amendment of law as to polling districts and polling places.
48. Conveyance of voters by sea in certain cases.
49. Election commissioners not to inquire into elections before the passing of this Act.

Legal Proceedings.

50. Trial in Central Criminal Court of indictment for corrupt practice at instance of Attorney-General.
51. Limitation of time for prosecution of offence.
52. Persons charged with corrupt practice may be found guilty of illegal practice.
53. Application of enactments of 17 & 18 Vict., c. 102., and 26 & 27 Vict., c. 29, relating to prosecutions for bribery.
54. Prosecution on summary conviction, and appeal to quarter sessions.
55. Application of Summary Jurisdiction and Indictable Offences Acts to proceedings before election courts.
56. Exercise of jurisdiction of High Court, and making of rules of court.
57. Director of Public Prosecutions, and expenses of prosecutions.
58. Recovery of costs payable by county or borough or by person.

Supplemental Provisions, Definitions, Savings, and Repeal.

59. Obligation of witness to answer, and certificate of indemnity.
60. Submission of report of election court or commissioners to Attorney-General.

Section.
61. Breach of duty by officer.
62. Publication and service of notices.
63. Definition of candidate, and saving for persons nominated without consent.
64. General interpretation of terms.
65. Short titles.
66. Repeal of Acts.
67. Commencement of Act.

Application of Act to Scotland.

68. Application of Act to Scotland.

Application of Act to Ireland.

69. Application of Act to Ireland.

Continuance.

70. Continuance.

SCHEDULES.

SECTIONS OF THE ACT.

Corrupt Practices.

What Is Treating.

1. Whereas under section four of the Corrupt Practices Prevention Act, 1854, persons other than candidates at Parliamentary elections are not liable to any punishment for treating, and it is expedient to make such persons liable; be it therefore enacted in substitution for the said section four as follows:—

(1.) Any person who corruptly by himself or by any other person, either before, during, or after an election, directly or indirectly gives or provides, or pays wholly or in part the expense of giving or providing, any meat, drink, entertainment or provision to or for any person, for the purpose of corruptly influencing that person or any other person to give or refrain from giving his vote at the election, or on account of such person or any other person having voted or refrained from voting, or being about to vote or refrain from voting at such election, shall be guilty of treating.

(2.) And every elector who corruptly accepts or takes any such meat, drink, entertainment or provision shall also be guilty of treating.

2. Every person who shall directly or indirectly, by himself or by any other person on his behalf, make use of or threaten to make use of any force, violence, or restraint, or inflict or threaten to inflict, by himself or by any other person, any temporal or spiritual injury, damage, harm, or loss upon or against any person in order to induce or compel such person to vote or refrain from voting, or on account of such person having voted or refrained from voting at any election, or who shall by abduction, duress, or any fraudulent device or contrivance impede or prevent the free exercise of the franchise of any elector, or shall thereby compel, induce, or prevail upon any elector either to give or to refrain from giving his vote at any election, shall be guilty of undue influence. *What is undue influence.*

3. The expression "corrupt practice" as used in this Act means any of the following offences, namely, treating and undue influence, as defined by this Act, and bribery and personation, as defined by the enactments set forth in Part III. of the Third Schedule to this Act, and aiding, abetting, counselling and procuring the commission of the offence of personation, and every offence which is a corrupt practice within the meaning of this Act shall be a corrupt practice within the meaning of the Parliamentary Elections Act, 1868. *What is corrupt practice. 31 & 32 Vict., c. 125.*

4. Where upon the trial of an election petition respecting an election for a county or borough the election court, by the report made to the Speaker in pursuance of section eleven of the Parliamentary Elections Act, 1868, reports that any corrupt practice other than treating or undue influence has been proved to have been committed in reference to such election by or with the knowledge and consent of any candidate at such election, or that the offence of treating or undue influence has been proved to have been committed in reference to such election by any candidate at such election, that candidate shall not be capable of ever being elected to or sitting in the House of Commons for the said county or borough, and if he has been elected, his election shall be void; and he shall further be subject to the same incapacities as if at the date of the said report he had been convicted on an indictment of a corrupt practice. *Punishment of candidate found, on election petition, guilty personally of corrupt practices, 31 & 32 Vict., c. 125.*

5. Upon the trial of an election petition respecting an election for a county or borough, in which a charge is made of any corrupt practice having been committed in reference to such election, the election court shall report in writing to the Speaker whether any of the candidates at such election has been guilty by his agents of any corrupt practice in reference to such election; and if the report is that any candidate at such election has been guilty by his agents of any corrupt practice in reference to such election, that candidate shall not be capable of being elected to or sitting in the House of *Punishment of candidate found, on election petition, guilty by agents of corrupt practices.*

Commons for such county or borough for seven years after the date of the report, and if he has been elected his election shall be void.

<small>Punishment of person convicted on indictment of corrupt practices.</small>

6. (1.) A person who commits any corrupt practice other than personation, or aiding, abetting, counselling, or procuring the commission of the offence of personation, shall be guilty of a misdemeanor, and on conviction on indictment shall be liable to be imprisoned, with or without hard labour, for a term not exceeding one year, or to be fined any sum not exceeding two hundred pounds.

(2.) A person who commits the offence of personation, or of aiding, abetting, counselling, or procuring the commission of that offence, shall be guilty of felony, and any person convicted thereof on indictment shall be punished by imprisonment for a term not exceeding two years, together with hard labour.

(3.) A person who is convicted on indictment of any corrupt practice shall (in addition to any punishment as above provided) be not capable during a period of seven years from the date of his conviction:

(*a*.) of being registered as an elector or voting at any election in the United Kingdom, whether it be a parliamentary election or an election for any public office within the meaning of this Act; or

(*b*.) of holding any public or judicial office within the meaning of this Act, and if he holds any such office the office shall be vacated.

(4.) Any person so convicted of a corrupt practice in reference to any election shall also be incapable of being elected to and of sitting in the House of Commons during the seven years next after the date of his conviction, and if at that date he has been elected to the House of Commons his election shall be vacated from the time of such conviction.

Illegal Practices.

<small>Certain expenditure to be illegal practice.</small>

7. (1.) No payment or contract for payment shall, for the purpose of promoting or procuring the election of a candidate at any election, be made—

(*a*.) on account of the conveyance of electors to or from the poll, whether for the hiring of horses or carriages, or for the railway fares, or otherwise; or

(*b*.) to an elector on account of the use of any house, land, building, or premises for the exhibition of any address, bill, or notice, or on account of the exhibition of any address, bill, or notice; or (*c.*) on account of any committee room in excess of the number allowed by the First Schedule to this Act.

(2.) Subject to such exception as may be allowed in pursuance to this Act, if any payment or contract for payment is knowingly made in contravention of this section either before, during, or after an election, the person making such payment or contract shall be guilty of an illegal practice, and any person receiving such payment or being a party to any such contract, knowing the same to be in contravention of this Act, shall also be guilty of an illegal practice.

(3.) Provided that where it is the ordinary business of an elector as an advertising agent to exhibit for payment bills and advertisements, a payment to or contract with such elector, if made in the ordinary course of business, shall not be deemed to be an illegal practice within the meaning of this section.

8. (1.) Subject to such exception as may be allowed in pursuance of this Act, no sum shall be paid and no expenses shall be incurred by a candidate at an election or his election agent, whether before, during, or after an election, on account of or in respect of the conduct or management of such election, in excess of any maximum amount in that behalf specified in the first schedule to this Act. Expense in excess of maximum be illegal practice.

(2.) Any candidate or election agent who knowingly acts in contravention of this section shall be guilty of an illegal practice.

9. (1.) If any person votes or induces or procures any person to vote at any election, knowing that he or such person is prohibited, whether by this or any other Act, from voting at such election, he shall be guilty of an illegal practice. Voting by prohibited persons and publishing of false statements of withdrawal to be illegal.

(2.) Any person who before or during an election knowingly publishes a false statement of the withdrawal of a candidate at such election for the purpose of promoting or procuring the election of another candidate shall be guilty of an illegal practice.

(3.) Provided that a candidate shall not be liable, nor shall his election be avoided, for any illegal practice under this section committed by his agent other than his election agent.

10. A person guilty of an illegal practice, whether under the foregoing sections or under the provisions hereinafter contained in this Act, shall on summary conviction be liable to a fine not exceeding one hundred pounds, and be incapable during a period of five years from the date of his conviction of being registered as an elector or voting at any election (whether it be a parliamentary election or an election for a public office within the meaning of this Act) held for or within the county or borough in which the illegal practice has been committed. Punishment on conviction of illegal practice.

Report of election court respecting Illegal practice, and punishment of candidate found guilty by such report. 31 & 32 Vict., c. 125.

11. Whereas by sub-section fourteen of section eleven of the Parliamentary Elections Act, 1868, it is provided that where a charge is made in an election petition of any corrupt practice having been committed at the election to which the petition refers, the judge shall report in writing to the Speaker as follows:

(*a.*) " Whether any corrupt practice has or has not been proved "to have been committed by or with the knowledge and con- " sent of any candidate at such election, and the nature of " such corrupt practice;

(*b.*) " The names of all persons, if any, who have been proved at " the trial to have been guilty of any corrupt practice;

(*c.*) " Whether corrupt practices have, or whether there is reason "to believe corrupt practices have, extensively prevailed at the "election to which the petition relates: "

And whereas it is expedient to extend the said sub-section to illegal practices:

Be it therefore enacted as follows:—

31 & 32 Vict., c. 125.

Sub-section fourteen of section eleven of the Parliamentary Elections Act, 1868, shall apply as if that sub-section were herein re-enacted with the substitution of illegal practice within the meaning of this Act for corrupt practice; and upon the trial of an election petition respecting an election for a county or borough, the election court shall report in writing to the Speaker the particulars required by the said sub-section as herein re-enacted, and shall also report whether any candidate at such election has been guilty by his agents of any illegal practice within the meaning of this Act in reference to such election, and the following consequences shall ensue upon the report by the election court to the Speaker; (that is to say,)

(*a.*) If the report is that any illegal practice has been proved to have been committed in reference to such election by or with the knowledge and consent of any candidate at such election, that candidate shall not be capable of being elected to or sitting in the House of Commons for the said county or borough for seven years next after the date of the report, and if he has been elected his election shall be void; and he shall further be subject to the same incapacities as if at the date of the report he had been convicted of such illegal practice; and

(*b.*) If the report is that a candidate at such election has been guilty by his agents of any illegal practice in reference to such election, that candidate shall not be capable of being elected to or sitting in the House of Commons for the said county or borough during the Parliament for which the election was held, and if he has been elected, his election shall be void.

12. Whereas by the Election Commissioners Act, 1852, as amended by the Parliamentary Elections Act, 1868, it is enacted that where a joint address of both Houses of Parliament represents to Her Majesty that an election court has reported to the Speaker that corrupt practices have, or that there is reason to believe that corrupt practices have, extensively prevailed at an election in any county or borough, and prays Her Majesty to cause inquiry under that Act to be made by persons named in such address (being qualified as therein mentioned), it shall be lawful for Her Majesty to appoint the said persons to be election commissioners for the purpose of making inquiry into the existence of such corrupt practices:

And whereas it is expedient to extend the said enactments to the case of illegal practices:

Be it therefore enacted as follows:—

When election commissioners have been appointed in pursuance of the Election Commissioners Act, 1852, and the enactments amending the same, they may make inquiries and act and report as if "corrupt practices" in the said Act and the enactments amending the same included illegal practices: and the Election Commissioners Act, 1852, shall be construed with such modifications as are necessary for giving effect to this section, and the expression "corrupt practice" in that Act shall have the same meaning as in this Act.

Extension of 15 & 16 Vict., c. 57, respecting election commissioners to illegal practices. 15 & 16 Vict., c. 57; 31 & 32 Vict., c. 125.

15 & 16 Vict., c. 57.

Illegal Payment, Employment, and Hiring.

13. Where a person knowingly provides money for any payment which is contrary to the provisions of this Act (or for any expenses incurred in excess of any maximum amount allowed by this Act), or for replacing any money expended in any such payment or expenses, except where the same may have been previously allowed in pursuance of this Act to be an exception, such person shall be guilty of illegal payment.

Providing of money for illegal practice or payment to be illegal payment.

14. (1.) A person shall not let, lend or employ for the purpose of the conveyance of electors to or from the poll, any public stage or hackney carriage, or any horse or other animal kept or used for drawing the same, or any carriage, horse, or other animal which he keeps or uses for the purpose of letting out for hire, and if he lets, lends, or employs such carriage, horse or other animal, knowing that it is intended to be used for the purpose of the conveyance of electors to or from the poll, he shall be guilty of an illegal hiring.

Employment of hackney carriages, or of carriages and horses kept for hire.

(2.) A person shall not hire, borrow, or use for the purpose of the conveyance of electors to or from the poll any carriage, horse, or other animal which he knows the owner thereof is prohibited by

Q

this section to let, lend, or employ for that purpose, and if he does so he shall be guilty of an illegal hiring.

(3.) Nothing in this Act shall prevent a carriage, horse, or other animal being let to or hired, employed, or used by an elector, or several electors at their joint cost, for the purpose of being conveyed to or from the poll.

(4.) No person shall be liable to pay any duty or to take out a licence for any carriage by reason only of such carriage being used without payment or promise of payment for the conveyance of electors to or from the poll at an election.

Corrupt withdrawal from a candidature.

15. Any person who corruptly induces or procures any other person to withdraw from being a candidate at an election, in consideration of any payment or promise of payment, shall be guilty of illegal payment, and any person withdrawing, in pursuance of such inducement or procurement, shall also be guilty of illegal payment.

Certain expenditure to be illegal payment.

16. (1.) No payment or contract for payment shall, for the purpose of promoting or procuring the election of a candidate at any election, be made on account of bands of music, torches, flags, banners, cockades, ribbons, or other marks of distinction.

(2.) Subject to such exception as may be allowed in pursuance of this Act, if any payment or contract for payment is made in contravention of this section, either before, during, or after an election, the person making such payment shall be guilty of illegal payment, and any person being a party to any such contract or receiving such payment shall also be guilty of illegal payment if he knew that the same was made contrary to law.

Certain employment to be illegal.

17. (1.) No person shall, for the purpose of promoting or procuring the election of a candidate at any election, be engaged or employed for payment or promise of payment for any purpose or in any capacity whatever, except for any purposes or capacities mentioned in the first or second parts of the First Schedule to this Act, or except so far as payment is authorised by the first or second parts of the First Schedule to this Act.

(2.) Subject to such exception as may be allowed in pursuance of this Act, if any person is engaged or employed in contravention of the section, either before, during, or after an election, the person engaging or employing him shall be guilty of illegal employment, and the person so engaged or employed shall also be guilty of illegal employment if he knew that he was engaged or employed contrary to law.

Name and address of printer on placards.

18. Every bill, placard, or poster having reference to an election shall bear upon the face thereof the name and address of the printer and publisher thereof; and any person printing, publishing, or posting, or causing to be printed, published, or posted, any such bill, placard, or poster as aforesaid, which fails to bear upon the face thereof the name and address of the printer and publisher, shall, if he is the candidate, or the election agent of the candidate, be guilty of an illegal practice, and if he is not the candidate, or the election agent of a candidate, shall be liable on summary conviction to a fine not exceeding one hundred pounds.

19. The provisions of this Act prohibiting certain payments and contracts for payments, and the payment of any sum, and the incurring of any expense in excess of a certain maximum, shall not affect the right of any creditor, who, when the contract was made or the expense was incurred, was ignorant of the same being in contravention of this Act. Saving for creditors.

20. (*a.*) Any premises on which the sale by wholesale or retail of any intoxicating liquor is authorised by a licence (whether the licence be for consumption on or off the premises), or

(*b.*) Any premises where any intoxicating liquor is sold, or is supplied to members of a club, society, or association other than a permanent political club, or

(*c.*) Any premises whereon refreshment of any kind, whether food or drink, is ordinarily sold for consumption on the premises, or

(*d.*) The premises of any public elementary school in receipt of an annual parliamentary grant, or any part of any such premises, shall not be used as a committee room for the purpose of promoting or procuring the election of a candidate at an election, and if any person hires or uses any such premises or any part thereof for a committee room, he shall be guilty of illegal hiring, and the person letting such premises or part, if he knew it was intended to use the same as a committee room, shall also be guilty of illegal hiring:

Provided that nothing in this section shall apply to any part of such premises which is ordinarily let for the purpose of chambers or offices or the holding of public meetings or of arbitrations, if such part has a separate entrance and no direct communication with any part of the premises on which any intoxicating liquor or refreshment is sold or supplied as aforesaid.

Use of committee room in house for sale of intoxicating liquor or refreshment, or in elementary school, to be illegal hiring.

21. (1.) A person guilty of an offence of illegal payment, employment or hiring shall, on summary conviction, be liable to a fine not exceeding one hundred pounds. Punishment of illegal payment, employment, or hiring.

(2.) A candidate or an election agent of a candidate who is personally guilty of an offence of illegal payment, employment, or hiring shall be guilty of an illegal practice.

Excuse and Exception for Corrupt or Illegal Practice or Illegal Payment, Employment, or Hiring.

Report exonerating candidate in certain cases of corrupt and illegal practice by agents.

22. Where, upon the trial of an election petition respecting an election for a county or borough, the election court report that a candidate at such election has been guilty by his agents of the offence of treating and undue influence, and illegal practice, or of any of such offences, in reference to such election, and the election court further report that the candidate has proved to the court—

(*a.*) That no corrupt or illegal practice was committed at such election by the candidate or his election agent, and the offences mentioned in the said report were committed contrary to the orders and without the sanction or connivance of such candidate or his election agent; and

(*b.*) That such candidate and his election agent took all reasonable means for preventing the commission of corrupt and illegal practices at such election; and

(*c.*) That the offences mentioned in the said report were of a trivial, unimportant, and limited character; and

(*d.*) That in all other respects the election was free from any corrupt or illegal practice on the part of such candidate and of his agents;

then the election of such candidate shall not, by reason of the offences mentioned in such report, be void, nor shall the candidate be subject to any incapacity under this Act.

Power of High Court and election court to except innocent act from being illegal practice, &c.

23. Where, on application made, it is shown to the High Court or to an election court by such evidence as seems to the Court sufficient—

(*a.*) that any act or omission of a candidate at any election, or of his election agent or of any other agent or person, would by reason of being a payment, engagement, employment, or contract in contravention of this Act, or being the payment of a sum or the incurring of expense in excess of any maximum amount allowed by this Act, or of otherwise being in contravention of any of the provisions of this Act, be but for this section an illegal practice, payment, employment, or hiring; and

(*b.*) that such act or omission arose from inadvertence or from accidental miscalculation or from some other reasonable cause of a like nature, and in any case did not arise from any want of good faith; and

(*c.*) that such notice of the application has been given in the county or borough for which the election was held as to the court seems fit;

and under the circumstances it seems to the Court to be just that the candidate and the said election and other agent and person, or any of them, should not be subject to any of the consequences under this Act of the said act or omission, the Court may make an order allowing such act or omission to be an exception from the provisions of this Act, which would otherwise make the same an illegal practice, payment, employment, or hiring, and thereupon such candidate, agent, or person shall not be subject to any of the consequences under this Act of the said act or omission.

Election Expenses.

24. (1.) On or before the day of nomination at an election a person shall be named by or on behalf of each candidate as his agent for such election (in this Act referred to as the election agent). Nomination of election agent.

(2.) A candidate may name himself as election agent, and thereupon shall, so far as circumstances admit, be subject to the provisions of this Act both as a candidate and as an election agent, and any reference in this Act to an election agent shall be construed to refer to the candidate acting in his capacity of election agent.

(3.) On or before the day of nomination the name and address of the election agent of each candidate shall be declared in writing by the candidate or some other person on his behalf to the returning officer, and the returning officer shall forthwith give public notice of the name and address of every election agent so declared.

(4.) One election agent only shall be appointed for each candidate, but the appointment, whether the election agent appointed be the candidate himself or not, may be revoked, and in the event of such revocation or his death, whether such event is before, during, or after the election, then forthwith another election agent shall be appointed, and his name and address declared in writing to the returning officer, who shall forthwith give public notice of the same.

25. (1.) In the case of the elections specified in that behalf in the First Schedule to this Act an election agent of a candidate may appoint the number of deputies therein mentioned (which deputies are in this Act referred to as sub-agents), to act within different polling districts. Nomination of deputy election agent as sub-agent.

(2.) As regards matters in a polling district the election agent may act by the sub-agent for that district, and anything done for the purposes of this Act by or to the sub-agent in his district shall be deemed to be done by or to the election agent, and any act or default of a sub-agent which, if he were the election agent, would be an illegal practice or other offence against this Act, shall be an illegal practice and offence against this Act committed by the sub-agent, and the sub-agent shall be liable to punishment accordingly; and the candidate shall suffer the like incapacity as if the said act or default had been the act or default of the election agent.

(3.) One clear day before the polling the election agent shall declare in writing the name and address of every sub-agent to the returning officer, and the returning officer shall forthwith give public notice of the name and address of every sub-agent so declared.

(4.) The appointment of a sub-agent shall not be vacated by the election agent who appointed him ceasing to be election agent, but may be revoked by the election agent for the time being of the candidate, and in the event of such revocation or of the death of a sub-agent another sub-agent may be appointed, and his name and address shall be forthwith declared in writing to the returning officer, who shall forthwith give public notice of the same.

26. (1.) An election agent at an election for a county or borough shall have within the county or borough (or within any county of a city or town adjoining thereto), and a sub-agent shall have within his district, or within any county of a city or town adjoining thereto, an office or place to which all claims, notices, writs, summons, and documents may be sent, and the address of such office or place shall be declared at the same time as the appointment of the said agent to the returning officer, and shall be stated in the public notice of the name of the agent.

(2.) Any claim, notice, writ, summons, or document delivered at such office or place and addressed to the election agent or sub-agent, as the case may be, shall be deemed to have been served on him, and every such agent may in respect of any matter connected with the election in which he is acting be sued in any court having jurisdiction in the county or borough in which the said office or place is situate.

27. (1.) The election agent of a candidate by himself or by his sub-agent shall appoint every polling agent, clerk, and messenger employed for payment on behalf of the candidate at an election, and hire every committee room hired on behalf of the candidate.

(2.) A contract whereby any expenses are incurred on account of or in respect of the conduct or management of an election shall not be enforceable against a candidate at such election unless made by the candidate himself or by 'his election agent either by himself or by his sub-agent; provided that the inability under this section to enforce such contract against the candidate shall not relieve the candidate from the consequences of any corrupt or illegal practice having been committed by his agent.

28. (1.) Except as permitted by or in pursuance of this Act, no payment and no advance or deposit shall be made by a candidate at an election or by any agent on behalf of the candidate or by any other person at any time, whether before, during, or after such election, in respect of any expenses incurred on account of or in respect of the conduct or management of such election, otherwise than by or through the election agent of the candidate, whether acting in person or by a sub-agent; and all money provided by any person other than the candidate for any expenses incurred on account of or in respect of the conduct or management of the election, whether as gift, loan, advance, or deposit, shall be *paid to* the candidate or his election agent and not otherwise;

Payment of expenses through election agent.

Provided that this section shall not be deemed to apply to a tender of security to or any payment by the returning officer or to any sum disbursed by any person out of his own money for any small expense legally incurred by himself, if such sum is not repaid to him.

(2.) A person who makes any payment, advance, or deposit in contravention of this section, or pays in contravention of this section any money so provided as aforesaid, shall be guilty of an illegal practice.

29. (1.) Every payment made by an election agent, whether by himself or a sub-agent, in respect of any expenses incurred on account of or in respect of the conduct or management of an election, shall, except where less than forty shillings, be vouched for by a bill stating the particulars and by a receipt.

Period for sending in claims and making payments for election expenses.

(2.) Every claim against a candidate at an election or his election agent in respect of any expenses incurred on account of or in respect of the conduct or management of such election which is not sent in to the election agent within the time limited by this Act shall be barred and shall not be paid; and, subject to such exception as may be allowed in pursuance of this Act, an election agent who pays a claim in contravention of this enactment shall be guilty of an illegal practice.

(3.) Except as by this Act permitted, the time limited by this Act for sending in claims shall be fourteen days after the day on which the candidates returned are declared elected

(4.) All expenses incurred by or on behalf of a candidate at an election, which are incurred on account of or in respect of the conduct or management of such election, shall be paid within the time limited by this Act and not otherwise; and, subject to such exception as may be allowed in pursuance of this Act, an election agent who makes a payment in contravention of this provision shall be guilty of an illegal practice.

(5.) Except as by this Act permitted, the time limited by this Act for the payment of such expenses as aforesaid shall be twenty-eight days after the day on which the candidates returned are declared elected.

(6.) Where the election court reports that it has been proved to such court by a candidate that any payment made by an election agent in contravention of this section was made without the sanction or connivance of such candidate, the election of such candidate shall not be void, nor shall he be subject to any incapacity under this Act by reason only of such payment having been made in contravention of this section.

(7.) If the election agent in the case of any claim sent in to him within the time limited by this Act disputes it, or refuses or fails to pay it within the said period of twenty-eight days, such claim shall be deemed to be a disputed claim.

(8.) The claimant may, if he thinks fit, bring an action for a disputed claim in any competent court; and any sum paid by the candidate or his agent in pursuance of the judgment or order of such court shall be deemed to be paid within the time limited by this Act, and to be an exception from the provisions of this Act, requiring claims to be paid by the election agent.

(9.) On cause shown to the satisfaction of the High Court, such court on application by the claimant or by the candidate or his election agent may by order give leave for the payment by a candidate or his election agent of a disputed claim, or of a claim for any such expenses as aforesaid, although sent in after the time in this section mentioned for sending in claims, or although the same was sent in to the candidate and not to the election agent.

(10.) Any sum specified in the order of leave may be paid by the candidate or his election agent, and when paid in pursuance of such leave shall be deemed to be paid within the time limited by this Act.

Reference to taxation of claim against candidates.

30. If any action is brought in any competent court to recover a disputed claim against a candidate at an election, or his election agent, in respect of any expenses incurred on account or in respect of the conduct or management of such election, and the defendant admits his liability, but disputes the amount of the claim, the said amount shall, unless the court, on the application of the plaintiff in the action, otherwise directs, be forthwith referred for taxation to the master, official referee, registrar, or other proper officer of the court, and the amount found due on such taxation shall be the amount to be recovered in such action in respect of such claim.

31. (1.) The candidate at an election may pay any personal expenses incurred by him on account of or in connection with or incidental to such election to an amount not exceeding one hundred pounds, but any further personal expenses so incurred by him shall be paid by his election agent. Personal expenses of candidate and petty expenses.

(2.) The candidate shall send to the election agent within the time limited by this Act for sending in claims a written statement of the amount of personal expenses paid as aforesaid by such candidate.

(3.) Any person may, if so authorised in writing by the election agent of the candidate, pay any necessary expenses for stationery, postage, telegrams, and other petty expenses, to a total amount not exceeding that named in the authority, but any excess above the total amount so named shall be paid by the election agent.

(4.) A statement of the particulars of payments made by any person so authorised shall be sent to the election agent within the time limited by this Act for the sending in of claims, and shall be vouched for by a bill containing the receipt of that person.

32. (1.) So far as circumstances admit, this Act shall apply to a claim for his remuneration by an election agent and to the payment thereof in like manner as if he were any other creditor, and if any difference arises respecting the amount of such claim, the claim shall be a disputed claim within the meaning of this Act, and be dealt with accordingly. Remuneration of election agent and returning officer's expenses.

(2.) The account of the charges claimed by the returning officer in the case of a candidate and transmitted in pursuance of section four of the Parliamentary Elections (Returning Officers) Act, 1875, shall be transmitted within the time specified in the said section to the election agent of the candidate, and need not be transmitted to the candidate. 38 & 39 Vict., c. 84.

33. (1.) Within thirty-five days after the day on which the candidates returned at an election are declared elected, the election agent of every candidate at that election shall transmit to the returning officer a true return (in this Act referred to as a return respecting election expenses), in the form set forth in the Second Schedule to this Act or to the like effect, containing, as respects that candidate,— Return and Declaration respecting election expenses.

(a.) A statement of all payments made by the election agent, together with all the bills and receipts (which bills and receipts are in this Act included in the expression "return respecting election expenses");

(*b*.) A statement of the amount of personal expenses, if any, paid by the candidate;

(*c*.) A statement of the sums paid to the returning officer for his charges, or, if the amount is in dispute, of the sum claimed and the amount disputed :

(*d*.) A statement of all other disputed claims of which the election agent is aware;

(*e*.) A statement of all the unpaid claims, if any, of which the election agent is aware, in respect of which application has been or is about to be made to the High Court :

(*f*.) A statement of all money, securities, and equivalent of money received by the election agent from the candidate or any other person for the purpose of expenses incurred or to be incurred on account of or in respect of the conduct or management of the election, with a statement of the name of every person from whom the same may have been received.

(2.) The return so transmitted to the returning officer shall be accompanied by a declaration made by the election agent before a justice of the peace in the form in the Second Schedule to this Act (which declaration is in this Act referred to as a declaration respecting election expenses).

(3.) Where the candidate has named himself as his election agent, a statement of all money, securities, and equivalent of money paid by the candidate shall be substituted in the return required by this section to be transmitted by the election agent for the like statement of money, securities, and equivalent of money received by the election agent from the candidate; and the declaration by an election agent respecting election expenses need not be made, and the declaration by the candidate respecting election expenses shall be modified as specified in the Second Schedule to this Act.

(4.) At the same time that the agent transmits the said return, or within seven days afterwards, the candidate shall transmit or cause to be transmitted to the returning officer a declaration made by him before a justice of the peace in the form, in the first part of the Second Schedule to this Act (which declaration is in this Act referred to as a declaration respecting election expenses).

(5.) If in the case of an election for any county or borough, the said return and declarations are not transmitted before the expiration of the time limited for the purpose, the candidate shall not,

after the expiration of such time, sit or vote in the House of
Commons as member for that county or borough until either
such return and declarations have been transmitted, or until the
date of the allowance of such an authorised excuse for the failure
to transmit the same, as in this Act mentioned, and if he sits or
votes in contravention of this enactment he shall forfeit one hundred
pounds for every day on which he so sits or votes to any person
who sues for the same.

(6.) If without such authorised excuse as in this Act mentioned,
a candidate or an election agent fails to comply with the requirements of this section he shall be guilty of an illegal practice.

(7.) If any candidate or election agent knowingly makes the
declaration required by this section falsely, he shall be guilty of an
offence, and on conviction thereof on indictment shall be liable to
the punishment for wilful and corrupt perjury; such offence shall
also be deemed to be a corrupt practice within the meaning of this
Act.

(8.) Where the candidate is out of the United Kingdom at the
time when the return is so transmitted to the returning officer, the
declaration required by this section may be made by him within
fourteen days after his return to the United Kingdom, and in that
case shall be forthwith transmitted to the returning officer, but
the delay hereby authorised in making such declaration shall not
exonerate the election agent from complying with the provisions
of this Act as to the return and declaration respecting election
expenses.

(9.) Where, after the date at which the return respecting election
expenses is transmitted, leave is given by the High Court for any
claims to be paid, the candidate or his election agent shall, within
seven days after the payment thereof, transmit to the returning
officer a return of the sums paid in pursuance of such leave, accompanied by a copy of the order of the court giving the leave, and
in default he shall be deemed to have failed to comply with the
requirements of this section without such authorised excuse as in
this Act mentioned.

34. (1.) Where the return and declarations respecting election *Authorised*
expenses of a candidate at an election for a county or borough have *compliance with*
not been transmitted as required by this Act, or being transmitted *provisions as to*
contain some error or false statement, then— *declaration*
respecting elec-
(*a*.) If the candidate applies to the High Court or an election *tion expenses.*
court and shows that the failure to transmit such return and
declarations, or any of them, or any part thereof, or any error
or false statement therein has arisen by reason of his illness, or

of the absence, death, illness, or misconduct of his election agent or sub-agent, or of any clerk or officer of such agent, or by reason of inadvertence or of any reasonable cause of a like nature, and not by reason of any want of good faith on the part of the applicant, or

(*b.*) If the election agent of the candidate applies to the High Court or an election court and shows that the failure to transmit the return and declarations which he was required to transmit, or any part thereof, or any error or false statement therein, arose by reason of his illness or of the death or illness of any prior election agent of the candidate, or of the absence, death, illness, or misconduct of any sub-agent, clerk, or officer of an election agent of the candidate, or of the absence, death, illness, or misconduct of any sub-agent, clerk, or officer of an election agent of the candidate, or by reason of inadvertence or of any reasonable cause of a like nature, and not by reason of any want of good faith on the part of the applicant, the court may, after such notice of the application in the said county or borough, and on production of such evidence of the grounds stated in the application, and of the good faith of the application, and otherwise as to the court seems fit, make such order for allowing an authorised excuse for the failure to transmit such return and declaration, or for an error or false statement in such return and declaration, as to the court seems just.

(2.) Where it appears to the court that any person being or having been election agent or sub-agent has refused or failed to make such return or to supply such particulars as will enable the candidate and his election agent respectively to comply with the provisions of this Act as to the return and declaration respecting election expenses, the court before making an order allowing the excuse as in this section mentioned shall order such person to attend before the court, and on his attendance shall, unless he shows cause to the contrary, order him to make the return and declaration, or to deliver a statement of the particulars required to be contained in the return, as to the court seem just, and to make or deliver the same within such time and to such person and in such manner as the court may direct, or may order him to be examined with respect to such particulars, and may, in default of compliance with any such order, order him to pay a fine not exceeding five hundred pounds.

(3.) The order may make the allowance conditional upon the making of the return and declaration in a modified form or within an extended time, and upon the compliance with such other terms as to the court seem best calculated for carrying into effect the objects of this Act; and an order allowing an authorised excuse shall relieve the applicant for the order from any liability or consequences under this Act in respect of the matter excused by the order; and where it is proved by the candidate to the court that any act or omission of the election agent in relation to the return and declaration respecting election expenses was without the sanction or connivance of the candidate, and that the candidate took all reasonable means for preventing such act or omission, the court shall relieve the candidate from the consequences of such act or omission on the part of his election agent.

(4.) The date of the order, or, if conditions and terms are to be complied with, the date at which the applicant fully complies with them, is referred to in this Act as the date of the allowance of the excuse.

35. (1.) The returning officer at an election within ten days after he receives from the election agent of a candidate a return respecting election expenses shall publish a summary of the return in not less than two newspapers circulating in the county or borough for which the election was held, accompanied by a notice of the time and place at which the return and declarations (including the accompanying documents) can be inspected, and may charge the candidate in respect of such publication, and the amount of such charge shall be the sum allowed by the Parliamentary Elections (Returning Officers) Act, 1875. Publication of summary of return of election expenses.
38 & 39 Vict., c. 84.

38 & 39 Vict. c. 84.

(2.) The return and declarations (including the accompanying documents) sent to the returning officer by an election agent shall be kept at the office of the returning officer, or some convenient place appointed by him, and shall at all reasonable times during two years next after they are received by the returning officer be open to inspection by any person on payment of a fee of one shilling, and the returning officer shall on demand furnish copies thereof or any part thereof at the price of twopence for every seventy-two words. After the expiration of the said two years the returning officer may cause the said return and declarations (including the accompanying documents) to be destroyed, or, if the candidate or his election agent so require shall return the same to the candidate.

Disqualification of Electors.

Prohibition of persons guilty of corrupt or illegal practices, &c., from voting.

36. Every person guilty of a corrupt or illegal practice, or of illegal employment, payment, or hiring at an election is prohibited from voting at such election, and if any such person votes his vote shall be void.

Prohibition of disqualified persons from voting.
35 & 36 Vict., c. 60.
45 & 46 Vict., c. 50.

37. Every person who, in consequence of conviction or of the report of any election court or election commissioners under this Act, or under the Corrupt Practices (Municipal Elections) Act, 1872, or under Part IV. of the Municipal Corporations Act, 1882, or under any other Act for the time being in force relating to corrupt practices at an election for any public office, has become incapable of voting at any election, whether a parliamentary election or an election to any public office, is prohibited from voting at any such election, and his vote shall be void.

Hearing of person before he is reported guilty of corrupt practice, and incapacity of person reported guilty.

38. (1.) Before a person, not being a party to an election petition nor a candidate on behalf of whom the seat is claimed by an election petition, is reported by an election court, and before any person is reported by election commissioners, to have been guilty, at an election, of any corrupt or illegal practice, the court or commissioners, as the case may be, shall cause notice to be given to such person, and if he appears in pursuance of the notice, shall give him an opportunity of being heard by himself and of calling evidence in his defence to show why he should not be so reported.

(2.) Every person reported by election commissioners to have been guilty at an election of any corrupt or illegal practice may appeal against such report to the next court of oyer and terminer or gaol delivery held in and for the county or place in which the offence is alleged to have been committed, and such court may hear and determine the appeal; and subject to rules of court such appeal may be brought, heard, and determined in like manner as if the court were a court of quarter sessions and the said commissioners were a court of summary jurisdiction, and the person so reported had been convicted by a court of summary jurisdiction for an offence under this Act, and notice of every such appeal shall be given to the Director of Public Prosecutions in the manner and within the time directed by rules of court, and subject to such rules then within three days after the appeal is brought.

(3.) Where it appears to the Lord Chancellor that appeals under this section are interfering, or are likely to interfere, with the ordinary business transacted before any courts of oyer and terminer or gaol delivery, he may direct that the said appeals, or any of them, shall be heard by the judges for the time being on the rota for election petitions, and in such case one of such judges shall proceed to the county or place in which the offences are alleged to have been committed, and shall there hear and determine the appeals in like manner as if such judges were a court of oyer and terminer.

(4.) The provisions of the Parliamentary Elections Act, 1868, with respect to the reception and powers of and attendance on an election court, and to the expenses of an election court, and of receiving and accommodating an election court, shall apply as if such judge were an election court.

(5.) Every person who, after the commencement of this Act, is reported by an election court or election commissioners to have been guilty of any corrupt or illegal practice at an election, shall, whether he obtained a certificate of indemnity or not, be subject to the same incapacity as he would be subject to if he had at the date of such election been convicted of the offence of which he is reported to have been guilty: Provided that a report of any election commissioners inquiring into an election for a county or borough shall not avoid the election of any candidate who has been declared by an election court on the trial of a petition respecting such election to have been duly elected at such election or render him incapable of sitting in the House of Commons for the said county or borough during the Parliament for which he was elected.

(6.) Where a person who is a justice of the peace is reported by any election court or election commissioners to have been guilty of any corrupt practice in reference to an election, whether he has obtained a certificate of indemnity or not, it shall be the duty of the Director of Public Prosecutions to report the case to the Lord High Chancellor of Great Britain with such evidence as may have been given of such corrupt practice, and where any such person acts as a justice of the peace by virtue of his being, or having been, mayor of a borough, the Lord High Chancellor shall have the same power to remove such person from being a justice of the peace as if he was named in a commission of the peace.

(7.) Where a person who is a barrister or a solicitor, or who belongs to any profession the admission to which is regulated by law, is reported by any election court or election commissioners to have been guilty of any corrupt practice in reference to an election, whether such person has obtained a certificate of indemnity or not, it shall be the duty of the Director of Public Prosecutions to bring the matter before the Inn of Court, High Court, or tribunal having power to take cognizance of any misconduct of such person in his profession, and such Inn of Court, High Court, or tribunal may deal with such person in like manner as if such corrupt practice were misconduct by such person in his profession.

(8.) With respect to a person holding a license or certificate under the Licensing Acts (in this section referred to as a licensed person) the following provisions shall have effect:

(*a.*) If it appears to the court by which any licensed person is convicted of the offence of bribery or treating that such offence was committed on his licensed premises, the court shall direct such conviction to be entered in the proper register of licenses.

(*b.*) If it appears to an election court or election commissioners that a licensed person has knowingly suffered any bribery or treating in reference to any election to take place upon his licensed premises, such court or commissioners (subject to the provisions of this Act as to a person having an opportunity of being heard by himself and producing evidence before being reported) shall report the same; and whether such person obtained a certificate of indemnity or not, it shall be the duty of the Director of Public Prosecutions to bring such report before the licensing justices from whom or on whose certificate the licensed person obtained his license, and such licensing justices shall cause such report to be entered in the proper register of licenses.

(*c.*) Where an entry is made in the register of licenses of any such conviction of or report respecting any licensed person as above in this section mentioned, it shall be taken into consideration by the licensing justices in determining whether they will or will not grant to such person the renewal of his license or certificate, and may be a ground, if the justices think fit, for refusing such renewal.

(9.) Where the evidence showing any corrupt practice to have been committed by a justice of the peace, barrister, solicitor, or other professional person, or any licensed person, was given before election commissioners, those commissioners shall report the case to the Director of Public Prosecutions, with such information as is necessary or proper for enabling him to act under this section.

(10.) This section shall apply to an election court under this Act, or under Part IV. of the Municipal Corporations Act, 1882, and the expression election shall be construed accordingly.

39. (1.) The registration officer in every county and borough shall annually make out a list containing the names and description of all persons who, though otherwise qualified to vote at a parliamentary election for such county or borough respectively, are not capable of voting by reason of having after the commencement of this Act been found guilty of a corrupt or illegal practice on conviction or by the report of any election court or election commissioners whether under this Act, or under Part IV. of the Municipal Corporations Act, 1882, or under any other Act for the time being in force relating to a parliamentary election or an election to any public office; and such officer shall state in the list (in this Act referred to as the corrupt and illegal practices list), the offence of which each person has been found guilty.

List in register of voters of persons incapacitated for voting by corrupt or illegal practices.

45 & 46 Vict. c. 50.

(2.) For the purpose of making out such list he shall examine the report of any election court or election commissioners who have respectively tried an election petition or inquired into an election where the election (whether a parliamentary election or an election to any public office) was held in any of the following places; that is to say,

(*a.*) if he is the registration officer of a county, in that county, or in any borough in that county; and

(*b.*) if he is the registration officer of a borough, in the county in which such borough is situate, or in any borough in that county.

(3.) The registration officer shall send the list to the overseers of every parish within his county or borough, together with his precept, and the overseers shall publish the list together with the list of voters, and shall also, in the case of every person in the corrupt and illegal practices list, omit his name from the list of persons entitled to vote, or, as circumstances require, add " objected " before his name in the list of claimants or copy of the register published by them, in like manner as is required by law in any other cases of disqualification.

(4.) Any person named in the corrupt and illegal practices list may claim to have his name omitted therefrom, and any person entitled to object to any list of voters for the county or borough may object to the omission of the name of any person from such list. Such claims and objections shall be sent in within the same time and be dealt with in like manner, and any such objection shall be served on the person referred to therein in like manner, as nearly as circumstances admit, as other claims and objections under the enactments relating to the registration of parliamentary electors.

(5.) The revising barrister shall determine such claims and objections and shall revise such list in like manner as nearly as circumstances admit as in the case of other claims and objections, and of any list of voters.

(6.) Where it appears to the revising barrister that a person not named in the corrupt and illegal practices list is subject to have his name inserted in such list, he shall (whether an objection to the omission of such name from the list has or has not been made, but) after giving such person an opportunity of making a statement to show cause to the contrary, insert his name in such list and expunge his name from any list of voters.

(7.) A revising barrister in acting under this section shall determine only whether a person is incapacitated by conviction or by the report of any election court or election commissioners, and shall not determine whether a person has or not been guilty of any corrupt or illegal practice.

(8.) The corrupt and illegal practices list shall be appended to the register of electors, and shall be printed and published therewith wherever the same is printed or published.

Proceedings on Election Petition.

Time for presentation of election petitions alleging illegal practice.
31 & 32 Vict. c. 125.

40. (1.) Where an election petition questions the return or the election upon an allegation of an illegal practice, then notwithstanding anything in the Parliamentary Elections Act, 1868, such petition, so far as respects such illegal practice, may be presented within the time following; (that is to say)

(a.) At any time before the expiration of fourteen days after the day on which the returning officer receives the return and declarations respecting election expenses by the member to whose election the petition relates and his election agent.

(b.) If the election petition specifically alleges a payment of money, or some other act to have been made or done since the said day by the member or an agent of the member, or with the privity of the member or his election agent in pursuance or in furtherance of the illegal practice alleged in the petition, the petition may be presented at any time within twenty-eight days after the date of such payment or other act.

31 & 32 Vict. c. 125.

(2.) Any election petition presented within the time limited by the Parliamentary Elections Act, 1868, may for the purpose of questioning the return or the election upon an allegation of an illegal practice be amended with the leave of the High Court within the time within which a petition questioning the return upon the allegation of that illegal practice can under this section be presented.

(3.) This section shall apply in the case of an offence relating to the return and declarations respecting election expenses in like manner as if it were an illegal practice, and also shall apply notwithstanding that the act constituting the alleged illegal practice amounted to a corrupt practice.

(4.) For the purposes of this section—

(a.) where the return and declarations are received on different days, the day on which the last of them is received, and

(b.) where there is an authorised excuse for failing to make and transmit the return and declarations respecting election expenses, the date of the allowance of the excuse, or if there was a failure as regards two or more of them, and the excuse was allowed at different times, the date of the allowance of the last excuse,

shall be substituted for the day on which the return and declarations are received by the returning officer.

(5.) For the purposes of this section, time shall be reckoned in like manner as it is reckoned for the purposes of the Parliamentary Elections Act, 1868.

41. (1.) Before leave for the withdrawal of an election petition is granted, there shall be produced affidavits by all the parties to the petition and their solicitors, and by the election agents of all of the said parties who were candidates at the election, but the High Court may on cause shown dispense with the affidavit of any particular person if it seems to the court on special grounds to be just so to do. *Withdrawal of election petition.*

(2.) Each affidavit shall state that, to the best of the deponent's knowledge and belief, no agreement or terms of any kind whatsoever has or have been made, and no undertaking has been entered into, in relation to the withdrawal of the petition; but if any lawful agreement has been made with respect to the withdrawal of the petition, the affidavit shall set forth that agreement, and shall make the foregoing statement subject to what appears from the affidavit.

(3.) The affidavits of the applicant and his solicitor shall further state the ground on which the petition is sought to be withdrawn.

(4.) If any person makes any agreement or terms, or enters into any undertaking, in relation to the withdrawal of an election petition, and such agreement, terms, or undertaking is or are for the withdrawal of the election petition in consideration of any payment, or in consideration that the seat shall at any time be vacated, or in consideration of the withdrawal of any other election petition, or is or are (whether lawful or unlawful) not mentioned in the aforesaid affidavits, he shall be guilty of a misdemeanour, and shall be liable on conviction on indictment to imprisonment for a term not exceeding twelve months, and to a fine not exceeding two hundred pounds.

(5.) Copies of the said affidavits shall be delivered to the Director of public prosecutions a reasonable time before the application for the withdrawal is heard, and the court may hear the Director of public prosecutions or his assistant or other representative (appointed with the approval of the Attorney-General), in opposition to the allowance of the withdrawal of the petition, and shall have power to receive the evidence on oath of any person or persons whose evidence the Director of Public Prosecutions or his assistant, or other representative, may consider material.

(6.) Where in the opinion of the court the proposed withdrawal of a petition was the result of any agreement, terms, or undertaking prohibited by this section, the court shall have the same power with respect to the security as under section thirty-five of the Parliamentary Elections Act, 1868, where the withdrawal is induced by a corrupt consideration.

31 & 32 Vict. c. 125.

(7.) In every case of the withdrawal of an election petition the court shall report to the Speaker whether, in the opinion of such court, the withdrawal of such petition was the result of any agreement, terms, or undertaking, or was in consideration of any payment, or in consideration that the seat should at any time be vacated, or in consideration of the withdrawal of any other election petition, or for any other consideration, and if so, shall state the circumstances attending the withdrawal.

(8.) Where more than one solicitor is concerned for the petitioner or respondent, whether as agent for another solicitor or otherwise, the affidavit shall be made by all such solicitors.

(9.) Where a person not a solicitor is lawfully acting as agent in the case of an election petition, that agent shall be deemed to be a solicitor for the purpose of making an affidavit in pursuance of this section.

Continuation of trial of election petition.

42. The trial of every election petition so far as is practicable, consistently with the interests of justice in respect of such trial, shall be continued de die in diem on every lawful day until its conclusion, and in case the rota of judges for the year shall expire before the conclusion of the trial, or of all the proceedings in relation or incidental to the petition, the authority of the said judges shall continue for the purpose of the said trial and proceedings.

43. (1.) On every trial of an election petition the Director of Public Prosecutions shall by himself or by his assistant, or by such representative as herein-after mentioned, attend at the trial, and it shall be the duty of such Director to obey any directions given to him by the election court with respect to the summoning and examination of any witness to give evidence on such trial, and with respect to the prosecution by him of offenders, and with respect to any person to whom notice is given to attend with a view to report him as guilty of any corrupt or illegal practice.

Attendance of Director of Public Prosecutions on trial of election petition, and prosecution by him of offenders.

(2.) It shall also be the duty of such Director, without any direction from the election court, if it appears to him that any person is able to give material evidence as to the subject of the trial, to cause such person to attend the trial, and with the leave of the court to examine such person as a witness.

(3.) It shall also be the duty of the said Director, without any direction from the election court, if it appears to him that any person who has not received a certificate of indemnity has been guilty of a corrupt or illegal practice, to prosecute such person for the offence before the said court, or if he thinks it expedient in the interests of justice before any other competent court.

(4.) Where a person is prosecuted before an election court for any corrupt or illegal practice, and such person appears before the court, the court shall proceed to try him summarily for the said offence, and such person, if convicted thereof upon such trial, shall be subject to the same incapacities as he is rendered subject to under this Act upon conviction, whether on indictment or in any other proceeding for the said offence; and further, may be adjudged by the court, if the offence is a corrupt practice, to be imprisoned, with or without hard labour, for a term not exceeding six months, or to pay a fine not exceeding two hundred pounds, and if the offence is an illegal practice, to pay such fine as is fixed by this Act for the offence.

Provided that, in the case of a corrupt practice, the court, before proceeding to try summarily any person, shall give such person the option of being tried by a jury.

(5.) Where a person is so prosecuted for any such offence, and either he elects to be tried by a jury or he does not appear before the court, or the court thinks it in the interests of justice expedient that he should be tried before some other court, the court, if of opinion that the evidence is sufficient to put the said person upon his trial for the offence, shall order such person to be prosecuted on indictment or before a court of summary jurisdiction, as the case may require, for the said offence; and in either case may order him to be prosecuted before such court as may be named in the order; and for all purposes preliminary and of and incidental to such prosecution the offence shall be deemed to have been committed within the jurisdiction of the court so named.

(6.) Upon such order being made,

(*a.*) if the accused person is present before the court, and the offence is an indictable offence, the court shall commit him to take his trial, or cause him to give bail to appear and take his trial for the said offence; and

(*b.*) if the accused person is present before the court, and the offence is not an indictable offence, the court shall order him to be brought before the court of summary jurisdiction before whom he is to be prosecuted, or cause him to give bail to appear before that court; and

(*c.*) if the accused person is not present before the court, the court shall as circumstances require issue a summons for his attendance, or a warrant to apprehend him and bring him before a court of summary jurisdiction, and that court, if the offence is an indictable offence, shall on proof only of the summons or warrant and the identity of the accused, commit him to take his trial, or cause him to give bail to appear and take his trial for the said offence, or if the offence is punishable on summary conviction, shall proceed to hear the case, or if such court be not the court before whom he is directed to be prosecuted, shall order him to be brought before that court.

(7.) The Director of Public Prosecutions may nominate, with the approval of the Attorney-General, a barrister or solicitor of not less than ten years' standing to be his representative for the purpose of this section, and that representative shall receive such remuneration as the Commissioners of Her Majesty's Treasury may approve. There shall be allowed to the Director and his assistant or representative, for the purposes of this section, such allowance for expenses as the Commissioners of Her Majesty's Treasury may approve.

(8.) The costs incurred in defraying the expenses of the Director of Public Prosecutions under this section (including the remuneration of his representative) shall, in the first instance, be paid by the Commissioners of Her Majesty's Treasury, and so far as they are not in the case of any prosecution paid by the defendant shall be deemed to be expenses of the election court; but if for any reasonable cause it seems just to the court so to do, the court shall order all or part of the said costs to be repaid to the Commissioners of Her Majesty's Treasury by the parties to the petition, or such of them as the court may direct.

44. (1.) Where upon the trial of an election petition respecting an election for a county or borough it appears to the election court that a corrupt practice has not been proved to have been committed in reference to such election by or with the knowledge and consent of the respondent to the petition, and that such respondent took all reasonable means to prevent corrupt practices being committed on his behalf, the court may make one or more orders with respect to the payment either of the whole or such part of the costs of the petition as the court may think right as follows; *[Power to election court to order payment by county or borough or individual of costs of election petition.]*

(*a.*) if it appears to the court that corrupt practices extensively prevailed in reference to the said election, the court may order the whole or part of the costs to be paid by the county or borough ; and

(*b.*) if it appears to the court that any person or persons is or are proved, whether by providing money or otherwise, to have been extensively engaged in corrupt practices, or to have encouraged or promoted extensive corrupt practices in reference to such election, the court may, after giving such person or persons an opportunity of being heard by counsel or solicitor and examining and cross-examining witnesses to show cause why the order should not be made, order the whole or part of the costs to be paid by that person, or those persons or any of them, and may order that if the costs cannot be recovered from one or more of such persons they shall be paid by some other of such persons or by either of the parties to the petition.

(2.) Where any person appears to the court to have been guilty of the offence of a corrupt or illegal practice, the court may, after giving such person an opportunity of making a statement to show why the order should not be made, order the whole or any part of the costs of or incidental to any proceeding before the court in relation to the said offence or to the said person to be paid by the said person.

(3.) The rules and regulations of the Supreme Court of Judicature with respect to costs to be allowed in actions, causes, and matters in the High Court shall in principle and so far as practicable apply to the costs of petition and other proceedings under the

Parliamentary Elections Act, 1868, and under this Act, and the taxing officer shall not allow any costs, charges, or expenses on a higher scale than would be allowed in any action, cause, or matter in the High Court on the higher scale, as between solicitor and client.

Miscellaneous.

<small>Inquiry by Director of Public Prosecutions into alleged corrupt or illegal practices.</small>

45. Where information is given to the Director of Public Prosecutions that any corrupt or illegal practices have prevailed in reference to any election, it shall be his duty, subject to the regulations under the Prosecution of Offences Act, 1879, to make such inquiries and institute such prosecutions as the circumstances of the case appear to him to require.

<small>Removal of incapacity on proof that it was procured by perjury.</small>

46. Where a person has, either before or after the commencement of this Act, become subject to any incapacity under the Corrupt Practices Prevention Acts or this Act by reason of a conviction or of a report of any election court or election commissioners, and any witness who gave evidence against such incapacitated person upon the proceeding for such conviction or report is convicted of perjury in respect of that evidence, the incapacitated person may apply to the High Court, and the Court, if satisfied that the conviction or report so far as respects such person was based upon perjury, may order that such incapacity shall thenceforth cease, and the same shall cease accordingly.

<small>Amendment of law as to polling districts and polling places.</small>

47. (1.) Every county shall be divided into polling districts, and a polling place shall be assigned to each district in such manner that, so far as is reasonably practicable, every elector resident in the county shall have his polling place within a distance not exceeding three miles from his residence, so nevertheless that a polling district need not in any case be constituted containing less than one hundred electors.

(2.) In every county the local authority who have power to divide that county into polling districts shall from time to time divide the county into polling districts, and assign polling places to those districts, and alter those districts and polling places in such manner as may be necessary for the purpose of carrying into effect this section.

(3.) The power of dividing a borough into polling districts vested in a local authority by the Representation of the People Act, 1867, and the enactments amending the same, may be exercised by such local authority from time time, and as often as the authority think fit, and the said power shall be deemed to include the power of altering any polling district, and the said local authority shall from time to time, where necessary for the purpose of carrying this section into effect, divide the borough into polling districts in such manner that—

(*a*.) Every elector resident in the borough, if other than one hereinafter mentioned, shall be enabled to poll within a distance not exceeding one mile from his residence, so nevertheless that a polling district need not be constituted containing less than three hundred electors; and

(*b*.) Every elector resident in the boroughs of East Retford, Shoreham, Cricklade, Much Wenlock, and Aylesbury, shall be enabled to poll within a distance not exceeding three miles from his residence, so nevertheless that a polling district need not be constituted containing less than one hundred electors.

(4.) So much of section five of the Ballot Act, 1872, and the enactments amending the same as in force and is not repealed by this Act, shall apply as if the same were incorporated in this section.

(5.) The expenses incurred by the local authority of a county or borough under this or any other Act in dividing their county or borough into polling districts, and, in the case of a county, assigning polling places to such districts, and in altering any such districts or polling places, shall be defrayed in like manner as if they were expenses incurred by the registration officer in the execution of the enactments respecting the registration of electors in such county or borough, and those enactments, so far as is consistent with the tenor thereof, shall apply accordingly.

48. Where the nature of a county is such that any electors residing therein are unable at an election for such county to reach their polling places without crossing the sea or a branch or arm thereof, this Act shall not prevent the provision of means for conveying such electors by sea to their polling place, and the amount of payment for such means of conveyance may be in addition to the maximum amount of expenses allowed by this Act. *Conveyance of voters by sea in certain cases.*

49. Notwithstanding the provisions of the Act 15 and 16 Vict., cap. 57, or any amendment thereof, in any case where, after the passing of this Act, any commissioners have been appointed, on a joint address of both Houses of Parliament, for the purpose of making inquiry into the existence of corrupt practices in any election, the said commissioners shall not make inquiries concerning any *Election commissioners not to inquire into elections before the passing of the Act.*

election that shall have taken place prior to the passing of this Act, and no witness called before such commissioners, or at any election petition after the passing of this Act, shall be liable to be asked or bound to answer any question for the purpose of proving the commission of any corrupt practice at or in relation to any election prior to the passing of this Act: Provided that nothing herein contained shall affect any proceedings that shall be pending at the time of such passing.

Legal Proceedings.

<small>Trial in Central Criminal Court of indictment for corrupt practice at instance of Attorney-General.</small>

50. Where an indictment as defined by this Act for any offence under the Corrupt Practices Prevention Acts or this Act is instituted in the High Court or is removed into the High Court by a writ of certiorari issued at the instance of the Attorney-General, and the Attorney-General suggests on the part of the Crown that it is expedient for the purposes of justice that the indictment should be tried in the Central Criminal Court, or if a special jury is ordered, that it should be tried before a judge and jury at the Royal Courts of Justice, the High Court may, if it think fit, order that such indictment shall be so tried upon such terms as the Court may think just, and the High Court may make such orders as appear to the Court necessary or proper for carrying into effect the order for such trial.

<small>Limitation of time for prosecution of offence.</small>

51. (1.) A proceeding against a person in respect of the offence of a corrupt or illegal practice or any other offence under the Corrupt Practices Prevention Acts or this Act shall be commenced within one year after the offence was committed, or if it was committed in reference to an election with respect to which an inquiry is held by election commissioners shall be commenced within one year after the offence was committed, or within three months after the report of such commissioners is made, whichever period last expires, so that it be commenced within two years after the offence was committed, and the time so limited by this section shall, in the case of any proceeding under the Summary Jurisdiction Acts for any such offence, whether before an election court or otherwise, be substituted for any limitation of time contained in the last-mentioned Acts.

(2.) For the purposes of this section the issue of a summons, warrant, writ, or other process shall be deemed to be a commencement of a proceeding, where the service or execution of the same on or against the alleged offender is prevented by the absconding or concealment or act of the alleged offender, but save as aforesaid the service or execution of the same on or against the alleged offender, and not the issue thereof, shall be deemed to be the commencement of the proceeding.

52. Any person charged with a corrupt practice may, if the circumstances warrant such finding, be found guilty of an illegal practice (which offence shall for that purpose be an indictable offence), and any person charged with an illegal practice may be found guilty of that offence, notwithstanding that the act constituting the offence amounted to a corrupt practice, and a person charged with illegal payment, employment, or hiring, may be found guilty of that offence, notwithstanding that the act constituting the offence amounted to a corrupt or illegal practice.

Persons charged with corrupt practice may be found guilty of illegal practice.

53. (1.) Sections ten, twelve and thirteen of the Corrupt Practices Prevention Act, 1854, and section six of the Corrupt Practices Prevention Act, 1863 (which relate to prosecutions for bribery and other offences under those Acts), shall extend to any prosecution on indictment for the offence of any corrupt practice within the meaning of this Act, and to any action for any pecuniary forfeiture for an offence under this Act, in like manner as if such offence were bribery within the meaning of those Acts, and such indictment or action were the indictment or action in those sections mentioned, and an order under the said section ten may be made on the defendant; but the Director of Public Prosecutions or any person instituting any prosecution in his behalf or by direction of an election court shall not be deemed to be a private prosecutor, nor required under the said sections to give any security.

Application of enactments of 17 & 18 Vict. c. 102, and 26 & 27 Vict. c. 29, relating to prosecutions for bribery.
17 & 18 Vict. c. 102.
26 & 27 Vict. c. 29.

(2.) On any prosecution under this Act, whether on indictment or summarily, and whether before an election court or otherwise, and in any action for a pecuniary forfeiture under this Act, the person prosecuted or sued, and the husband or wife of such person, may, if he or she think fit, be examined as an ordinary witness in the case.

(3.) On any such prosecution or action as aforesaid it shall be sufficient to allege that the person charged was guilty of an illegal practice, payment, employment, or hiring within the meaning of this Act, as the case may be, and the certificate of the returning officer at an election that the election mentioned in the certificate was duly held, and that the person named in the certificate was a candidate at such election, shall be sufficient evidence of the facts therein stated.

Prosecution on summary conviction, and appeal to quarter sessions.

54. (1.) All offences under this Act punishable on summary conviction may be prosecuted in manner provided by the Summary Jurisdiction Acts.

(2.) A person aggrieved by a conviction by a court of summary jurisdiction for an offence under this Act may appeal to general or quarter sessions against such conviction.

Application of Summary Jurisdiction and Indictable Offences Acts to proceedings before election courts.

55. (1.) Except that nothing in this Act shall authorize any appeal against a summary conviction by an election court, the Summary Jurisdiction Acts shall, so far as is consistent with the tenor thereof, apply to the prosecution of an offence summarily before an election court, in like manner as if it were an offence punishable only on summary conviction, and accordingly the attendance of any person may be enforced, the case heard and determined, and any summary conviction by such court be carried into effect and enforced, and the costs thereof paid, and the record thereof dealt with under those Acts in like manner as if the court were a petty sessional court for the county or place in which such conviction took place.

(2.) The enactments relating to charges before justices against persons for indictable offences shall, so far as is consistent with the tenor thereof, apply to every case where an election court orders a person to be prosecuted on indictment in like manner as if the court were a justice of the peace.

Exercise of jurisdiction of High Court, and making of rules of court.

56. (1.) Subject to any rules of court, any jurisdiction vested by this Act in the High Court may, so far as it relates to indictments or other criminal proceedings, be exercised by any judge of the Queen's Bench Division, and in other respects may either be exercised by one of the judges for the time being on the rota for the trial of election petitions, sitting either in court or at chambers, or may be exercised by a master of the Supreme Court of Judicature in manner directed by and subject to an appeal to the said judges:

Provided that a master shall not exercise jurisdiction in the case either of an order declaring any act or omission to be an exception from the provisions of this Act with respect to illegal practices, payments, employments, or hirings, or of an order allowing an excuse in relation to a return or declaration respecting election expenses.

(2.) Rules of court may from time to time be made, revoked, and altered for the purposes of this Act, and of the Parliamentary Elections Act, 1868, and the Acts amending the same, by the same authority by whom rules of court for procedure and practice in the Supreme Court of Judicature can for the time being be made.

57. (1.) The Director of Public Prosecutions in performing any duty under this Act shall act in accordance with the regulations under the Prosecution of Offences Act, 1879, and subject thereto in accordance with the directions (if any) given to him by the Attorney General; and any assistant or representative of the Director of Public Prosecutions in performing any duty under this Act shall act in accordance with the said regulations and directions, if any, and with the directions given to him by the Director of Public Prosecutions.

<small>Director of Public Prosecutions, and expenses of prosecutions. 42 & 43 Vict. c. 22.</small>

(2.) Subject to the provisions of this Act, the costs of any prosecution on indictment for an offence punishable under this Act, whether by the Director of Public Prosecutions or his representative or by any other person, shall, so far as they are not paid by the defendant, be paid in like manner as costs in the case of a prosecution for felony are paid.

58. (1.) Where any costs or other sums (not being costs of a prosecution on indictment) are, under an order of an election court, or otherwise under this Act, to be paid by a county or borough, the Commissioners of Her Majesty's Treasury shall pay those costs or sums, and obtain repayment of the amount so paid, in like manner as if such costs and sums were expenses of election commissioners paid by them, and the Election Commissioners Expenses Acts, 1869 and 1871, shall apply accordingly as if they were herein re-enacted and in terms made applicable to the above-mentioned costs and sums.

<small>Recovery of costs payable by county or borough or by person. 32 & 33 Vict. c. 21. 34 & 35 Vict. c. 61.</small>

(2.) Where any costs or other sums are, under the order of an election court or otherwise under this Act, to be paid by any person, those costs shall be a simple contract debt due from such person to the person or persons to whom they are to be paid, and if payable to the Commissioners of Her Majesty's Treasury shall be a debt to Her Majesty, and in either case may be recovered accordingly.

Supplemental Provisions, Definitions, Savings, and Repeal.

59. (1.) A person who is called as a witness respecting an election before any election court shall not be excused from answering any question relating to any offence at or connected with such election, on the ground that the answer thereto may criminate or tend to criminate himself or on the ground of privilege;

<small>Obligation of witness to answer, and certificate of indemnity.</small>

Provided that—

(a.) a witness who answers truly all questions which he is required by the election court to answer shall be entitled to receive a certificate of indemnity under the hand of a member of the court stating that such witness has so answered : and

(b.) an answer by a person to a question put by or before any election court shall not, except in the case of any criminal proceeding for perjury in respect of such evidence, be in any proceeding, civil or criminal, admissible in evidence against him.

(2.) Where a person has received such a certificate of indemnity in relation to an election, and any legal proceeding is at any time instituted against him for any offence under the Corrupt Practices Prevention Acts or this Act committed by him previously to the date of the certificate at or in relation to the said election, the court having cognisance of the case shall on proof of the certificate stay the proceeding, and may in their discretion award to the said person such costs as he may have been put to in the proceeding.

(3.) Nothing in this section shall be taken to relieve a person receiving a certificate of indemnity from any incapacity under this Act or from any proceeding to enforce such incapacity (other than a criminal prosecution).

(4.) This section shall apply in the case of a witness before any election commissioners, in like manner as if the expression "election court" in this section included election commissioners.

(5.) Where a solicitor or person lawfully acting as agent for any party to an election petition respecting any election for a county or borough has not taken any part or been concerned in such election, the election commissioners inquiring into such election shall not be entitled to examine such solicitor or agent respecting matters which came to his knowledge by reason only of his being concerned as solicitor or agent for a party to such petition.

Submission of report of election court or commissioners to Attorney-General

60. An election court or election commissioners, when reporting that certain persons have been guilty of any corrupt or illegal practice, shall report whether those persons have or not been furnished with certificates of indemnity; and such report shall be laid before the Attorney-General (accompanied in the case of the commissioners with the evidence on which such report was based) with a view to his instituting or directing a prosecution against such persons as have not received certificates of indemnity, if the evidence should, in his opinion, be sufficient to support a prosecution.

61. (1.) Section eleven of the Ballot Act, 1872, shall apply to a returning officer or presiding officer or clerk who is guilty of any wilful misfeasance or wilful act or omission in contravention of this Act in like manner as if the same were in contravention of the Ballot Act, 1872.

Breach of duty by officer. 35 & 36 Vict. c. 33.

(2.) Section ninety-seven of the Parliamentary Registration Act, 1843, shall apply to every registration officer who is guilty of any wilful misfeasance or wilful act of commission or omission contrary to this Act in like manner as if the same were contrary to the Parliamentary Registration Act, 1843.

6 Vict. c. 18.

62. (1.) Any public notice required to be given by the returning officer under this Act shall be given in the manner in which he is directed by the Ballot Act, 1872, to give a public notice.

Publication and service of notices. 35 & 36 Vict. c. 33.

(2.) Where any summons, notice, or document is required to be served on any person with reference to any proceeding respecting an election for a county or borough, whether for the purpose of causing him to appear before the High Court or any election court, or election commissioners, or otherwise, or for the purpose of giving him an opportunity of making a statement, or showing cause, or being heard by himself, before any court or commissioners, for any purpose of this Act, such summons, notice, or document may be served either by delivering the same to such person, or by leaving the same at, or sending the same by post by a registered letter to his last known place of abode in the said county or borough, or if the proceeding is before any court or commissioners, in such other manner as the court or commissioners may direct, and in proving such service by post it shall be sufficient to prove that the letter was prepaid, properly addressed, and registered with the post office.

(3.) In the form of notice of a parliamentary election set forth in the Second Schedule to the Ballot Act, 1872, the words "or any illegal practice" shall be inserted after the words "or other corrupt practices," and the words the "Corrupt and Illegal Practices Prevention Act, 1883," shall be inserted after the words "Corrupt Practices Prevention Act, 1854."

63. (1.) In the Corrupt Practices Prevention Acts, as amended by this Act, the expression "candidate at an election" and the expression "candidate" respectively mean, unless the context otherwise requires, any person elected to serve in Parliament at such election, and any person who is nominated as a candidate at such election, or is declared by himself or by others to be a candidate, on or after the day of the issue of the writ for such election,

Definition of candidate, and saving for persons nominated without consent.

or after the dissolution or vacancy in consequence of which such writ has been issued:

(2.) Provided that where a person has been nominated as a candidate or declared to be a candidate by others, then—

(*a*.) If he was so nominated or declared without his consent, nothing in this Act shall be construed to impose any liability on such person, unless he has afterwards given his assent to such nomination or declaration or has been elected; and

(*b*.) If he was so nominated or declared, either without his consent or in his absence, and he takes no part in the election, he may, if he thinks fit, make the declaration respecting election expenses contained in the second part of the Second Schedule to this Act, and the election agent shall, so far as circumstances admit, comply with the provisons of this Act with respect to expenses incurred on account of or in respect of the conduct or management of the election in like manner as if the candidate had been nominated or declared with his consent.

General interpretation of terms.

64. In this Act, unless the context otherwise requires—

The expression "election" means the election of a member or members to serve in Parliament:

31 & 32 Vict. c. 125.

The expression "election petition" means a petition presented in pursuance of the Parliamentary Elections Act, 1868, as amended by this Act:

The expression "election court" means the judges presiding at the trial of an election petition, or, if the matter comes before the High Court, that court:

15 & 16 Vict. c. 57.

The expression "Election Commissioners" means commissioners appointed in pursuance of the Election Commissioners Act, 1852, and the enactments amending the same:

The expression "High Court" means Her Majesty's High Court of Justice in England.

42 & 43 Vict. c. 49.

The expressions "court of summary jurisdiction," "petty sessional court," and "Summary Jurisdiction Acts" have the same meaning as in the Summary Jurisdiction Act, 1879:

The expression "the Attorney General" includes the Solicitor General in cases where the office of the Attorney General is vacant or the Attorney General is interested or otherwise unable to act:

The expression "registration officer" means the clerk of the peace in a county, and the town clerk in a borough, as respectively defined by the enactments relating to the registration of parliamentary electors:

The expression " elector " means any person whose name is for the time being on the register roll or book containing the names of the persons entitled to vote at the election with reference to which the expression is used:

The expression " register of electors " means the said register roll or book:

The expression " polling agent " means an agent of the candidate appointed to attend at a polling station in pursuance of the Ballot Act, 1872, or of the Acts therein referred to or amending the same: 35 & 36 Vict. c. 33.

The expression " person " includes an association or body of persons, corporate or unincorporate, and where any act is done by any such association or body, the members of such association or body who have taken part in the commission of such act shall be liable to any fine or punishment imposed for the same by this Act:

The expression "committee room " shall not include any house or room occupied by a candidate at an election as a dwelling, by reason only of the candidate there transacting business with his agents in relation to such election; nor shall any room or building be deemed to be a committee room for the purposes of this Act by reason only of the candidate or any agent of the candidate addressing therein electors, committeemen, or others:

The expression " public office " means any office under the Crown or under the charter of a city or municipal borough or under the Acts relating to Municipal Corporations, or to the Poor Law, or under the Elementary Education Act, 1870, or under the Public Health Act, 1875, or under any Acts amending the above-mentioned Acts, or under any other Acts for the time being in force (whether passed before or after the commencement of this Act) relating to local government, whether the office is that of mayor, chairman, alderman, councillor, guardian, member of a board, commission, or other local authority in any county, city, borough, union, sanitary district, or other area, or is the office of clerk of the peace, town clerk, clerk or other officer under a council, board, commission, or other authority, or is any other office to which a person is elected or appointed under any such charter or Act as above-mentioned, and includes any other municipal or parochial office; and the expressions " election," " election petition," " election court," and " register of electors," shall, where expressed to refer to an election for any such public office, be construed accordingly: 33 & 34 Vict. c. 75.   38 & 39 Vict. c. 55.

The expression "judicial office" includes the office of justice of the peace and revising barrister:

S

The expression "personal expenses" as used with respect to the expenditure of any candidate in relation to any election includes the reasonable travelling expenses of such candidate, and the reasonable expenses of his living at hotels or elsewhere for the purposes of and in relation to such election:

The expression "indictment" includes information:

The expression "costs" includes costs, charges, and expenses:

The expression "payment" includes any pecuniary or other reward; and the expressions "pecuniary reward" and "money" shall be deemed to include any office, place or employment, and any valuable security or other equivalent for money, and any valuable consideration, and expressions referring to money shall be construed accordingly:

The expression "Licensing Acts" means the Licensing Acts, 1872 to 1874:

Other expressions have the same meaning as in the Corrupt Practices Prevention Acts.

Short titles.

65. (1.) The enactments described in the Third Schedule to this Act are in this Act referred to as the Corrupt Practices Prevention Acts.

(2.) The Acts mentioned in the Fourth Schedule to this Act are in this Act referred to and may be cited respectively by the short titles in that behalf in that schedule mentioned.

(3.) This Act may be cited as the Corrupt and Illegal Practices Prevention Act, 1883.

(4.) This Act and the Corrupt Practices Prevention Acts may be cited together as the Corrupt Practices Prevention Acts, 1854 to 1883.

Repeal of Acts.

66. The Acts set forth in the Fifth Schedule to this Act are hereby repealed as from the commencement of this Act to the extent in the third column of that schedule mentioned, provided that this repeal or the expiration of any enactment not continued by this Act shall not revive any enactment which at the commencement of this Act is repealed, and shall not affect anything duly done or suffered before the commencement of this Act, or any right acquired or accrued or any incapacity incurred before the commencement of this Act, and any person subject to any incapacity under any enactment hereby repealed or not continued shall continue subject thereto, and this Act shall apply to him as if he had become so subject in pursuance of the provisions of this Act.

67. This Act shall come into operation on the fifteenth day of October, one thousand eight hundred and eighty-three, which day is in this Act referred to as the commencement of this Act.

Commencement of Act.

Application of Act to Scotland.

68. This Act shall apply to Scotland, with the following modifications:

Application of Act to Scotland.

(1.) The following expressions shall mean as follows:—
The expression "misdemeanour" shall mean crime and offence:
The expression "indictment" shall include criminal letters:
The expression "solicitor" shall mean enrolled law agent:
The expression "revising barrister" shall mean sheriff:
The expression "barrister" shall mean advocate:
The expression "petty sessional court" shall mean sheriff court:
The expression "quarter sessions" shall mean the Court of Justiciary:
The expression "registration officer" shall mean an assessor under the enactments relating to the registration of parliamentary voters:
The expression "municipal borough" shall include royal burgh and burgh of regality and burgh of barony:
The expression "Acts relating to municipal corporations" shall include the General Police and Improvement (Scotland) Act, 1862, and any other Act relating to the constitution and government of burghs in Scotland:
The expression "mayor" shall mean provost or chief magistrate:
The expression "alderman" shall mean bailie:
The expression "Summary Jurisdiction Acts" shall mean the Summary Jurisdiction (Scotland) Acts, 1864 and 1881, and any Acts amending the same.

(2.) The provisions of this Act with respect to polling districts and the expenses of dividing a county or borough into polling districts shall not apply to Scotland.

(3.) The provisions respecting the attendance at the trial of an election petition of a representative of the Director of Public Prosecutions shall not apply to Scotland, and in place thereof the following provisions shall have effect:

(a.) At the trial of every election petition in Scotland Her Majesty's advocate shall be represented by one of his deputies or by the procurator-fiscal of the sheriff court of the district, who shall attend such trial as part of his official duty, and shall give all necessary assistance to the judge with respect to the citation of witnesses and recovery of documents:

(*b.*) If the judge shall grant a warrant for the apprehension, commitment, or citation of any person suspected of being guilty of a corrupt or illegal practice, the case shall be reported to Her Majesty's advocate in order that such person may be brought to trial before the High Court of Justiciary or the sheriff, according to the nature of the case:

(*c.*) It shall be the duty of the advocate depute or, in his absence, the procurator-fiscal, if it appears to him that a corrupt or illegal practice within the meaning of this Act has been committed by any person who has not received a certificate of indemnity, to report the case to Her Majesty's advocate in order to such person being brought to trial before the proper court, although no warrant may have been issued by the judge.

(4.) The jurisdiction of the High Court of Justice under this Act shall, in Scotland, be exercised by one of the Divisions of the Court of Session, or by a judge of the said court to whom the same may be remitted by such division, and subject to an appeal thereto, and the Court of Session shall have power to make Acts of sederunt for the purposes of this Act.

(5.) Court of Oyer and Terminer shall mean a circuit court of Justiciary, and the High Court of Justiciary shall have powers to make acts of adjournal regulating the procedure in appeals to the circuit court under this Act.

(6.) All offences under this Act punishable on summary conviction may be prosecuted in the sheriff court in manner provided by the Summary Jurisdiction Acts, and all necessary jurisdictions are hereby conferred on sheriffs.

(7.) The authority given by this Act to the Director of Public Prosecutions in England shall in Scotland be exercised by Her Majesty's advocate, and the reference to the Prosecution of Offences Act, 1879, shall not apply.

25 & 26 Vict. c. 55. 39 & 40 Vict. c. 26.

(8.) The expression "Licensing Acts" shall mean "The Public Houses Acts Amendment (Scotland) Act, 1862," and "The Publicans' Certificates (Scotland) Act, 1876," and the Acts thereby amended and therein recited.

(9.) The expression "register of licences" shall mean the register kept in pursuance of section twelve of the Act of the ninth year of the reign of King George the Fourth, chapter fifty-eight.

(10.) The references to the Public Health Act, 1875, and to the Elementary Education Act, 1870, shall be construed to refer to the Public Health (Scotland) Act, 1867, and to the Elementary Education (Scotland) Act, 1872.

(11.) Any reference to the Parliamentary Elections Returning Officers Act, 1875, shall not apply.

(12.) The provision with respect to the registration officer sending the corrupt and illegal practices list to overseers and the dealing with such list by overseers shall not apply, and in lieu thereof it is hereby enacted that the assessor shall in counties include the names of such persons in the list of persons who have become disqualified, and in boroughs shall omit the names of such persons from the list of persons entitled to vote.

(13.) The power given by this Act to the Lord Chancellor in England shall in Scotland, except so far as relates to the justices of the peace, be exercised by the Lord Justice General.

(14.) Any reference to the Attorney-General shall refer to the Lord Advocate.

(15.) The provisions with respect to the removal of cases to the Central Criminal Court or to the trial of cases at the Royal Courts of Justice shall not apply.

(16.) Section thirty-eight of the County Voters Registration (Scotland) Act, 1861, shall be substituted for section ninety-seven of the Parliamentary Registration Act, 1843, where reference is made to that section in this Act. 24 & 25 Vict. c. 83.

(17.) The provision of this Act with regard to costs shall not apply to Scotland, and instead thereof the following provision shall have effect :

> The costs of petitions and other proceedings under "The Parliamentary Elections Act, 1868," and under this Act, shall, subject to any regulations which the Court of Session may make by act of sederunt, be taxed as nearly as possible according to the same principles as costs between agent and client are taxed in a cause in that court, and the auditor shall not allow any costs, charges, or expenses on a higher scale.

Application of Act to Ireland.

69. This Act shall apply to Ireland, with the following modifications :— Application of Act to Ireland.

(1.) No person shall be tried for any offence against this Act under any of the provisions of "The Prevention of Crime (Ireland) Act, 1882."

(2.) The expression "Summary Jurisdiction Acts" means, with reference to the Dublin Metropolitan Police District, the Acts regulating the powers and duties of justices of the peace and of the police in such district; and with reference to other parts of Ireland means the Petty Sessions (Ireland) Act, 1851, and any Acts amending the said Act.

(3.) Section one hundred and three of the Act of the session of the thirteenth and fourteenth years of the reign of Her present Majesty, chapter sixty-nine, shall be substituted for section ninety-seven of the Parliamentary Registration Act, 1843, where reference is made to that section in this Act.

(4.) The provision with respect to the registration officer sending the corrupt and illegal practices list to overseers and the dealing with such list by overseers shall not apply, and in lieu thereof it is hereby enacted that the registration officer shall, after making out such list, himself publish the same in the manner in which he publishes the lists referred to in the twenty-first and the thirty-third sections of the Act of the session of the thirteenth and fourteenth years of the reign of Her present Majesty, chapter sixty-nine; and shall also in the case of every person in the corrupt and illegal practices list enter " objected to " against his name in the register and lists made out by such registration officer in like manner as he is by law required to do in other cases of disqualification.

(5.) The Supreme Court of Judicature in Ireland shall be substituted for the Supreme Court of Judicature.

(6.) The High Court of Justice in Ireland shall be substituted for the High Court of Justice in England.

(7.) The Lord High Chancellor of Ireland shall be substituted for the Lord High Chancellor of Great Britain.

(8.) The Attorney-General for Ireland shall be substituted for the Director of Public Prosecutions, and the reference to the prosecution of the Offences Act, 1879, shall not apply.

(9.) The provisions of this Act relative to polling districts shall not apply to Ireland, but in the county of the town of Galway there shall be a polling station at Barna, and at such other places within the parliamentary borough of Galway as the town commissioners may appoint.

(10.) Any reference to Part IV. of the Municipal Corporations Act, 1882, shall be construed to refer to the Corrupt Practices (Municipal Elections) Act, 1872.

(11.) Any reference to the Licensing Acts shall be construed to refer to the Licensing Acts (Ireland), 1872-1874.

(12.) The Public Health (Ireland) Act, 1878, shall be substituted for the Public Health Act, 1875. 11 & 12 Vict. c. 52.

(13.) The provisions with respect to the removal of cases to the Central Criminal Court, or to the trial of cases at the Royal Courts of Justice, shall not apply to Ireland.

Continuance.

70. This Act shall continue in force until the thirty-first day of December one thousand eight hundred and eighty-four, and no longer, unless continued by Parliament; and such of the Corrupt Practices Prevention Acts as are referred to in Part One of the Third Schedule to this Act shall continue in force until the same day, and no longer, unless continued by Parliament. Continuance.

SCHEDULES.

FIRST SCHEDULE.

PART I.

Persons Legally Employed for Payment.

(1.) One election agent and no more.

(2.) In counties one deputy election agent (in this Act referred to as a sub-agent) to act within each polling district and no more.

(3.) One polling agent in each polling station and no more.

(4.) In a borough one clerk and one messenger, or if the number of electors in the borough exceeds five hundred, a number of clerks and messengers not exceeding in number one clerk and one messenger for every complete five hundred electors in the borough, and if there is a number of electors over and above any complete five hundred or complete five hundreds of electors, then one clerk and one messenger may be employed for such number, although not amounting to a complete five hundred.

(5.) In a county for the central committee room one clerk and one messenger, or if the number of electors in the county exceeds five thousand, then a number of clerks and messengers not exceeding in number one clerk and one messenger for every complete five thousand electors in the county; and if there is a number of electors over and above any complete five thousand or complete five thousands of electors, then one clerk and one messenger may be employed for such number, although not amounting to a complete five thousand.

(6.) In a county a number of clerks and messengers not exceeding in number one clerk and one messenger for each polling district in the county, or where the number of electors in a polling district exceeds five hundred, one clerk and one messenger for every complete five hundred electors in the polling district, and if there is a number of electors over and above any complete five hundred or complete five hundreds of electors, then one clerk and one messenger may be employed for such number, although not amounting to a complete five hundred: Provided always, that the number of clerks and messengers so allowed in any county may be employed in any polling district where their services may be required.

(7.) Any such paid election agent, sub-agent, polling agent, clerk, and messenger may or may not be an elector but may not vote.

(8.) In the case of the boroughs of East Retford, Shoreham, Cricklade, Much Wenlock, and Aylesbury, the provisions of this part of this schedule shall apply as if such borough were a county.

PART II.

Legal Expenses in Addition to Expenses under Part I.

(1.) Sums paid to the returning officer for his charges not exceeding the amount authorised by the Act 38 & 39 Vict. c. 84.

(2.) The personal expenses of the candidate.

(3.) The expenses of printing, the expenses of advertising, and the expenses of publishing, issuing, and distributing addresses and notices.

(4.) The expenses of stationery, messages, postage, and telegrams.

(5.) The expenses of holding public meetings.

(6.) In a borough the expenses of one committee room, and if the number of electors in the borough exceeds five hundred then of a number of committee rooms not exceeding the number of one committee room for every complete five hundred electors in the borough, and if there is a number of electors over and above any complete five hundred or complete five hundreds of electors, then of one committee room for such number, although not amounting to a complete five hundred.

(7.) In a county the expenses of a central committee room, and in addition of a number of committee rooms not exceeding in number one committee room for each polling district in the county, and where the number of electors in a polling district exceeds five hundred one additional committee room may be hired for every complete five hundred electors in such polling district over and above the first five hundred.

PART III.

Maximum for Miscellaneous Matters.

Expenses in respect of miscellaneous matters other than those mentioned in Part I. and Part II. of this schedule not exceeding in the whole the maximum amount of two hundred pounds, so nevertheless that such expenses are not incurred in respect of any matter or in any manner constituting an offence under this or any other Act, or in respect of any matter or thing, payment for which is expressly prohibited by this or any other Act.

PART IV.

Maximum Scale.

(1.) In a borough the expenses mentioned above in Parts I., II., and III. of this schedule, other than personal expenses and sums paid to the returning officer for his charges, shall not exceed in the whole the maximum amount in the scale following :—

If the number of electors on the register—   The maximum amount shall be—

Does not exceed 2,000 - 350*l.*

Exceeds 2,000 - - 380*l.*, and an additional 30*l.* for every complete 1,000 electors above 2,000.

Provided that in Ireland if the number of electors on the register—   The maximum amount shall be—

Does not exceed 500 - 200*l.*

Exceeds 500, but does not exceed 1,000 - - 250*l.*

Exceeds 1,000, but does not exceed 1,500 - 275*l.*

(2.) In a county the expenses mentioned above in Parts I., II., and III. of this schedule, other than personal expenses and sums paid to the returning officer for his charges, shall not exceed in the whole the maximum amount in the scale following :—

If the number of electors on the register—	The maximum amount shall be –
Does not exceed 2,000	650*l.* in England and Scotland, and 500*l.* in Ireland.
Exceeds 2,000	710*l.* in England and Scotland, and 540*l.* in Ireland; and an additional 60*l.* in England and Scotland, and 40*l.* in Ireland, for every complete 1,000 electors above 2,000.

PART V.

General.

(1.) In the case of the boroughs of East Retford, Shoreham, Cricklade, Much Wenlock, and Aylesbury, the provisions of Parts II., III., and IV. of this schedule shall apply as if such borough were a county.

(2.) For the purposes of this schedule the number of electors shall be taken according to the enumeration of the electors in the register of electors.

(3.) Where there are two or more joint candidates at an election the maximum amount of expenses mentioned in Parts III. and IV. of this schedule shall, for each of such joint candidates, be reduced by one-fourth, or if there are more than two joint candidates by one-third.

(4.) Where the same election agent is appointed by or on behalf of two or more candidates at an election, or where two or more candidates, by themselves or any agent or agents, hire or use the same committee rooms for such election, or employ or use the services of the same sub-agents, clerks, messengers, or polling agents at such election, or publish a joint address or joint circular or notice at such election, those candidates shall be deemed for the purposes of this enactment to be joint candidates at such election.

Provided that

(*a.*) The employment and use of the same committee room, sub-agent, clerk, messenger, or polling agent, if accidental or casual, or of a trivial and unimportant character, shall not be deemed of itself to constitute persons joint candidates.

(*b.*) Nothing in this enactment shall prevent candidates from ceasing to be joint candidates.

(*c.*) Where any excess of expenses above the maximum allowed for one of two or more joint candidates has arisen owing to his having ceased to be a joint candidate, or to his having become a joint candidate after having begun to conduct his election as a separate candidate, and such ceasing or beginning was in good faith, and such excess is not more than under the circumstances is reasonable, and the total expenses of such candidate do not exceed the maximum amount allowed for a separate candidate, such excess shall be deemed to have arisen from a reasonable cause within the meaning of the enactments respecting the allowance by the High Court or election court of an exception from the provisions of this Act which would otherwise make an act an illegal practice, and the candidate and his election agent may be relieved accordingly from the consequences of having incurred such excess of expenses.

SECOND SCHEDULE.

PART I.

FORM OF DECLARATIONS AS TO EXPENSES.

Form for Candidate.

I   , having been a candidate at the election for the county [*or* borough] of   on the   day of   , do hereby solemnly and sincerely declare that I have examined the return of election expenses [about to be] transmitted by my election agent [*or if the candidate is his own election agent* "by me"], to the returning officer at the said election, a copy of which is now shown to me and marked   , and to the best of my knowledge and belief that return is correct;

And I further solemnly and sincerely declare that, except as appears from that return, I have not, and to the best of my knowledge and belief no person, nor any club, society, or association, has, on my behalf made, any payment, or given, promised, or offered any reward, office, employment, or valuable consideration, or incurred any liability on account of or in respect of the conduct or management of the said election;

And I further solemnly and sincerely declare that I have paid to my election agent [*if the candidate is also his own election agent, leave out* " to my election agent "] the sum of   pounds and no more for the purpose of the said election, and that except as specified in the said return, no money, security, or equivalent for money has to my knowledge or belief been paid, advanced, given, or deposited by anyone to or in the hands of my election agent [*or if the candidate is his own election agent,* " myself "] or any other person for the purpose of defraying any expenses incurred on my behalf on account of or in respect of the conduct or management of the said election ;

And I further solemnly and sincerely declare that I will not, except so far as I may be permitted by law, at any future time make or be party to the making or giving of, any payment, reward office, employment, or valuable consideration for the purpose of defraying any such expenses as last mentioned, or provide or be party to the providing of any money, security, or equivalent for money for the purpose of defraying any such expenses.

Signature of declarant.   *C.D.*

Signed and declared by the above-named declarant on the day of   , before me.

(Signed)   *E.F.*

Justices of the Peace for

Form for Election Agent.

I,   , being election agent to   , candidate at the election for the county [*or* borough] of   , on the   day of   , do hereby solemnly and sincerely declare that I have examined the return of election expenses about to be transmitted by me to the returning officer at the said election, and now shown to me and marked   , and to the best of my knowledge and belief that return is correct ;

And I hereby further solemnly and sincerely declare that, except as appears from that return, I have not and to the best of my knowledge and belief no other person, nor any club, society, or association has on behalf of the said candidate made any payment, or given, promised or offered any reward, office, employment, or valuable consideration, or incurred any liability on account of or in respect of the conduct or management of the said election :

And I further solemnly and sincerely declare that I have received from the said candidate   pounds and no more [*or* nothing] for the purpose of the said election, and that, except as specified in the said return sent by me, no money, security, or equivalent for money has been paid, advanced, given, or deposited by any one to me or in my hands, or, to the best of my knowledge and belief, to or in the hands of any other person for the purpose of defraying any expenses incurred on behalf of the said candidate on account of, or in respect of the conduct or management of the said election.

Signature of declarant.   A.B.

Signed and declared by the above-named declarant on the day of   before me.

(Signed)   E.F.
Justice for the peace for

FORM OF RETURN OF ELECTION EXPENSES.

I, *A.B.*, being election agent to *C.D.*, candidate at the election for the county [*or* borough] of   on the day of   , make the following return respecting election expenses of the said candidate at the said election [*or where the candidate has named himself as election agent*, "I, *C.D.*, candidate "at the election for the county [*or* borough] of   on the "   day of   , acting as my own election agent, "make the following return respecting my election expenses at the "said election"].

Receipts.

Received of [*the above-named candidate*] [*or where the candidate is his own election agent,* "Paid by me"] - - - - - - - } £

Received of *J.K.*   -   -   -   -   - £

[*Here set out the name and description of every person, club, society, or association, whether the candidate or not, from whom any money, securities, or equivalent of money was received in respect of expenses incurrred on account of or in connexion with or incidental to the above election, and the amount received from each person, club, society, or association separately.*]

Expenditure.

Paid to *E E.*, the returning officer for the said county [*or* borough] for his charges at the said election - } £

Personal expenses of the said *C.D.*, paid by himself [*or if the candidate is his own election agent,* " Paid by me as candidate "] - - - - £

Do. do. paid by me [*or if the candidate is his own election agent, add* " acting as election agent "] - - - - £

Received by me for my services as election agent at the said election [*or if the candidate is his own election agent, leave out this item*] - - - £

Paid to *G.H.* as sub-agent to the polling district of - £

[*The name and description of each sub-agent and the sum paid to him must be set out separately.*]

Paid to   as polling agent - - - £
Paid to   as clerk for   days' services - £
Paid to   as messenger for days' services - £

[*The names and descriptions of every polling agent, clerk, and messenger, and the sum paid to each, must be set out separately either in the account or in a separate list annexed to and referred to in the account, thus, "Paid to polling agent (or as the case may be) as per annexed list £   ."*]

Paid to the following persons in respect of goods supplied or work and labour done:

 To *P.Q.* (printing) - - - - - £
 To *M.N.* (advertising) - - - - £
 To *R.S.* (stationery) - - - - £

[*The name and description of each person, and the nature of the goods supplied, or the work and labour done by each, must be set out separately either in the account or in a separate list annexed to and referred to in the account.*]

Paid for postage - - - - - - £
Paid for telegrams - - - - - £
Paid for the hire of rooms as follows:—
 For holding public meetings - - - £
 For committee rooms - - - - £

[*A room hired for a public meeting or for a committee room must be named or described so as to identify it; and the name and description of every person to whom any payment was made for each such room, together with the amount paid, must be set out separately either in the account or in a separate list annexed to and referred to in the account.*]

Paid for miscellaneous matters, namely—

[*The name and description of each person to whom any sum is paid, and the reason for which it was paid to him, must be set out separately either in the account or in a separate list annexed to and referred to in the account.*]

In addition to the above, I am aware, as election agent for *C.D.*, [*or if the candidate is his own election agent*, leave out "as election agent for *C.D.*"] of the following disputed and unpaid claims; namely,—

Disputed claims.

By *T.U.* for   -   -   -   -   -   £

[*Here set out the name and description of each person whose claim is disputed, the amount of the claim, and the goods, work, or other matter on the ground of which the claim is based.*]

Unpaid claims allowed by the High Court to be paid after the proper time or in respect of which application has been or is about to be made to the High Court.

By *M.O.* for -   -   -   -   -   £

[*Here state the name and description of each person to whom any such claim is due, and the amount of the claim and the goods, work, and labour or other matter on account of which the claim is due.*]

(Signed)   *A.B.*

PART II.

Form of Declaration as to Expenses.

Form for candidate where declared a candidate or nominated in his absence and taking no part in the election.

I,   , having been nominated [*or* having been declared by others] in my absence [to be] a candidate at the election for the county or borough of
held on the   day of   , do hereby solemnly and sincerely declare that I have taken no part whatever in the said election.

And I further solemnly and sincerely declare that [*or* with the exception of   ] I have not, and no person, club, society, or association at my expense has, made any payment or given, promised, or offered, any reward, office, employment, or valuable consideration, or incurred any liability on account of or in respect of the conduct or management of the said election.

And I further solemnly and sincerely declare that [or with the exception of   ] I have not paid any money or given any security or equivalent for money to the person acting as my election agent at the said election, or to any other person, club, society, or association on account of or in respect of the conduct or management of the said election, and that [or with the exception of   ] I am entirely ignorant of any money security or equivalent for money having been paid, advanced, given, or deposited by any one for the purpose of defraying any expenses incurred on account of or in respect of the conduct or management of the said election.

And I further solemnly and sincerely declare that I will not, except so far as I may be permitted by law, at any future time make or be party to the making or giving of any payment, reward, office, employment, or valuable consideration for the purpose of defraying any such expenses as last mentioned, or provide or be party to the providing of any money, security, or equivalent of money for the purpose of defraying any such expenses.

Signature of declarant   C.D.

Signed and declared by the above-named declarant on the   day of   , before me,

(Signed)   E.F.
Justice of the Peace for

THIRD SCHEDULE.

Corrupt Practices Prevention Acts.

PART ONE.—*Temporary.*

Session and Chapter.	Title of Act.	Enactments referred to as being the Corrupt Practices Prevention Acts.
17 & 18 Vict. c. 102.	The Corrupt Practices Prevention Act, 1854.	The whole Act so far as unrepealed.
26 & 27 Vict. c. 29.	An Act to amend and continue the law relating to corrupt practices at elections of members of Parliament.	The whole Act so far as unrepealed.
31 & 32 Vict. c. 125.	The Parliamentary Elections Act, 1868.	The whole Act so far as unrepealed.
35 & 36 Vict. c. 33.	The Ballot Act, 1872.	Part III. so far as unrepealed.
42 & 43 Vict. c. 75.	The Parliamentary Elections and Corrupt Practices Act, 1879.	The whole Act so far as unrepealed.

T

THIRD SCHEDULE—*continued*.

PART TWO.

Permanent.

Session and Chapter.	Title of Act.	Enactments referred to as being the Corrupt Practices Prevention Acts.
30 & 31 Vict. c. 102.	The Representation of the People Act, 1867.	Sections eleven, forty-nine, and fifty.
31 & 32 Vict. c. 48.	The Representation of the People (Scotland) Act, 1868.	Sections eight and forty-nine.
31 & 32 Vict. c. 49.	The Representation of the People (Ireland) Act, 1868.	Sections eight and thirteen.
44 & 45 Vict. c. 40.	The Universities Elections Amendment (Scotland) Act, 1881.	Sub-section seventeen of section two.

PART THREE.

ENACTMENTS DEFINING THE OFFENCES OF BRIBERY AND PERSONATION.

The Corrupt Practices Prevention Act, 1854, *17 & 18 Vict., c. 102, ss. 2, 3.*

Bribery defined.   s. 2. The following persons shall be deemed guilty of bribery, and shall be punishable accordingly :—

(1.) Every person who shall, directly or indirectly, by himself, or by any other person on his behalf, give, lend, or agree to give or lend, or shall offer, promise, or promise to procure or to endeavour to procure, any money or valuable consideration to or for any voter or to or for any person on behalf of any voter, or to or for any other person in order to induce any voter to vote or refrain from voting, or shall corruptly do any such act as aforesaid on account of such voter having voted or refrained from voting at any election :

(2.) Every person who shall, directly or indirectly, by himself, or by any other person on his behalf, give or procure, or agree to give or procure, or offer, promise, or promise to procure or to endeavour to procure, any office, place, or employment to or for any voter, or to or for any person on behalf of any voter, or to or for any other person in order to induce such voter to vote or refrain from voting, or shall corruptly do any such act as aforesaid on account of any voter having voted or refrained from voting at any election :

(3.) Every person who shall, directly or indirectly, by himself, or by any other person on his behalf, make any such gift, loan, offer, promise, procurement, or agreement as aforesaid to or for any person, in order to induce such person to procure or endeavour to procure the return of any person to serve in Parliament, or the vote of any voter at any election :

(4.) Every person who shall, upon or in consequence of any such gift, loan, offer, promise, procurement, or agreement, procure or engage, promise, or endeavour to procure the return of any person to serve in Parliament, or the vote of any voter at any election :

(5.) Every person who shall advance or pay, or cause to be paid, any money to or to the use of any other person with the intent that such money or any part thereof shall be expended in bribery at any election, or who shall knowingly pay or cause to be paid any money to any person in discharge or repayment of any money wholly or in part expended in bribery at any election. Provided always, that the aforesaid enactment shall not extend or be construed to extend to any money paid or agreed to be paid for or on account of any legal expenses bonâ fide incurred at or concerning any election.

s. 3. The following persons shall also be deemed guilty of bribery, and shall be punishable accordingly :— *Bribery further defined.*

(1.) Every voter who shall, before or during any election, directly or indirectly, by himself or by any other person on his behalf, receive, agree, or contract for any money, gift, loan, or valuable consideration, office, place, or employment, for himself or for any other person, for voting or agreeing to vote, or for refraining or agreeing to refrain from voting at any election :

(2.) Every person who shall, after any election, directly or indirectly, by himself or by any other person on his behalf, receive any money or valuable consideration on account of any person having voted or refrained from voting, or having induced any other person to vote or refrain from voting at any election.

The Representation of the People Act, 1867, 30 and 31 Vict., c. 102, s. 49.

Corrupt payment of rates to be punishable as bribery.

49. Any person, either directly or indirectly, corruptly paying any rate on behalf of any ratepayer for the purpose of enabling him to be registered as a voter, thereby to influence his vote at any future election, and any candidate or other person, either directly or indirectly, paying any rate on behalf of any voter for the purpose of inducing him to vote or refrain from voting, shall be guilty of bribery, and be punishable accordingly; and any person on whose behalf and with whose privity any such payment as in this section is mentioned is made shall also be guilty of bribery, and punishable accordingly.

The Representation of the People (Scotland) Act, 1868, 31 & 32 Vict., c. 48, s. 49.

Corrupt payment of rates to be punishable as bribery.

49. Any person, either directly or indirectly, corruptly paying any rate on behalf of any ratepayer for the purpose of enabling him to be registered as a voter, thereby to influence his vote at any future election, and any candidate or other person, either directly or indirectly, paying any rate on behalf of any voter for the purpose of inducing him to vote or refrain from voting, shall be guilty of bribery, and be punishable accordingly; and any person on whose behalf and with whose privity any such payment as in this section mentioned is made shall also be guilty of bribery, and punishable accordingly.

The Universities Elections Amendment (Scotland) Act, 1881, 44 & 45 Vict., c. 40, s. 2.

Corrupt payment of registration fee to be punishable as bribery.

17. Any person, either directly or indirectly, corruptly paying any fee for the purpose of enabling any person to be registered as a member of the general council, and thereby to influence his vote at any future election, and any candidate or other person, either directly or indirectly, paying such fee on behalf of any person for the purpose of inducing him to vote or to refrain from voting, shall be guilty of bribery, and shall be punishable accordingly; and any person on whose behalf and with whose privity any such payment as in this section mentioned is made, shall also be guilty of bribery and punishable accordingly.

The Ballot Act, 1872, 35 & 36 Vict., c. 33, s. 24.

A person shall for all purposes of the laws relating to parlia- Personation mentary and municipal elections be deemed to be guilty of the defined. offence of personation who, at an election for a county or borough, or at a municipal election, applies for a ballot paper in the name of some other person, whether that name be that of a person living or dead, or of a fictitious person, or who, having voted once at any such election, applies at the same election for a ballot paper in his own name.

FOURTH SCHEDULE.

SHORT TITLES.

Session and Chapter.	Long Title.	Short Title.
15 & 16 Vict. c. 57.	An Act to provide for more effectual inquiry into the existence of corrupt practices at the election of members to serve in Parliament.	Election Commissioners Act, 1852.
26 & 27 Vict. c. 29.	An Act to amend and continue the law relating to corrupt practices at elections of members of Parliament.	The Corrupt Practices Prevention Act, 1863.

FIFTH SCHEDULE.

ENACTMENTS REPEALED.

NOTE.—Portions of Acts which have already been specifically repealed are in some instances included in the repeal in this Schedule in order to preclude henceforth the necessity of looking back to previous Acts.

A description or citation of a portion of an Act is inclusive of the words, section, or other part first or last mentioned, or otherwise referred to as forming the beginning or as forming the end of the portion comprised in the description or citation.

FIFTH SCHEDULE—*continued.*

Session and Chapter.	Title or Short Title.	Extent of Repeal.
60 Geo. 3. & 1 Geo. 4, c. 11.	An Act for the better regulation of polls, and for making further provision touching the election of members to serve in Parliament for Ireland	Section thirty-six.
1 & 2 Geo. 4, c. 58.	An Act to regulate the expenses of election of members to serve in Parliament for Ireland.	The whole Act except section three
4 Geo. 4. c. 55.	An Act to consolidate and amend the several Acts now in force so far as the same relate to the election and return of members to serve in Parliament for the counties of cities and counties of towns in Ireland.	Section eighty-two.
17 & 18 Vict. c. 102.	The Corrupt Practices Prevention Act, 1854.	Section one. Section two, from "and any person so offending" to "with full costs of suit." Section three, from "and any person so offending" to the end of the section. Section four. Section five. Section six. Section seven, from "and all payments" to the end of the section. Section nine, section fourteen, section twenty-three, section thirty-six, section thirty-eight, from "and the words personal expenses" to the end of the section, and section thirty-nine and Schedule A.

FIFTH SCHEDULE—continued.

Session and Chapter.	Title or Short Title.	Extent of Repeal.
21 & 22 Vict. c. 87.	An Act to continue and amend the Corrupt Practices Preventi'n Act, 1854	The whole Act.
26 & 27 Vict. c. 29.	An Act to amend and continue the law relating to corrupt practices at elections of Members of Parliament.	The whole Act, except section six.
30 & 31 Vict. c. 102.	The Representation of the People Act, 1867.	Section thirty-four, from "and in other boroughs the justices" to "greater part thereof is situate" and section thirty-six.
31 & 32 Vict. c. 48.	The Representation of the People (Scotland) Act, 1868.	Section twenty-five.
31 & 32 Vict. c. 49.	The Representation of the People (Ireland) Act, 1868	Section twelve.
31 & 32 Vict. c. 58.	The Parliamentary Electors Registration Act, 1868.	Section eighteen, "from the power of dividing their county" to the end of the section.
31 & 32 Vict. c. 125.	The Parliamentary Elections Act, 1868.	So much of section three as relates to the definitions of "candidate." Section sixteen. Section thirty-three. Section thirty-six. Section forty-one, from "but according to the same principles" to "the High Court of Chancery." Section forty-three. Section forty-five. Section forty-six. Section forty-seven. Section fifty-eight, from "The principles" down to "in the court of session," being subsection sixteen.

FIFTH SCHEDULE—*continued.*

Session and Chapter.	Title or Short Title.	Extent of Repeal.
35 & 36 Vict. c. 33.	The Ballot Act, 1872	Section five, from the beginning down to "one hundred registered electors." Section twenty-four, from "The offence of "personation, or of aiding," to "hard labour," and from "The offence of personation shall be deemed to be" to the end of the section.
42 & 43 Vict. c. 75.	The Parliamentary Elections and Corrupt Practices Act, 1879.	Section three and schedule.
43 Vict. c. 18.	The Parliamentary Elections and Corrupt Practices Act, 1880.	The whole Act, except sections one and three.

47 & 48 VIC., CHAP. 34.   A.D. 1884.

An Act to extend the Hours of Polling at Parliamentary and Municipal Elections in certain Boroughs.

[28th July, 1884.]

1. (1.) At every parliamentary or municipal election to which this Act applies the poll (if any) shall commence at eight o'clock in the forenoon and be kept open until eight o'clock in the afternoon of the same day and no longer. *Hours of polling in boroughs with more than three thousand electors.*

(2.) A parliamentary election to which this Act applies shall be an election of a member or members to serve in Parliament for any parliamentary borough within the meaning of this Act which has, for the time being, as appears from the number of names entered in the register of electors for the time being in operation in such borough, a number of registered *electors exceeding three thousand*. *31 and 32 Vict., c. 125.*

(3.) A municipal election to which this Act applies shall be an election of a councillor, commissioner of police, auditor, or revising assessor in any municipal borough within the meaning of this Act or in any ward thereof, where the whole or part of the area of such borough is co-extensive with, or included in the area of a parliamentary borough with such number of registered electors as above in this section mentioned.

2. In this Act—   *Definitions.*

The expression "parliamentary borough" means any city, borough, place, or combination of places (not being a county at large or division of a county at large, or university or universities) which returns a member or members to serve in Parliament; and

The expression "municipal borough" means, as regards England, a borough subject to the Municipal Corporations Act, 1882, and as regards Scotland, means a burgh or town which has a town council or police commissioners, and as regards Ireland means a borough subject to the Act of the session of the third and fourth years of the reign of Her present Majesty, chapter one hundred and eight, intituled "An Act for the regulation of municipal Corporations in Ireland" and the Acts amending the same:

The word "councillor" shall, in Ireland, be taken to include alderman.

3. This Act may be cited as the Elections (Hours of Poll) Act, 1884.

SUMMARY OF ELECTION OFFENCES.

OFFENCES.	PENALTIES.
Corrupt Practices.	
BRIBERY.—No gift, loan, or promise of money, or money's worth, must be made to a voter to induce him either to vote or abstain from voting. The offer or promise of a situation or employment to a voter or anyone connected with him, if made with the same object, is also bribery. The consequences are the same whether bribery is committed before, during, or after an election. Giving or paying money for the purpose of bribery is equivalent to the offence itself. A gift or promise to a third person to procure a vote is bribery. Payments for loss of time, wages, or travelling expenses are equal to bribery. *Anyone who receives a bribe, or bargains for employment or reward in consideration of his vote is guilty of bribery.*	To the briber or the person bribed, twelve months' imprisonment, with or without hard labour, or a fine of £200. Deprivation of the right of voting for seven years. Removal from, and disqualification for, any public office. Payment of costs of an election enquiry in certain cases. If committed by the Candidate he also loses his seat, if elected, and is disqualified for ever from representing the Constituency. If committed by any Agent, the election is void, and the Candidate is disqualified for seven years.
TREATING.—No meat, drink, entertainment or provision can be paid for or provided for any person, at any time, in order to induce him, or any other person, to vote or abstain from voting. Treating the wives or relations of voters is equally forbidden. The gift of tickets to be exchanged for refreshment is treating. *The receiver of any meat, drink, &c., is equally guilty, and liable to the same consequences.*	The same as for Bribery.

| OFFENCES. | PENALTIES. |

Corrupt Practices—continued.

UNDUE INFLUENCE.—No force, restraint, or fraud may be used to compel an elector to vote or abstain.

Using or threatening any spiritual or temporary injury is undue influence.

The withdrawal of custom, or a threat to do so, comes under this prohibition. A threat to evict a tenant will also be undue influence.

The same as for Bribery.

PERSONATION.—*Applying for* a ballot paper in the name of another person whether living or dead.

Voting twice at the same election.

Aiding or abetting the commission of the offence of personation.

Forging or counterfeiting a ballot paper.

To the offender, two years' imprisonment, with hard labour.

Seven years' incapacity to vote, or hold any public office.

If committed by any Agent, the Candidate loses his seat.

Illegal Practices.

CONVEYANCE. — Paying or receiving money for conveyance of voters to or from the poll.

(Private conveyances lent gratuitously can alone be employed; hackney carriages are prohibited except when hired by voters for their own exclusive use).

ADVERTISING.—Paying money to an elector for exhibiting bills, &c. The *receiver* is also guilty.

COMMITTEE ROOMS.—Hiring unauthorised Committee Rooms. (The Election Agent *alone* may hire Committee Rooms, and the number is strictly limited.)

VOTING when prohibited, or inducing a prohibited elector to vote. (Electors employed for payment cannot vote.)

FALSE STATEMENT.—Publishing a false statement of the withdrawal of any Candidate.

A fine of £100.

Incapacity to vote for five years.

If committed by an Agent, the election may be rendered void.

OFFENCES.	PENALTIES.

Illegal Payment, Employment and Hiring.

PUBLISHING BILLS, placards or posters without the printer's name and address. (The Election Agent *alone* must issue any printed matter at the election).	
PAYMENTS FOR BANDS OF MUSIC, torches, flags, banners, ribbons, &c.	
LENDING OR USING, for the conveyance of voters, ANIMALS or VEHICLES usually kept for hire.	A fine of £100.
EMPLOYMENT of any person beyond the numbers allowed. (No person can be employed for payment at an election except by the Election Agent, who is strictly limited as to the numbers he may engage.)	
USING A COMMITTEE ROOM in any licensed house, refreshment house, or public elementary school.	

MISCELLANEOUS.

NOTE.— Any of the above offences, if committed by a Candidate, Election Agent (or Sub-Agent, in Counties), will render the election void.

The term "agent," as used above, *may*, under certain circumstances, include members of an Election Committee or voluntary canvassers.

No expense must be incurred by anybody without the Election Agent's written authority, as the maximum expense allowed by law for each Candidate cannot be exceeded without rendering the election void.

The person incurring any unauthorised expense will be personally liable for its repayment, as well as for the consequences of having broken the law.

LIST OF FORMS.

		Page.	Corresponding Conservative Central Office Forms.	
Form. No.			County.	Boro'.
1.	Appointment of Election Agent ...	7	A.	1
2.	Appointment of Sub-agents	10	K.	
3.	Election Agents' Preliminary Notice ...	11	B.	2
4.	List of Volunteer Clerks or Messengers	18		
5.	List of Paid Clerks or Messengers ...	20		
6.	Printer's Estimate	23		
7.	Notice for Private Posting Stations ...	25		
8.	Schedule of Advertisement Charges... ...	26		
9.	Agreement for Hire of Committee Room...	30	O.	13
10.	Agreement for Committee Rooms in Clubs	31		
11.	Notice to Licensed Victuallers... ...	32	Z.	21
12.	Election Expenses Book	35	E.	5
13.	Form of Order Book	37	C.	3
14.	Authority for Petty Disbursements... ...	38	S.	17
14a.	Ward or District Book	45		
15.	List of Outvoters...	47	V.	
16.	List of Non-Resident Voters	49	U.	
16a & 16b.—Canvass Books and Instructions to Canvassers		50–4		
17	Canvassers' Return Sheets	55		
18	List of Removals	56	X.	19
19	Ward or District Return Sheets	58	R.	16
20	Central Committee's Canvass Ledger ...	59	Q.	15
21	Canvass Cards	59		
22	Special Canvass Cards	60		
23	Circulars for Ward Committees	60		
24	Special do. do. ...	61		
25	Circular to Electors ...	62	J.	10
26	Form of Reply to do. ...	63	J.	10

LIST OF FORMS *continued*.

Form.		Page.	County.	Boro'.
27	Circular as to Canvass of Outvoters	64	W.	
28	Private Instructions to Sub-agents	65	L.	
29	List of Committee Rooms	73		11
30	Instructions to Ward or District Committees	78	M.	12
31	Instructions to Clerks in Charge	82		
32	Instructions to Canvassers	84		
33	Circular and Instructions to Voters ...	91	BB.	23
34	Voters' Polling Card	92	BB.	23
35	Canvassers' Instructions for Polling Day...	93	AA.	22
36	Wall Number Sheets	95-6		
37 & 38.—Polls Returns Book		97-8		
39	Do. (Slip Book) ...	100		
40	Do. (Inside)	101		
41	Do. to Central Committee	102		
42	Do. or do. ...	103		
43	Notice of Appointment of Polling Agents	104	DD.	25
44	Appointment of Polling Agents...	105	N.	11
45	Instructions to Polling Agents...	106	FF.	27
46	Appointment of Country Agents & Notice	111	GG.	28
47	Declaration of Secrecy	112	EE.	26
48	Instructions to Ward or District Committees on Polling Day	113	AA.	22
49	Inspector of Refreshments' Instructions ...	116		
50	Unpolled Voters Cards	117	KK.	30
51	List of Voluntary Conveyances...	124	T.	18
52	Carriage Poster	125		
53	Nomination Paper	131		
54	Notice to Creditors to send in Bills and Claims	146	LL.	31

INDEX.

	PAGE.
ADDRESSES of candidate for distribution	61
ADDRESSED envelopes	61
Post wrappers	61
ADMIRALTY COURT, judge of, cannot be a candidate	1
ADVERTISING—	
Persons who can contract for	25
To be carefully considered and charges arranged for	26
Form for settling cost of	26
AGREEMENTS for hire of committee rooms, &c., to be in writing	30
BALLOT PAPER—	
What are objections to	142
Objection to be decided by returning officer	141
,, when to be made	140—142
How to be kept	143
BANKRUPT cannot be a candidate	2
BILL POSTING, when payment can be made for	24
BOROUGHS excepted from Corrupt Practices Act, 1883, as to expenses	11
CANDIDATE—	
Objections to own	1
,, opposite	1
Status of	1
Qualification of	1
Disqualifications of	1
,, as to a particular place	2
Must appoint an election agent before nomination	4
May appoint himself as election agent	4
Must give office address for notices, &c.	4
To notify to returning officer appointment of agent	4
His own election agent to appoint clerks, messengers, polling agents, &c.	4
To make returns of his receipts and expenditure	4
Canvassing to be attended by special agent	4
Personal expenses of	5—148
To send written statement of personal expenses to election agent	5
Personal expenses, what are	5
Subscriptions may be received by	5
Definition of personal expenses of	5
May withdraw or be withdrawn	6
Dying between nomination and poll	6
Dying immediately before or whilst election proceeding	6
Maximum amount allowed where more than one	11
Disqualified by acts at municipal election	3
Disqualified by acts at a previous election	3
Disqualified by corrupt practices of agent at a previous election	3
Disqualified by consenting to illegal practices at a previous election	4
Disqualified by illegal practices of agent at a previous election	4
Objection to description of, when to be made	134
Election of, without a poll	135
Dying before poll commences	135—136
Dead when nominated, or dying during election	136
Elected without a poll	138
How return to be made of elected	144
Address of	152

U

	PAGE.
CANDIDATE (continued)—	
When his own agent to make return of expenses and statutory declaration.	150
Penalties incurred by, for breach of Act	150
CANDIDATES, JOINT	14
CANVASS—	
Object of	42
What books, forms, &c., agent to provide	42—43
Book, ward or district form of	45
,, ,, use of	49
Out-voters in counties, how to	46—47
Out-voters' list in boroughs, for	48
Non-resident voters' list for boroughs and counties	48
Object of non-resident voters' list	48
List of committee rooms, &c., to be posted in all committee rooms	49
Form for non-resident voters	49
Book, form of blank	51
How prepared	52
Book, as prepared	53
,, how used by canvasser	54
Books, list of, to be kept	54
Return sheets of	55
Sheets, use of return	55
Return of, form of	55
Daily returns of, to be made	57
Form of daily return sheets	58
Ledger, use of	59
Candidate's addresses to be distributed, during	61—62
Form of circular to be sent with candidate's addresses	62
Reply circular may be used during	63
Form of reply circular used during	63
Circulars to out-voters, or voters removed, to be sent during	64
Form of circular to be sent to agent to canvass out-voters or voters removed	64
Agent to receive daily return of	86
To be taken in account before poll	86
Necessary to have a second	88
CANVASS CARDS—	
Use of	59
Form of	59
Special Form of	60
Circulars	60—61
CANVASSERS—	
Instructions to	84—85
,, on polling day	93—94
CANVASSERS' RETURN SHEETS—	
Use of	55
Form of	55
CANVASSER'S CANVASS BOOK—	
Uses of	49
Form of	51
How prepared	52
List of, to be made	54
Return sheets, form and use of	55
Care to be taken in distribution of	77
Number of voters limited in each	77
CARRIAGE SUPERINTENDENT—	
Duties in boroughs of	125
,, in counties of	126
CENTRAL COMMITTEE—	
Canvass Ledger	58
,, how kept	58
,, use of	58
,, form of	59
Should be most central and convenient	71
Polls return book, form of	103
Review of Staff of	128—129

	PAGE.
CIRCULARS—	
Form of	60
Special canvassing	60—61—62
Register number to be filled in before sending	63
Stamped envelope to be sent with	63
Form of to be sent to agents in other towns	64
CLERKS—	
Number employed limited	18
If paid, cannot vote	18
Unpaid	18
List and addresses of unpaid to be kept	18
Declaration by unpaid to be signed	18
Form of declaration by unpaid	18
Number allowed, if paid	19
,, (in boroughs)	19—21
,, (in counties)	19—21
May work in any part of a borough	19
,, ,, a county	19—20
List to be made of paid	20
Declaration to be signed by paid	20
Form of declaration by paid	20
Election agent's	20
Law stationer's	20
To election agent may vote	21
To law stationer may vote	21
Slip and wallsheet	100
COMMISSIONER of POLICE, cannot be a candidate	2
COMMITTEE ROOMS—	
Hire of	27
To be near polling stations	27
List to be made of	27—73
Permanent political clubs may be used as	27
,, ,, definition of	28—29
Rooms may be lent for	26—29—27
No limit to rooms lent for	27
Number allowed for payment	27
,, ,, (in a borough)	27
,, ,, (in a county)	27
Where rooms can not be used as	27—28
Definition of premises used as	28
,, of committee room	29
Should be in the same building where more rooms used than one	29
Must be hired by election agent personally in boroughs	29
Must be hired by election agent personally or by sub-agents personally in counties	29
Agreements for hire of to be in writing	30
Agreements to include all charges	30
Form of agreement for hire of	30
To be under exclusive control of election agent, if in permanent political club	30
Form of agreement for hire of in clubs	31
Ward or district	72
List of, to be made	72
Form of list of	73
No refreshments to be allowed in	73
Additional on day of poll	73
COMMITTEES (ELECTION)—	
How composed	73
All members of political clubs or associations not to form	74
How formed	75
Should be a special body	75
List of, to be kept by agent	75
COMMITTEES (WARD OR DISTRICT)—	
How formed	75
Duty of chairman at first meeting	76
Qualification of chairman	76
,, clerk in charge	76
Appointment of clerk in boroughs to	77
,, ,, counties to	77

	PAGE.
COMMITTEES (WARD OR DISTRICT) continued—	
Election agent to attend meetings of	77
Instructions on canvassing	78—82
„ to clerks	82—84
„ on polling day	113
CONTRACT—	
Who can contract for advertising	25
Form of	23
CONTRACTOR FOR PUBLIC SERVICE—	
What is	2
Cannot be a candidate	2
CONVEYANCE OF VOTERS TO POLL—	
Illegal to pay for conveyance of voters to poll, except where arm of sea to be crossed	122
Voters may pay for own conveyance	122
Carriages may be lent to candidate gratuitously on election day	123
Carriages lent to candidate not liable to duty or a licence	123
Illegal to hire or lend carriages or horses kept for hire	124
Carriages jobbed *bonâ fide* may be lent gratuitously	124
List of persons willing to lend private carriages to be made	124
Cabs for use of messengers may be hired by candidate	125
Notice to be attached to messengers' cab	125
COUNTING AGENTS—	
Candidate to appoint	110
Names and addresses to be sent to returning officer	110
Form of appointment of	111
Declaration of secrecy to be made by	111
Death of, before counting	112
Form of notice to, and declaration of secrecy of	112
COUNTING VOTES—	
How done	138
Persons to be present on	139
Persons not to be employed in	139
Secrecy to be maintained in	139
Adjournment of	139
What to be done on completion of	143
COUNTY COURT JUDGE, cannot be a candidate	1
DEACON, cannot be a candidate	2
DEAD VOTERS, how returned by canvassers	50
DEFINITION of " premises "	28
„ " permanent political club "	28—29
„ " personal expenses "	5
„ " committee room "	29
DETECTIVE COMMITTEE—	
Use of	127
How composed	127
Qualifications and duties of persons forming	127
DISQUALIFICATION OF CANDIDATE	1
„ „ as to a particular place	2
DISTRICT OR WARD—	
Return sheets, use of	57
Form of	58
ELECTION—	
Preparation for	89
What required for	89—90
Duty of out-door superintendent and election agent at	136
Duty of Central Committee at	137
Duty of returning officer before counting votes	138
Agent, duty of, on close of poll	137

	PAGE.
ELECTION AGENT	7
First duty of	7
Each candidate must appoint only one	7
Candidate may appoint himself	7
Name and address to be sent to returning officer	7
Office address to be sent to returning officer	7
Candidate may revoke appointment of	8
If paid cannot vote	8—21
Who may or may not be an	8
Penalty for employing a disqualified	8
Duty of an	8—9
Place of business of	9
May appoint a sub-agent for each polling district in county or division	9
Sub-agents' acts deemed to be acts of	10
Name and address of sub-agents to be sent to returning officer by	10
To take every means to prevent corrupt practices	11
Notices to be published in newspapers by	11
Notices to be posted in committee rooms by	12
Expenditure to be under absolute control of	12
Fees	16—17
Fee to be returned with other expenses	17
Fee to be reduced if maximum sum exceeded	17
Fee to include services of own clerks	20
Duty of, at close of poll	137
Remuneration of	148
ENVELOPES (ADDRESSED)	61
EXPENSES (ELECTION)—	
Apportionment of	13—12
Gratuitous aid to be sought to keep down	13
Apportionment to be made prior to election	13
What amount can be legally spent as	13
Record of estimated, to be kept	13—14
What are covered by maximum sum	14
Of joint candidates	14
Maximum sum allowed for	13—14
,, to be apportioned	16
Miscellaneous payments for	34
Refreshments for *bona fide* clerks, &c., may be paid for as	34
Book to be kept for	34
,, ,, form of	35
Book to be entered up daily	36
Book to be for central committee room, and each polling district in counties	36
Margin allowed for unforeseen	36
Cash Book	36
Orders on account of, to be in writing	36
Form of book for orders	37
Book to be checked by order book	37
Election agent may authorize payment of petty	37
Authority must be in writing	37
Form of authority	38
Weekly account of wages to be sent to election agent	38
Duty of visiting clerk to committee rooms	38
Actual cost of borough elections (York and Ipswich)	38—39
What are election	39
Definition of "person" includes clubs, &c.	40
Cost of requisition to person to become candidate not	40
Election expenses where no candidate selected	40—41
Gratuitous aid not regarded as	41
Registration books &c., may be lent gratuitously	41
Registration books, &c., may be hired by candidate and included in	41
Candidate's subscriptions to a club or other association, if given without corrupt intent, not	42
Meetings to hear member or intended candidate, not	42
Boroughs excepted from Corrupt Practices Act, 1883, as to	144
To be paid only through agent	145
Accounts of, to be sent in to election agent	145
None to be made except through agent	145
Contributions towards, to be paid either to candidate or agent	145
Form of notice to public to send in accounts to agent	146
Disputed claims, how dealt with	146
Time limited for sending in claims of	147

	PAGE.
EXPENSES (ELECTION) continued—	
Time limited for payment of	147
Who authorized to pay petty	148
When receipt necessary for	148
Return to be made of	149
What must be returned as	149
Return to be accompanied by statutory declaration	150
Form of return of	150
Payment of, after return made	151
Return of, not made as required, application to High Court necessary	151
FELON—	
Cannot be a candidate	2
FORMS (LIST OF)	286—287
HIGH COURT OF JUSTICE (Applications to)	151—152
ILLEGAL PRACTICE—	
Innocent act not an offence	151
Application to High Court for excuse, to be supported by affidavits or other evidence	152
INSTRUCTIONS—	
To canvassers in canvass book	50—54
,, Sub-agents	65
,, Ward or district committees	78
,, Clerks in charge	82
,, Canvassers on canvass	84
,, Voters	91
,, Canvassers for polling day	93
,, Polling agents	106
,, Ward or district committees for polling day	113
,, Inspector of refreshments	116
JOINT CANDIDATES—	
Who are to be deemed	15
May become or cease to be	15
Maximum sum allowed for	14
JUDGE cannot be a candidate	1
LICENSED PREMISES, meetings on	4—31
MAXIMUM SUM allowed for election expenses	13—14
MEETINGS, &c.—	
Cost of, to hear member or intended candidate not election expenses	42
MESSENGERS—	
Number employed as, limited	18
If paid, cannot vote	18
Unpaid, can vote	18
List and addresses to be kept of unpaid	18
Declaration to be signed by unpaid	18
Form of declaration	18
Number of, allowed, if paid	19
,, ,, (in boroughs)	19
,, ,, (in counties)	19
May work in any part of a borough	19—21
,, ,, county	19—20
List to be made of paid	20
Declaration to be signed by paid	20
MINISTER of Church of Scotland cannot be a candidate	2
MISDEMEANANT convicted of fraud cannot be a candidate	2

	PAGE.
NOMINATION—	
Objections to opposite candidate, not to be made until after	1
Paper, how subscribed	130
,, how filled up	131
,, how assented to	131
Form of assent to	131
Paper, who to sign	132
,, how delivered	132
,, how candidate described in	132
,, objection to, when to be made	132—133
,, to be published	133
,, what names to be inserted in	133
Objection to, when to be made	134
Who to make objection to	134—135
NON-RESIDENT VOTERS LIST	48
NOTICE IN NEWSPAPERS—	
Agents and sub-agents to publish on appointment	11
Form of	11
OBJECTION to opposite candidate not to be made until after nomination	1
Who to make, to nomination	134
Returning officer to decide validity of	134
OFFENCES (LIST OF)	283
OFFICE under Crown, if created since 1705, person holding cannot be a candidate	2
OFFICES—what, disqualify persons holding, from being candidates	2
OUT-DOOR SUPERINTENDENT—	
Qualifications and duties of	126—127
OUT-VOTERS—	
How dealt with	46
How to be canvassed	46
Committee to attend to	46—47
List of	47
Form of list	47
PAYMENT—	
To a voter for services disqualifies him from voting	18
PENSION, what disqualifies person holding, from being a candidate	2
PERSONATION AGENTS—	
Each candidate may appoint one or more	104
Appointed by candidate must not be paid	104
Form of appointment of	105
PEER cannot be a candidate unless of Ireland	1
PLACARDS—	
Name and address of printer to appear on	12
Penalty for omission	12
To be examined by agent before posting	12
Arrangement with opposite side for number of	22
Number required	22
Price list	24
May be posted on walls, barns, &c., gratuitously	25
List to be made of places where posted	25
Notice to be placed on all posting stations	25
Form of notice	25
Arrangements for posting	25
POLICE MAGISTRATE cannot be a candidate	1
" POLITICAL CLUB "—	
Definition of permanent	28—29

	PAGE.

POLLS—
 Return books, forms and uses of .... 97—98
  ,, outside 98
  ,, inside 101
 Where two candidates, how state of poll arrived at 99
 Where more than two candidates.. 99
 Return and slip clerks 121

POLLING AGENTS—
 Fee to.. 21
 Duties of 21
 Gratuitous aid to be obtained to act as... 21
 Election agent to arrange list of 21
 Number limited of 21
 If paid cannot vote .... 21—104
 Appointment of... 104
 Register for use of.. 106
 Instructions to ....106—110
 Form of appointment of ....104—105
 Notice to be given to returning officer or deputy, of appointment of... 104
 If paid to be appointed by election agent 104
 Object of register for use of 106
 Form of notice to, and declaration of secrecy by......................... 112
 Suitability of persons as 119
 Qualifications of 119

POST WRAPPERS (ADDRESSED) 61

POSTAGE—
 When and how used... 26—27
 Estimated cost of... 26—27

POSTING (BILLS)—
 Who may or may not be paid for 24
 Notice to be placed on all stations for 25
 Form of Notice 25
 Arrangements for bill posting... 25

PRIEST cannot be a candidate 2

PRINTING—
 Expenses of... 22
 Election agent to exercise careful supervision over 22
 Tenders to be obtained for 22-23
 Form of tender for 23

PROFIT, place of, under Crown, created since 1705, person holding cannot be a candidate 2

PUBLIC HOUSE—notice to be given to landlord, where public meetings held in 32

PUBLIC MEETINGS—
 Expenses of... 31
 May be held anywhere 31
 If on licensed premises, notice to landlord................................. 31
 Form of notice to landlord of licensed premises 31
 Provisions of C.P. Act, 1883, with regard to licensed premises ......32—33—34
 Payment for use of room to be agreed upon prior to holding 34

QUALIFICATION of Candidate 1

RECORDER cannot be elected for place for which he is recorder 3

REFRESHMENTS—
 Clerks, &c., engaged bond fide for election, not prohibited having 34
 Inspector of, instructions to..116—117
 Inspectors of, qualifications of..121—122

REGISTERS OF VOTERS—
 Use of 43
 Charge for 43
 What number required 43
 How prepared .... 43—44

	PAGE.
REGISTRAR of deeds cannot be a candidate	2
REMOVALS LIST	55
Form of	56
To be canvassed book	57
Committee for canvassing	57
To be reported by canvassers	56
RETURN OF CANVASS to be made daily	55
RETURN SHEETS—	
Ward or district	57
Form and use of	58
RETURNING OFFICER—	
Name and address of election agents and situation of offices to be published by	7—8
To decide validity of objection to nomination paper	134
Charges of, are limited, and can be taxed	140
Duty of, on receipt of writ for election	129
Cannot be a candidate for the place for which he acts	3
REVISING BARRISTER cannot be a candidate for place for which he was appointed within 18 months of appointment	3
ROME—Person in holy orders in Church of, cannot be a candidate	2
SHERIFF cannot be elected for county for which he acts	3
SLIP BOOK—	
Form of	100
Clerk	97—101—100—121
STATUS OF CANDIDATE	1
STATUTES (TABLE OF)	viii
STATUTORY DECLARATION, Form of	150
STAFF—	
Positions and duty of, on election day	118
List to be prepared by committees of	118
If paid, should not be voters	118
Committee room	118
Polling booth	118
SUB-AGENT—	
Appointment not revoked by election agent ceasing to act	10
Care in the selection of	11
If paid, cannot vote	11
Notices to be published in newspapers by	11
,, posted in committee rooms by	12
May act for two or more districts in counties	18
Instructions to	65—71
Form of appointment of	65
Fee to	17
SUBSCRIPTIONS may be received by candidate	5
,, by candidate to clubs, &c.	41—42
TELEGRAMS—	
Not to be used unless absolutely necessary	26
TENDERS—	
To be obtained for printing and stationery	22
TREATING—	
Penalty for corruptly	82
UNPOLLED VOTERS CARDS—	
Use and object of	117
Form of	117
VISITING CLERK—	
To visit each committee room daily	58
Duty of	85

	PAGE.
VOTER—	
Employment of, disqualifies him from voting	8—11—18—21
Polled clerks and messengers	97—120
VOTERS—	
Registers of	43
Out, how to be dealt with	46
Out, to be canvassed, list of	46—47
Out, committee for	46—47
Left town, &c., how dealt with	46
Out, list of, to be kept	48
Dead or gone abroad, &c.	50
Instruction card to	90—91
Form of card for	92
Private mark on card for	93
WAGES—	
Account to be made out weekly	38
WALL SHEETS—	
Object of	94
Form and use of	95
How arranged on polling day	95
How prepared	96—97
Clerks of	120
Duty and qualification of clerks of	120—121
WARD OR DISTRICT BOOK—	
Use of	44
Form of	45
WARD OR DISTRICT RETURN SHEETS—	
How prepared	57
Use of daily	57
Form of	58
WITHDRAWAL of candidate	6 & 135

www.ingramcontent.com/pod-product-compliance
Lightning Source LLC
Chambersburg PA
CBHW030814230426
43667CB00008B/1207